"Marybeth Hicks reminds us that it is more important to be our children's parents than it is to be their friends. Her book is a go-to guide when it's time to set limits on how much and what our children are exposed to in this world of celebrity, mass media, and affluence."

—Chris Hansen, *Dateline NBC* correspondent and author of
*To Catch a Predator: Protecting Your Kids from
Online Enemies Already in Your Home*

"Every so often a book comes along that I tell my friends they absolutely must read.... Read this book, declare your status as a 'geek' mom or dad, and create a better life for your family.... This is the time for us to take back our children's childhoods, and in doing so to claim our role as strong, protective parents."

—Dr. Kimberly M. Thompson, associate professor and director of the
Kids Risk Project, Harvard School of Public Health

"Today's popular culture is robbing from an entire generation of children their most treasured possession—the sweet innocence of youth. *Bringing Up Geeks* is a breath of fresh air, and we owe Marybeth Hicks a debt of gratitude. It's required reading for any parent struggling to raise a child in a society that's lost its moral compass."

—L. Brent Bozell, president, Media Research Center and
founder, Parents Television Council

continued...

"In an era when children are being systematically robbed of their childhood, Marybeth Hicks offers sound advice on how to let kids be kids and still grow up to be fulfilled, responsible, well-rounded adults. *Bringing Up Geeks* makes more sense than anything I've ever read on the subject of raising children."

—Pat Sajak, father, husband, and host of *Wheel of Fortune*

"Marybeth Hicks writes with a keen eye and a mother's loving heart in this hilarious guide to raising a child you can actually take out in public without cringing. Brava to Marybeth and her original and comedic voice."

—Adriana Trigiani, *New York Times* bestselling author

"*Bringing Up Geeks* is the most reassuring and valuable thing I have read concerning my most important job...being a parent. I want to raise my kids to embrace the right values, and not to simply seek out the 'cool' route. I want them to have the confidence and conviction to follow their hearts and recognize what is truly important to them. *Bringing Up Geeks* brings real clarity to a complicated process."

—Jay Bilas, husband, father, lawyer, and ESPN basketball analyst

"Let's cut to the chase: Every parent in America should own and read this book. Parents who don't will be at a huge disadvantage, because it brilliantly helps them understand and deal effectively and wisely with raising a child in our culture today. That's *the* most important and difficult job there is—and this book is simply an ENORMOUS help. It *could* have just been titled *The Parent's Handbook*. Do yourself *and your kids* a big favor: Get this book and USE it! You'll be thanking the author for many years to come."

—Eric Metaxas, VeggieTales writer and author of *Amazing Grace: William Wilberforce and the Heroic Campaign to End Slavery* and *Everything You Always Wanted to Know About God (but were afraid to ask)*

"Marybeth Hicks has provided readers of the *Washington Times* with years of parenting wisdom, and her new book *Bringing Up Geeks* promises to add to that extraordinary body of sage advice for every family seeking to engage the hearts, souls, and minds of their children in the midst of the current culture wars."

—John Solomon, editor in chief, *The Washington Times*

"Hooray for Marybeth Hicks! In her funny, original, and engaging new book, she shows us everything good about parenting against the culture. Far from being a nerd, this mom inspires us to raise GEEK kids by helping us see how they will be so much more cool than their peers when it comes to finding *real* joy in today's world—and tomorrow's."

—Betsy Hart, syndicated columnist, and author of *It Takes a Parent: How the Culture of Pushover Parenting Is Hurting Our Kids— And What to Do About It*

"Right on to raising happy, independent GEEKS! Rules and limits don't stultify children any more than strict iambic pentameter stultified Shakespeare. Marybeth Hicks encourages parents to stick to their guns and buck the sexy/cynical/smart-alec kiddie culture that most parents actually hate, but feel powerless to fight. I just hope it's not too late for me and my own kids!"

—Lenore Skenazy, columnist, *New York Sun*

"Marybeth Hicks has raised the bar for families. *Bringing Up Geeks* boldly challenges adults to act like their children's parents instead of their buddies. Geeks are the new cool."

—Lori Borgman, *Indianapolis Star* columnist and author of *I Was a Better Mother Before I Had Kids*

continued...

"*Bringing Up Geeks* puts a positive spin on being a geek. Hicks offers insightful rationale for raising brainy, sheltered, and principled children, along with an arsenal of helpful anecdotes and sound advice. It's cool to be uncool, and incorporating this paradigm shift will allow kids to enjoy the innocence of their childhoods, rather than be swept into our highly sexualized mainstream culture."

—Rebecca Hagelin, vice president, The Heritage Foundation and author of *Home Invasion: Protecting Your Family in a Culture That's Gone Stark Raving Mad*

"At last, someone is telling parents it's better to raise a kid for success in life than to be cool in the seventh grade. If your family is teetering at the brink of today's culture of cool (or even if you've been swallowed whole), pick up this book. Marybeth Hicks has emerged from the trenches to endorse common sense and courage in parenting."

—Jen Singer, founder, Mommasaid.net and author of *You're a Good Mom (and Your Kids Aren't So Bad Either)*

"If you're worried about your kids growing up too fast and struggle to keep your kids from the potentially harmful effects of MySpace, MTV, and racy music lyrics, *Bringing Up Geeks* has the answers you've been looking for. Hicks's practical, reassuring, and commonsense advice is a Godsend for moms and dads, whether they're just starting a family or have already hit the teen years."

—Tim Bete, director, Erma Bombeck Writers' Workshop and author of *Guide to Pirate Parenting*

"*Bringing Up Geeks* by Marybeth Hicks serves as a compass for finding and nurturing the good character in children. Parents stand to regain their bearings for doing the right thing from Hicks's clarity, kindness, and well-researched facts."

—Suzette Martinez Standring, syndicated columnist, GateHouse News Service and author of *The Art of Column Writing: Insider Secrets from Art Buchwald, Dave Barry, Arianna Huffington, Pete Hamill and Other Great Columnists*

"Finally! *Bringing Up Geeks* is the book I've been waiting for. In it, Marybeth Hicks—in her practical, unassuming, hilarious way—encourages parents and kids to leave our social-consciousness and worldly values behind and embrace being geeky. I, for one, couldn't be happier that Hicks is willing to tell the truth about what our goals as parents *should* be, as well as the awesome rewards of parenting the 'geeky' way. If you long to raise Genuine, Enthusiastic, Empowered Kids (and who doesn't?!), read this book."

—Dena Dyer, coauthor of *The Groovy Chicks' Road Trip to Peace*

Bringing Up Geeks

HOW TO PROTECT YOUR KID'S
CHILDHOOD IN A
GROW-UP-TOO-FAST WORLD

Marybeth Hicks

BERKLEY BOOKS, NEW YORK

THE BERKLEY PUBLISHING GROUP
Published by the Penguin Group
Penguin Group (USA) Inc.
375 Hudson Street, New York, New York 10014, USA
Penguin Group (Canada), 90 Eglinton Avenue East, Suite 700, Toronto, Ontario M4P 2Y3, Canada
(a division of Pearson Penguin Canada Inc.)
Penguin Books Ltd., 80 Strand, London WC2R 0RL, England
Penguin Group Ireland, 25 St. Stephen's Green, Dublin 2, Ireland (a division of Penguin Books Ltd.)
Penguin Group (Australia), 250 Camberwell Road, Camberwell, Victoria 3124, Australia (a division
of Pearson Australia Group Pty. Ltd.)
Penguin Books India Pvt. Ltd., 11 Community Centre, Panchsheel Park, New Delhi—110 017, India
Penguin Group (NZ), 67 Apollo Drive, Rosedale, North Shore 0632, New Zealand (a division of
Pearson New Zealand Ltd.)
Penguin Books (South Africa) (Pty.) Ltd., 24 Sturdee Avenue, Rosebank, Johannesburg 2196,
South Africa

Penguin Books Ltd., Registered Offices: 80 Strand, London WC2R 0RL, England

While the author has made every effort to provide accurate telephone numbers and Internet addresses
at the time of publication, neither the publisher nor the author assumes any responsibility for errors,
or for changes that occur after publication. Further, publisher does not have any control over and does
not assume any responsibility for author or third-party websites or their content.

The definition of the Six Pillars of Character are reprinted with permission.
© 2008 Josephson Institute. www.charactercounts.org

PRINTING HISTORY
Berkley trade paperback edition: July 2008

Library of Congress Cataloging-in-Publication Data

Hicks, Marybeth.
  Bringing up geeks : how to protect your kid's childhood in a grow-up-too-fast world / Marybeth
Hicks.
    p. cm.
  Includes bibliographical references.
  ISBN 978-0-425-22156-3
  1. Child rearing—Handbooks, manuals, etc. 2. Parenting—Handbooks, manuals, etc. I. Title.

  HQ769.H555 2008
  649'.7—dc22

                                                              2008001063

PRINTED IN THE UNITED STATES OF AMERICA

10 9 8 7 6 5 4 3 2 1

For
Pauline M. Brennan
and in memory of
Anita G. Hicks

*Two extraordinary women and gifted teachers
who taught me the power of a mother's love*

Acknowledgments

The thing about a book is that only the author's name goes on the cover. Yet I've concluded most books are the result of a fair amount of collaboration and this one is no exception. I have been blessed beyond measure by the efforts, interest, and commitment of many people as I wrote *Bringing Up Geeks*, so I'll start by acknowledging and thanking God for leading me to them and inspiring them to help me.

Chief among those collaborative souls is literary agent Jody Rein of Jody Rein Books. From the moment she read my query letter about raising geeks, Jody committed herself to making this book a reality. By sharing my vision and her expertise, Jody brilliantly and patiently taught me all I needed to know to produce the work you now hold in your hands. She is the consummate professional, not to mention a treasured friend and an awesome geek mom.

With literally thousands of potential titles to choose from each year, the folks at Berkley Books offered a coveted spot on their list to me; a vote of confidence for which I am most grateful. Thanks to Leslie Gelbman, Denise Silvestro, Meredith Giordan, Mary Ann Zissimos, Pamela Barricklow, and the grammatically gifted Marty Karlow.

I learned quickly that having a literary agent and a publisher would only get me so far. If you want to be successful as an author, you need "people." Publicist Robin Blakely of Livingston Communications has offered me her creativity and can-do attitude, plus more energy and enthusiasm than even I can muster some days. Robin sees the possibilities in all situations and dreams big. Better yet, she knows how to turn dreams into reality. That's what my kids call "skeels."

You aren't born knowing how to find a publicist. Well, most people aren't but Jen Singer was. In fact, I have come to believe that Jen, founder of mommasaid.net and author of several wonderful parenting books, was born knowing how to do everything. She was also born with the kindest, most generous spirit I have ever encountered, not to mention an iron will. Some people will offer a hand when you need it; Jen offers a ladder and instructions to reach beyond your best hopes for yourself. She sets the standard for true friendship.

Along my writing journey, I've been blessed with the support, insight, and friendship of many folks who deserve thanks: Maria Stainer, Patrick O'Brien, Elizabeth Solsburg, Sean Herriott, Wendy Weiss, Binyamin Jolkovsky, Lisa Hendy, Debbie Griffith, Tim Bete, and the entire Christian Humor Writers Yahoo group. I'm indebted as well to Fr. Charlie Irvin, Fr. Larry Delaney, Cindy Pastula, Mary Tardiff, and everyone at St. Francis Retreat Center in Dewitt, Michigan, for giving me a place to write and for their prayers. Thanks also to Dr. Kimberly Thompson for her advocacy on behalf of children and for joining my geek parenting crusade; to Michigan State University men's basketball coach Tom Izzo for a thirty-minute interview that lasted three hours; and to Fr. Joe Krupp for winter nights around the fire pit.

My husband and I have been blessed on our parenting journey with the wisdom and support of our wonderful families. Thanks to all our siblings, aunts, uncles, and cousins: the Brennans, Campbells, Radelets, Bernards, Pedisiches, O'Reillys, Gereks, and Gruns. Jim's late mom and dad, Anita and Jim Hicks, set wonderful examples for him, which are evident in his tremendous parenting abilities. We miss them. Special thanks to my parents, Pauline and Thomas Brennan, for your constant love and encouragement.

Thanks as well to a host of fantastic friends for the help you offer us and our children and the fun you bring to our lives, especially the

Schneiders, Swains, Freunds, Watsons, Lemmers, Davises, Winters, Lawrences, Kuhnmuenches, Lapines, Butkis, Nabers, Chisolms, Stringers, Todds, McDowells, Hinzes, Heberleins, Dewans, Clements, Japingas, Brogans, Kanes, Vercelli-Kennedys, and Loretta Subhi. Special thanks to Chris Janson and Tim Simpson. Our lives are richer for the friendship of two special couples: Theresa and Fred Foote and Mary Pat and Paul Sullivan.

Finally, for obvious reasons, I could not have written this book without the boundless love, selfless participation, and stalwart commitment of my family. Love and thanks to Scotty the dog, for warming my feet; to Amy, for your wit and your tender heart—you are the exclamation point in our lives; to Jimmy, for giving me the extraordinary experience of a son's love—you are my "Boy Wanted"; to Betsy, for a connection as natural as breathing, and for insights that make me a better mom and a better person; and to Kate—my teacher—you changed me forever on the day you were born and I am eternally grateful. To my husband, Jim, mere thanks are insufficient. Your devotion, support, confidence, and love are the real reasons I could write this book. I love you with all my heart.

Contents

Foreword

Every so often a book comes along that I tell my friends they absolutely must read. In the case of the book you now hold in your hand, my advice is that everyone should: buy it, read it, revisit it frequently, and live it! Raising "GEEKs"—genuine, enthusiastic, empowered kids—represents an enormous challenge in today's world. At last, Marybeth Hicks has provided a much-needed guide to help us do it. This book will undoubtedly become a leading resource for all parents who are committed to raising the truly wonderful children who will become successful adults. And if you're a geek mom or dad like me, take heart—this book proves that we are not alone.

As director of the Kids Risk Project at the Harvard School of Public Health, I spend a lot of time thinking about and studying children's risks and the ways that we can do our best for children. Yet as a parent, I believe one of the biggest risks facing our children is the unwillingness of many parents to step up and protect our children from a world that would exploit their innocence.

If you question the need for this book, take a close look at just one aspect of our modern world: the media. Once a shared activity and source of information (recall families sharing sections of the morning paper or huddled around a single radio or TV in the living room), media now segment and target us. Instead of bringing us together, today's media often divide families by age, gender, and interests. This means that many parents have no idea about the content in the media effectively teaching their children about life and what is "cool."

Should you worry? In 2008, the leaders of "cool" recognized Amy Winehouse with five Grammy Awards. Her autobiographical song "Rehab" offered an alarming twist on a major public health message: "just say no to drug rehab." Yikes. Maybe your child is more into award-winning video games. BioShock, rated "M" for mature players, with content descriptors for "Blood and Gore, Drug Reference, Intense Violence, Sexual Themes, Strong Language," received the Game Critics Award as the top game in 2007. While most parents use the Entertainment Software Rating Board game ratings to help them make decisions about content, most don't realize that the ESRB does not actually play the games before assigning its ratings. The ratings alone are not enough—parents need to consume media with their kids to truly appreciate the content.

This is just one part of the environment in which we geek moms and dads are trying to raise genuine, enthusiastic, empowered kids. It's not easy! Bringing up geeks requires a huge commitment. As parents, we have to be present in our children's lives and exercise authority. We must teach our children to make good choices both now and in the future.

Through the Kids Risk Project, colleagues and I quantify the risks posed to children from a variety of hazards, including messages in the media. One theme that emerges repeatedly in my work is the critical role that adults play in protecting kids and preventing bad outcomes, and the need for adults to pay attention to what is happening in children's lives. Let Marybeth Hicks help open your eyes and empower YOU to take action.

As you read through this book, you will appreciate the challenges of being a geek parent, but you'll also be reassured that you're not alone. This book offers simple instructions, and it will help you appreciate the value of bringing up a geek. I hope that you will use the great ideas in this book to strengthen your family and to support your journey as a geek parent.

The best part is that geeks are happy kids. They have strong values and passion for life. They have hope and promise. They're kids that adults like, and more importantly, they become the kind of adults we need more of in our world.

This is the time for us to take back our children's childhoods, and in doing so to claim our roles as strong, protective parents. We need dictionaries to include another definition of the word *geek*—as "a genuine, enthusiastic, empowered kid"—and leaders to call for more geeks and to commit to their growth and development. Read this book, declare your status as a geek supporter or geek parent, and create a better life for your family.

I join Marybeth Hicks in proclaiming loudly and proudly that: "I'm bringing up geeks!" and I hope that you will join us too!

Dr. Kimberly M. Thompson
Associate Professor and Director of the Kids Risk Project
Harvard School of Public Health
Boston, Massachusetts
March 2008

Bringing Up Geeks

Introduction

SO WHAT IF
WE'RE GEEKS

A few years ago I found myself at an all-school picnic—one of those harried, obligatory functions where children run amok and parents stand around having fragments of conversation. I can't remember if it was the beginning of the year or the end—as the mom of four children, my memories of these functions tend to blur—but I'll never forget a conversation that took place at this one particular event.

I'm standing in a circle of mothers, chatting about—what else?—our kids. At some point in the conversation I admitted that my children are geeks. I said this to be funny, but it's true. I know it. My kids know it. Most everyone who knows us knows it. And we're okay with that.

But one mom in the circle was shocked. "Oh, noooooo," she comforted me. "Your kids are very popular! Reeeally." She told me this as though, (a) I don't know what it means to *be* popular, and (b) this is my goal in raising my children. It's not.

I argued the point—with a smile, of course—but I got pretty quickly that she thought I was insulting my own children. "Why would you say such a thing?" she said indignantly.

"It's okay," I explained. "We like that our kids are geeks." I mean, as long as I'm comfortable with it, why wasn't she?

"That just isn't true," the mom insisted. Now she was getting upset with me. I'm thinking, *This is absurd. So what if we're geeks?* What started as a punch line quickly turned into a full-blown discussion about popularity and social status in children. (Is there a more dangerous topic among mothers? I think not.)

If I recall right, one of my children initiated a fortuitous meltdown (how often does *that* happen?), giving me a reason for a hasty exit. I trudged out to the van, all the while wondering why it was so important to that mom that my children be popular.

That was the first time I asked myself, *What's wrong with bringing up geeks?* We were doing it on purpose—and quite successfully, I might add.

The fact is, raising uncool children takes effort. As parents, my husband and I spend a lot more time than you might think thwarting the path to a robust social life in the fast lane. Are we sadistically imposing miserable childhoods on our four offspring just for the sport of it? Heck no.

We're simply committed to raising our children to have good characters and strong values. We are not raising them to be popular in elementary school and beyond. And the longer I'm a parent, the more I'm convinced these two goals often are mutually exclusive.

It's not like I set out to determine in advance which path would be best for our children—cool or geeky—and then snuck into some dark, dank parenting laboratory to cook up concoctions for an uncool life. Rather, over time and with each child, as my husband and I set our priorities, it has become clear that our parenting definitely plays a role in the social status of our children.

Our parenting style puts an imprint on our children—the label *geek*—because we resist things that would allow our kids to be considered "cool." As you'll learn in this book, we have reasons to eschew instant messaging, clothes from Abercrombie, iPods for preteens, and cell phones for children so young that we're legally responsible to know their whereabouts at all times—things most cool kids possess. While our children sometimes suffer the trials of being unpopular, we have determined not to change course because we put our values ahead of the social result those values might produce.

For example, at about the time the Spice Girls were the hot pop group, my daughter Katie started fifth grade. This meant she and her classmates got their first school lockers. Naturally, the girls decorated their lockers as though they intended to sleep in them at night, and the must-have locker decor turned out to be Spice Girls posters—or at least every photo of the group one could find in teen magazines, cut out and displayed in furry, pink magnetic picture frames.

Typically, I wouldn't have a problem with a celebrity photo taped to a locker door. But if you recall, the Spice Girls' outlandish and skimpy attire ran the gamut from tacky to tasteless. Call me crazy, but I didn't think it was appropriate to post photos of "Scary Spice" in her leather bustier on the inside of a fifth grader's school locker. I didn't permit Spice Girls, so instead, Katie taped photos of our family on vacation in New York City, along with a magnet of the Statue of Liberty.

Katie's locker was very uncool, but she liked it.

Who's Cool at School?

If it seems implausible that something as benign as decorating a school locker could have an impact on a child's social life, guess again. It does—and it's indicative of an overarching reality.

Social caste systems within schools have been around as long as children have defined themselves in the context of their peers. From elementary school through high school, certain children have always been crowned "cool" or "popular," and others are expected to admire and emulate these charmed children.

But being on the top rung of the childhood social ladder is different for today's kids from what it was for those of us now negotiating the rough waters of parenting. If the "cool crowd" once was good-looking, athletic, and socially successful, today's adolescent "A-list" is bold and cynical, and even jaded.

These days, popularity results less from sports success or personal attractiveness, and more from being immersed in the "culture of cool," a media-saturated, consumer-driven state of pseudo adulthood. From their clothes, toys, and gadgets to the attitudes and values reflected in their behavior, popular kids in twenty-first-century America are "in the know," conforming to the fads and trends transmitted through the media. Childhood popularity now is dictated by materialism, competition, and exposure to the adult world.

Being popular seems like the road to happiness, especially to a young girl, but popularity can lead to some poor choices. Research confirms that popular kids are more likely to engage in experimental or deviant behaviors in order to keep their elevated status. They succumb more easily to peer pressure than their unpopular counterparts and they're more willing to take behavioral risks in order to impress their friends.

A study by the National Institute of Mental Health confirmed that popular adolescents are likely to show greater levels of delinquency and drug use. "In short," the study said, "the more popular the teens, the more likely they were to get into trouble during the year in which they were followed."

What struck me as common sense—that as they get older, cool kids are more likely to drink, do drugs, have sex, and seek out dangerous adventure—turns out to be true. This is reason enough to discourage the cool lifestyle for my children.

What's the alternative to pursuing popularity and social prominence? In my home, the answer is: bringing up geeks.

The Geek Alternative to the "Culture of Cool"

The encounter at the school picnic those many years ago forced me to consider the reasons why I labeled my kids "geeks." If I think about it, I suppose it's not exactly flattering since the term has long described the outcasts of the social scene who have little understanding of trends and fads, and instead pursue their own quirky and often intellectual passions. Geeks have hardly any sophistication and even less savvy.

But is this a bad thing? Not for a child.

In my mind, a geek is an empowered kid enjoying an innocent childhood, and a parent raising a geek is choosing and doing the *right* things: promoting a family system in which innocence is protected, media is limited, pop culture is regulated, consumerism is held in check, relationships are fostered, spirituality is encouraged, and an ideal of excellent behavior is taught and expected.

In a culture where being cool is the ultimate goal, what does the geek alternative look like? Here are a few examples:

* My son Jimmy and his best pal enjoy a sleepover at our house. Rather than chat online with friends or make prank phone calls (common practices at middle school sleepovers that we don't allow), they get my husband to join them in a round of Risk—*Lord of the Rings* Edition. Their strategy game goes until well after midnight.

* In her sophomore year, my daughter Katie hosts a party for roughly twenty-five boys and girls from her class. After pizza and pop, they collect in small groups all over the basement—some play cards, some board games; some just chat and hang out. Eventually they decide to perform for one another the songs they're planning to sing at the upcoming auditions for the school's spring musical. We watch the show along with two couples who have joined my husband and me to chaperone the party. (No one cares that there are parents in the room.)

* Daughter Betsy wants a tenth-birthday party but we're reticent; we think the level of gift giving at kids' parties has gotten out of hand. Instead, she asks her guests to bring a housewarming gift for a refugee family. The girls enjoy a wrapping party to package up their contributions, and then go caroling in the neighborhood.

* Amy contends she is the only girl in her third grade class without pierced ears. Our family policy is no pierced ears until age
ten, and then only if other aspects of personal care are handled
appropriately. When she occasionally complains about this rule
we remind her that our goal is to keep her from growing up too
quickly.

These are just a few glimpses into the geek lifestyle—there will be
more in the chapters to follow. As you can see, it's not exactly radical
or even remotely unreasonable. But it is a lifestyle that hinges on raising children to be "late bloomers" in a culture when most kids hit "full
bloom" in their tweens.

Because of this, geek parenting, when viewed against the cultural
norm, may at first seem strict or tough. As you're about to see, I'm
asserting that adults *can* and *should* create standards for their children—and those standards should reflect our best hopes and dreams
for our kids. Contrary to some comments I've heard as I have developed the geek parenting strategies outlined in the chapters that follow,
this way of raising children is not strident. They may not be culturally
"cool," but my kids are happy and well adjusted, and they will be the
first to tell you that their parents are loving, affectionate, and fun! In
fact, here's an irony—I'm "the cool mom" according to my children's
friends. And yet I'm certainly known as a demanding parent who sets
the bar high and expects kids to reach it.

Where I set that bar is the foundation for the geek lifestyle. Just how
do I get from this theoretical concept to the notion that it all boils down
to bringing up geeks? Well, first you need to understand what I mean by
the term *geek*.

REDEFINING WHAT IT MEANS TO BE A G.E.E.K

In my vernacular, a geek isn't the stereotypical dork or nerd of days
gone by. No horn-rim glasses, pocket protectors, short pants, or body
odor. A geek isn't a "loner" or "loser"; and he's not without strong

social skills. In fact, a geek exhibits social competence based on excellent manners, knowledge of etiquette, consideration of others, and genuine self-confidence.

Since my goal is to engender positive self-esteem, I wanted my own children to see the term *geek* as a good thing. So we redefined what this label means by creating an acronym for the letters *G-E-E-K*—it stands for *Genuine, Enthusiastic, Empowered Kid.*

* **G**enuine: Geeks are kids who are wholly themselves, free to explore their interests and passions without worrying about what they "should" or "shouldn't" be doing according to the dictates of the popular crowd. Genuine geeks aren't wannabes, conforming to what's cool for the sake of acceptance, but instead are confident to pursue their individuality.

* **E**nthusiastic: Unconcerned about being ostracized by the cool kids, geeks embrace life with enthusiasm. They get excited about science projects, great works of literature, visiting a museum, having dinner with relatives, or singing at the school concert. They don't act condescendingly disinterested, but rather accept any experience as an opportunity for fun and learning. They're not "too cool" for anything.

* **E**mpowered: Geeks are empowered because they develop on all levels—intellectually, emotionally, socially, physically, and spiritually. As they enjoy the benefits of a happy, uncool childhood, they learn about the world beyond their immediate experience. They grow to care about issues and ideas; they're idealistic and passionate about their beliefs. Though they sometimes struggle with exclusion or feeling out of sync with peers, geeks understand that growing up sometimes is hard, but rewards await them in the future.

* **K**ids: Geeks truly enjoy their childhoods. Protected by their parents from a world that asks them to grow up too fast, they mature appropriately through the natural passing of time, not artificially

by immersion in a harsh or vulgar culture. Geeks are kids until they emerge into adulthood armed with knowledge, wisdom, and authentic character.

AGES AND STAGES FOR GEEK DEVELOPMENT

At every age, you'll discover that geek parenting is a matter of reordering your priorities to reflect your values and summoning the courage to make decisions that are different from many—if not most—of the parents you know (perhaps trusting your instincts more than you previously have). Throughout this book, you'll see that geek parenting is relevant at virtually every stage of a child's life. However, I've discovered a few watershed stages that seem to lend themselves to charting the course for the geek lifestyle. (Exact ages may vary for your kids.) At these times the decisions and choices you make will have a major impact on your child's social status:

* **Kindergarten** Kindergarten is an exciting new beginning, but it's also an eye-opening time for parents. When the school bell rings, it signals not only the start of the highly competitive world of academic achievement (yes, even in kindergarten!), but also the social positioning process. If preschool was a time when most parents taught their kids to play nicely with all the boys and girls in the classroom, kindergarten is the time when children— with the help of their parents—begin to form cliques and social structures.

* **Third/fourth grade** Social hierarchy is fully established at about this time. Self-awareness and intellect have developed enough by age nine for children to understand that there is a popular group and to know if they are part of it or not. If they are, children at this age start to assert power ("you can't play here," etc). If they aren't in the popular group, children at this age begin developing strategies to cope—either by embarking on the ardu-

ous task of becoming cooler, or by finding other uncool friends. For parents, this is the time to encourage children to explore their many and varied interests and to help them seek out kindred spirits.

* **Seventh grade** This is the year I have deemed "the line in the sand." Seventh graders on the social fast track have full access to the culture of cool—freedom to absorb media messages about sex, violence, and partying through TV, movies, Web sites, and music lyrics; freedom to communicate via the Internet and with personal cell phones; freedom to adopt the predominate value system of consumerism and instant gratification. Parenting at this age is crucial in determining the path of the geek lifestyle. If, to this point, some social boundaries have remained fluid, seventh grade is the time when you finally must draw a line and choose which side of it you're going to stand on. It's sometimes shocking and often disappointing to realize that many of the families you thought were similar to yours now are making choices you can't support.

* **Sophomore year** The transition to high school having already taken place, sophomore year is a watershed because it includes the added mobility offered by a driver's license. For popular, cool kids, this means the freedom to further push the behavioral envelope. For uncool kids who want to be included in the cool crowd, it could mean taking on the role of designated driver. For geeks who are happily uncool, it means the freedom to get ice cream on the way home from the library. Around this time many parents believe the majority of their parenting job is done ("kids are going to do what they want anyway," etc). In the geek lifestyle, the exercise of parental authority is not concluded just because a child has reached his or her adult height. Geek parents believe a high schooler still has a lot of growing up to do—and a lot of active parenting is needed to help foster true maturity.

Cool and Uncool Parents

Naturally, our parenting platforms begin with our life experiences. As we develop our parenting styles, we tend to adopt or reject the styles of our own parents. Classically, we women sometimes find after a number of years that we one day open our mouths and our mothers come out in a freakish, familiar reincarnation. Just as we can't escape the imprint our parents made on us, we also can't forget the experiences of our childhood social lives.

Whenever I speak to parent groups about raising geeks, the first question I ask the audience is "Were you cool as a child or were you a geek?" There have been times when my entire presentation could have focused on this question and the impact it had in life. This is because every adult—no matter how old or mature or successful—can still tell you who was popular in the seventh grade and whether that person was a friend or foe.

Asking about parents' childhood popularity elicits some interesting responses. Some folks are defensive, assuming I'm pointing a critical finger in their direction. Others are sheepish—they know they were popular and they're not totally comfortable with their social history. Still others shoot their hands in the air when I ask who in the audience was a geek—it's almost as if they want a prize for being survivors. What's fascinating to me is the similarity in responses from group to group, city to city.

What follows is in no way scientific—it's merely an anecdotal observation on my part—but my informal research (if you can call "can I see a show of hands?" research) has taught me that parental attitudes about childhood popularity play out in four prevailing parent types:

* **Parents who were popular as children and who want popular kids** These parents expect their children to follow in their cool, popular footsteps. Popularity equates with success and is sometimes so important to these parents that they cultivate

friendships with the parents of other cool kids and use parenting decisions to promote their children's social status. In the extreme, these can become so-called toxic parents who buy their kids booze and pot, host prom-night sleepovers, and generally play the role of "über-buddies," not parents.

* **Parents who were unpopular as kids but want their children to be popular** These parents may have endured taunts or exclusion and are determined their own children will enjoy more socially successful childhoods than they had. They make decisions that allow their children access to the culture of cool.

* **Parents who were popular as children but don't want this status for their own kids** These parents realize that being popular wasn't important after all. Looking back on their popular status as children, they may regret some of their own behaviors or attitudes, or else they recall their youths as painful and unpleasant despite the outward appearance of being happy. They make decisions that assure their kids' experiences are different from their own.

* **Parents who were geeks as kids and want their kids to be geeks too** Whether out of a sense of resignation or a genuine understanding that popularity in childhood had little to do with happiness in life, these parents know that their social status as children isn't a plague that their offspring should avoid at all costs. They may be empathetic with their kids' social situations, yet their parenting reflects a desire to instill genuine self-confidence and nurture their children's authentic personalities.

THE MEANING OF CHILDREN

There's another question I pose when speaking to parent groups. While it isn't the main focus of this book, it's a crucial self-study question as you consider the attitudes that drive your parenting decisions. Ask yourself: "What do my children mean in my life?"

What does my question imply?

Presumably, we have children in order to enjoy the innumerable benefits of family life. Yet sadly, our culture has produced parents for whom children are not just a family, but an accomplishment. Driven by their children's achievements, these mothers and fathers engage in parenting as a competitive endeavor in which every aspect of life is open to comparison and improvement. They tout their children's successes in school and on standardized tests, in sports, music, and the arts as reflections of their parental acumen (or their gene pool or the money they spend on lessons and tutors—you get the idea). The notion that children are twenty-first-century "trophies" continues to gain attention in psychological and parenting literature, and it's honestly too big an issue to tackle here. Suffice to say, the attitude that children represent an adult achievement can create parental pressure for kids to be socially superior. This is a major reason why some children quite literally *need* to be popular and cool.

Taken to its most extreme levels, this kind of parenting is resulting in a tragic trend according to psychological and psychiatric professionals. In her book *The Price of Privilege,* Dr. Madeline Levine chronicles her findings after concluding that her pediatric therapy practice had become rife with affluent children and adolescents whose parents are providing material possessions and freedom, but whose families are defined by emptiness, depression, and hopelessness. Dr. Levine notes that parents, especially in affluent communities, often focus on "what a child does, not who he is." The result is a generation at risk for long-term psychological struggle as it tries to find real happiness and contentment.

Wanting good things for your children doesn't necessarily mean you have impure motives. We all want our kids to succeed academically and in other areas and to be well regarded by friends, teachers, and the community. As we help our kids "do their best," we're all subject to the pressures around us that tell us how to measure ourselves as parents and how to analyze the well-being of our kids.

But if we start to believe that our children reflect our social status, or if we feel more successful because of their abilities and accomplishments or because of the stuff we can give them, we may unwittingly be promoting the cool lifestyle. Ultimately, we can find ourselves making choices and decisions that don't reflect our best hope for our children—that they become the people they were meant to be—but instead support the goals of popularity and social dominance.

PARENTING BY PROXY

If some parents manipulate their kids' popularity, others seem not to understand that the issue can be cause for concern. They make decisions by proxy, simply going along with whatever it seems "everyone else" is doing. It's a form of benign consent that causes families to drift into a lifestyle mandated by the whims and desires of popular child leaders and the culture in which they are immersed.

The more I talk to people—especially young moms of preschoolers—the more I understand that many of today's parents aren't implementing lifestyle choices that reflect their own values and beliefs, but rather they're adopting values practiced by "everyone" they know. While their children are young, they may be in complete accord with each other about what constitutes appropriate media, for example. Then one day they discover that their five-year-old has seen an episode of *The Simpsons* while at a friend's house, and suddenly there's a decision to make about whether to go along with this standard of media supervision or take a different path.

A child's upbringing ought not to be accidental or thoughtless. As a culture, we ought not to ride a collective wave of parental capitulation, conforming to behaviors and attitudes we aren't choosing or even evaluating. And just because "everyone" thinks it's impossible to achieve an ideal environment for children doesn't mean we should drop our standards of what the ideal could be—it just means we should work harder to figure out how to do a better job of parenting despite the challenges our culture presents. Giving up means we can rightly fear that the sheer force of the cultural current will wash our children into a torrent of behaviors and attitudes that reflect a whole lot of stuff we may find abhorrent.

Taking Charge: Geeks and Parental Authority

I once read an article about a middle school girl who was the victim of cyber-bullying by a classmate. The story chronicled months of abuse and relational aggression on the part of an eighth grader. In the article, the reporter asked the mother of the victim what steps she had taken to protect her daughter. The mother said, "I wanted to call the school or the other girl's parents but my daughter *wouldn't let me*." (Italics emphasize my general outrage.)

I know what this mom meant—that her daughter probably begged and pleaded for her not to get involved for fear it would make matters worse. But the phrase struck me like a "bolt of enlightenment." This mom put the decision about her role as a parent in the midst of a difficult and potentially dangerous situation into the hands of her thirteen-year-old daughter. She wanted to assert herself as the adult authority figure in her daughter's life, but she instead surrendered her authority to her child.

Um... "my daughter wouldn't let me"? Sorry. No.

Suffice to say, establishing and exercising parental authority in the home is the first and most important job of every parent. Without authority—and the respect that ensues from it—implementing the geek lifestyle will be a challenge. This is because children's respect will be crucial when the time comes to make decisions and choices that are contrary to what they want (and totally unlike the choices most other parents make).

When I speak to mom and dads' groups, I usually remind them that God created parents for a reason—because kids don't know what's good for them. Left to their own devices, most children would feast each night on Froot Loops, pizza, and Mountain Dew and quit school after the fifth grade. Step one in establishing parental authority is to remember that this is how families were meant to be structured. *Parental authority is yours to claim.*

Am I suggesting you adopt a militaristic demeanor and run your household like a drill sergeant at boot camp? Of course not! (In fact, the result of asserting appropriate authority in your home is that you ultimately spend less time on issues of conduct and responsiveness, and more time on the good stuff.) Yet oddly, when I talk about authority, some people immediately assume I'm advocating a hypercontrolling, unyielding, and unemotional parenting style. That's just not true.

In psychological literature, parental authority generally is illustrated as a continuum from permissive parents who seek to be buddies with their children to authoritarian parents who are inflexible and unyielding. In the center are *authoritative* parents who are both appropriately warm and attached to their children, as well as appropriately demanding. Authoritative parents set high standards for behavior and implement consistent discipline, but they also are nurturing, understanding, and supportive even when their children fail to meet those standards (which, as all of us will admit, is pretty much all the time).

In her book, Dr. Levine counsels parents to assert their authority firmly. "Various studies have found that firm parental control is associated with children who can take care of themselves, who are academically successful, who are emotionally well developed and who are happier." (She could have said "who are geeks"—it would have been quicker!) While some folks shudder at the idea of exercising authority, believing it's a throwback to the parental Stone Age, it's the lack of authority in the home that clearly is chipping away at healthy family structures and the capacity for parents to play a useful role in the formation of their children.

OBEDIENCE IS NOT SUCH A BAD THING

In geek parenting, Mom and Dad's rules, judgments, and decisions must be regarded and obeyed simply because mom and dad know what's best for children. I use the word *obey* around my house—my kids know that this is our expected standard of compliance. It doesn't mean we're raising "Stepford children" who may never assert their opinions or ideas. It means that obedience is something we value, and conversely, disobedience will meet with correction and discipline.

Apparently, some experts think obedience is bad, while cooperation is good. For example, Dr. John Gray, author of *Children Are from Heaven,* says, "Past parenting approaches sought to create obedient children. The goal of positive parenting is to create strong-willed but cooperative children. A child's will doesn't have to be broken in order to create cooperation. Children are from Heaven. When their hearts are open and their will is nurtured, they actually are more willing to cooperate." I have to say the only sentence in that paragraph by the expert Dr. Gray with which I agree is the idea that children are from heaven.

For some reason, the word *obedience* conjures images of robotic children, overbearing, unreasonable parents, and negative approaches such as yelling and hitting. This is just ridiculous! In fact, a home in which children learn to obey mom and dad is a home where there is less conflict, less emotionalism, and more harmony.

In my view, raising obedient kids is a great thing—especially when you're yelling "Stop!" to a toddler who is heading toward the street, or when you ask your high school senior to meet his midnight curfew. In these cases, obedience assures safety.

Children first need to understand what it means to be obedient. When my kids were little, I quizzed them with a fill-in-the-blank question: "To obey means..." I'd let my voice trail off, whereupon their little voices would respond in unison, "to do what you are told." (Okay, it was a little bit "Stepford," but it worked.) The point is, I taught them a simple definition that they could understand and follow.

When they are small, we naturally require obedience and assert parental authority over our kids when we hold their hands across a parking lot, maneuver their wriggling bodies into a car seat, or respond with a forceful "no" when they climb on the bathroom sink. In these simple ways, we demonstrate to our children that we're in control and we expect compliance and respect. Usually, we do these things firmly yet lovingly, not angrily, thereby creating a sense of comfort in the fact that we're protecting them.

As they grow and their expectations of our authority are established, we can ease up. Obviously, I long ago stopped my pop quiz on the definition of obedience! Still, when I sought their cooperation, I relied on my children's experiences of my authority. Over time, they learned to obey as they were praised for satisfying our requests and commands, and when they suffered consequences (including punishment) for ignoring or refusing us. Sometimes I explained myself ("we're saving the juice boxes for lunches, so please don't drink them for snacks"); at other times, I just lay down the law ("turn off the TV and go outside to play"). "Because I said so" also works.

WE DON'T LOSE AUTHORITY, WE GIVE IT AWAY

As they grow, children test our authority—this is *their* job. This is how they figure out what the limits are and what happens to them if they challenge our boundaries. Just because children test our parental authority doesn't mean we've lost it—rather, it means we need to continually prove to them where the authority rests.

We never really lose our authority unless we give it away. Negotiating with children, bargaining for the behavior we want, threatening but failing to follow through with discipline, ignoring behaviors that ought to be unacceptable—these are the habits we can fall into that gradually chip away at the perception that we are the ultimate arbiters for behavioral standards. Inconsistency is another problem that results in a lack of respect for parental authority. When we're inconsistent we send two crucial messages: "sometimes I care about this behavior and sometimes I don't"; and "sometimes you have to listen to me, and sometimes you don't."

Perhaps the most damaging way we give away parental authority is for mom and dad to exhibit two conflicting values about it. Kids figure out quickly which parent is more demanding and which one can be counted on to let things go, and they tend to use this observation to their own advantage. So, for example, when Junior wants to stay up late on a school night using the computer, he might go to dad for permission because he knows mom will say no. Later, while his parents are busy bickering about whether he should be in bed already, Junior is happily playing interactive games with people the world over. No point arguing about who has the authority in the family. Junior does.

Like the mom who allowed her daughter to decide whether she should get involved in the cyber-bullying problem, parents lose authority when we don't stand up and act as responsible adults. Afraid to face the ire of children who know they can simply pitch a fit and get what they want, many parents promote the very behavior that frustrates and confounds them.

THE PITFALLS OF PERMISSIVENESS

I'm not a sociologist or a research psychologist, so I don't have statistics on the phenomenon of parents as "über-buddies." I just know, because I've been at it for a while, that the world is full of parents who are intent on being their kids' best friends rather than the primary authority figures in their lives. They think the only thing that matters is to foster closeness and this is much more important to them than setting appropriate limits or demanding compliance with behavioral standards. They often think this approach makes them "cool parents," but as I said earlier, you don't have to be permissive to be cool.

To get close, buddy parents often exhibit the worst possible judgment an adult can have, especially as children grow into teenagers. The worst-case examples of parent buddies are "toxic parents" who provide alcohol and drugs for their teens' parties, "supervise" gatherings of teens by collecting the car keys while handing out beers, and blindly head off to bed leaving slumber parties of young people to crash (or do whatever) in all the rooms of their homes. Parent buddies reason that their kids are going to do things regardless of what they, the parents, recommend (there's that standard of mediocrity), so why not keep them drinking and smoking pot at home rather than out and about where someone can get hurt? They also reason that they themselves behaved similarly when in high school, so where's the harm? Partying is just what all teens do.

Actually, there's plenty of harm. Several states now are holding parents legally responsible for the underage drinking they permit in their homes, and in some states, when drugs and alcohol have been implicated in car wrecks involving teens, the adults who provided the substances have been held accountable and even jailed. It's a big deal to ply kids with alcohol, not only because it puts teens at risk but because it undermines the parental authority of other parents.

Buddy parents also tend to make excuses for their kids' poor choices and step in to fix things when their kids make mistakes. These practices also erode authority because they send the message that children needn't be accountable for their actions—mom or dad can always come to the rescue.

Not to mention, permissiveness breeds bad habits. The reason a toddler throws a temper tantrum to get what he wants is that he knows his mommy will do anything to make his screaming stop. The reason, at age ten, this same boy buzzes off his mother's directive to turn off the Xbox 360 and come to dinner is that he knows she'll zap his meal in the microwave whenever he decides to eat it. And the reason, at sixteen, he is unconcerned about his eleven-o'clock curfew and instead rolls into the driveway at 2 A.M. is that he has concluded, over his brief lifetime, that nothing really bad is going to come of it. Grounded? *Whatever.*

In parenting groups, I'm often asked how to establish authority. The simple answer is to *claim it.* State your expectations and the consequences for noncompliance, mete out discipline *consistently* (in two-parent homes, consistently *as a couple*), and remind yourself that while children may balk (okay, children *will* balk), deep down they want limits. Limits are how they know you're paying attention to them. Limits are how children feel your love.

SETTING LIMITS, DEFINING EXPECTATIONS

Throughout the past eighteen years, I've learned that the discipline strategies and tactics I use in parenting my children must naturally evolve as my kids grow and as our family matures. At various ages, I've used different tricks and tools of the trade, and these change since you can't exactly send a high school senior to the corner for a time-out, can you? Myriad resources exist on best practices for discipline, and at different times I've probably employed any number of them to drive home the message that my parental authority prevails.

If my methods of discipline have varied, what hasn't changed—and what my children have grown to count on—is my commitment to consistently set standards and limits, and to make decisions that reflect what we value in our home. For this reason, no matter what age or stage they reach, my kids generally figure mom and dad will have geeky responses to whatever issues arise.

Of course the premise here is that my children know what we value. In teaching them our moral, ethical, religious, and social beliefs, my husband and I have created the framework within which we set standards and limits for our children. This is why, in the fifth grade, my daughter knew there wasn't any point in asking if I would take her to see the Backstreet Boys in concert at $60 per person, as most of her friends were doing. She already had learned that I didn't value the group's lyrics about sex and that I wouldn't pay $120 to take a ten-year-old to a major concert at a football stadium.

Beyond limits and the rules we set for our children, we parents also need to define our expectations. If limits are the way we say no to our kids, standards and expectations are the way we say yes—as in, yes, you can win the geography bee; yes, you are capable of pleasant conversation on the phone with dad's boss; yes, you are smart and mature enough to read the novel I just finished. Generally, I think we can do much more to raise the bar of parental expectations and, ultimately, to improve the outcome of our parenting efforts. I'm not talking about raising the level of competition for grades and test scores, or heaping pressure on kids to be starters on the basketball team or the fastest runners on the track.

Rather, I'm talking about elevating our expectations of respect, maturity, accountability, and responsibility in the next generation. Instead of accepting the notion that children are incapable of better behavior, especially as they enter adolescence, I'm convinced our kids will meet us where we expect to find them. For this reason, I have eschewed the myth that all teenagers become monsters who "dis" their parents as they separate and become emotionally independent.

As my kids got older, I started to dread their teen years because I was warned time and again that our relationships absolutely would suffer. Yet I stubbornly refused to believe that I had to endure being treated like a potted plant by my own children just because they were entering high school. Instead, my husband and I have asked our young teens to make a commitment to treat us with courtesy and respect. We've told them that growing up means exhibiting maturity, not indulging in moodiness and eye rolling. They're free to disagree with our decisions and to tell us how they feel about things, but they're not free to raise their voices or slam doors.

I'm proud to say we're busting that myth about teenage monsters. Disagreements can and do occur, and we all get frustrated from time to time, but the foundation of courtesy and respect always remains. The reason is that we expect something better than what our culture tells us is typical teen behavior (more on this issue in Rule Number Four).

I'm not alone in believing children will reach the bar we set for them. Judge Glenda Hatchett, TV jurist and author of the book *Say What You Mean and Mean What You Say,* says we must "expect greatness…it's not the greatness that matters, but the expectation of it, the reaching for it, the setting it out as a goal or ideal." Her experiences as both a parent and as the authority figure in the lives of young people at risk have convinced her that our culture too readily accepts mediocrity as the standard for behavior in children. I agree. Our kids are capable of much more. Believing this—and setting my expectations accordingly— is a cornerstone of bringing up geeks.

HANDS-ON PARENTING

Something else that has stayed the same as my parenting journey
has unfolded is the sort of "hands-on" parenting my husband and I
employ. Simply put, we are intimately involved in the lives of our four
children, from their school to our neighborhood, from their extracurricular activities to their social lives. Being involved doesn't mean we're
out to raise dependent children who can't think or act for themselves.
We're not "helicopter" parents hovering over our kids' every move,
intent on following them to college and beyond! Instead, being "hands-
on" means we're always around in some appropriate, supervisory
capacity.

We're the drivers to their school dances, we attend their sporting
competitions and sometimes coach their teams, we talk about homework assignments and give help when needed, we go to teacher con-
ferences. We know who their friends are—and just as importantly, we
know the parents of their friends. We spend time just talking about
what's going on—listening and learning about the day-to-day events
that shape their young lives.

I'm not going to lie. Parenting this way is relentlessly time-
consuming. I haven't watched an uninterrupted episode of *Law &
Order* in years. To be "hands-on," you truly have to be willing to sacrifice your time and expend the physical and emotional energy that it
takes to stay completely focused and involved with your kids each and
every day.

But the way I figure it, the risks posed by any alternative style are
simply too great. This is because a lack of involvement on the part of
parents leaves a gaping hole that is quickly filled by an overactive social
life and the influence of an unyielding media whose messages corrupt
and confuse our children. Staying "hands-on" is our insurance policy
against the prevailing popular culture.

What's Really Cool Anyway?

Ultimately, I'm asking you to reconsider what's really cool. Do we have to buy into the fads and trends that fill the media and preoccupy modern American children? Must we define ourselves by what we own, or worse, by what others think about what we own? Does immersion in popular culture make us happier, more powerful, more successful?

In my home, here's what we think is cool: being who you really are, doing stuff you love to do and are passionate about, having faith in yourself and in God, sharing your gifts and talents with the world, respecting and accepting others and celebrating them as individuals, resisting the urge to conform for its own sake, being authentically *you*.

Yet you would be astonished at the people who say this view of children and the parenting style that achieves it is simply *unrealistic*. What a sad, sardonic conclusion! Parents who believe it's not possible to influence their children in this way are in one sense giving up on them, leaving the culture to determine what's best, or at least what is common.

Bringing up geeks is a parenting style that can't be pigeonholed in any particular political or religious point of view. It's a way of life that works for families of every faith and any political outlook. In fact, I often point out that it doesn't matter if an eighteen-year-old canvasses your neighborhood on behalf of Rock the Vote or the National Rifle Association; they've both been raised very similarly—as geeks.

Ever since I launched my newspaper column and started writing about my geek-parenting journey, I've heard from countless mothers and fathers who share my belief that the culture war now is being fought in their own homes and the culture is "cool." They're not satisfied that immersion in this culture is worth the price of innocence and the outcome of cynicism, and they want support in maintaining a parenting system that results in good kids—great kids.

Geeks are great kids, the kinds of kids you admire and respect. They're sometimes the quarterbacks of the football team or the stars of the school musical; but just as often they're the secretaries of the Spanish club or members of the debate team. They're high achievers in whatever they choose because they choose to do things that light a fire in their hearts, not just what's considered cool or trendy. They're "teacher's pets," the kids coaches enjoy coaching, the ones you can count on as babysitters and community volunteers. They may be overlooked when it's time for their fellow high school seniors to vote for "best smile" or "most likely to be famous." But just wait and see who's smiling in ten years; and wait to see who actually gets famous.

At our house, we remind our kids, "geeks rule the world."

My goal with these ten geek strategies is to launch a child-rearing movement that promotes innocence over exploitation, substance over style, and genuine self-esteem over superficial acceptance. I hope they inspire you toward your most courageous, effective, and satisfying parenting experience.

Rule #1

RAISE A BRAINIAC

One day my daughter Amy announced to me, "Mom, the word of the day is *behold*."

"Behold?"

"Yes. As in, behold, I am eating my Froot Loops." This is how my morning unfolds with Amy, aka "Vocabulary Girl."

Once, the word of the day was *huzzah*, the term of approval and glee used in colonial times. Another day, the word was *authorized*, as in, "Mom, you are authorized to use the word of the day, which could be *authorized* or *unauthorized*."

Huzzah. I am authorized.

A varied vocabulary is a good thing—a result of reading and listening and usually a sign of a brainiac, so we encourage the use of new words. But mostly we encourage it because words interest Amy—she collects vocabulary the way some kids collect bugs or bracelets or stickers.

Of course the difference is, unlike displaying your sticker collection, using big words in the fourth grade is a surefire way to get labeled a geek. In fact, an advanced vocabulary seems to be the plight of the uncool. Eventually, your friends say things to you like the comment one child made to Amy: "You're so mini-ful, but you use such big words." (Amy didn't know whether to be insulted about her small stature or her unusual expressions.)

But Amy doesn't really care. She loves unusual words more than she loves the idea of being just like all the other kids. One day when I asked her what the word of the day was, her eyes lit up as if a spark had caught flame. "I don't have one," she said. "Got any suggestions?"

"I like the word *propensity*," I said, "as in: your propensity to use interesting words makes you a brainiac." We talked about what the word *propensity* means and how to use it in conversation. She thinks she has a propensity to wiggle around in her seat. She's right. She does.

Beyond Performance: What It Means to Be a Brainiac

Just what is a brainiac, anyway? *In my geek vernacular, a brainiac is a child who believes he's smart, who loves the process of learning, and who indulges his natural curiosity for the sake of satisfying his need to know new things.*

Note I did NOT say a brainiac is a superior student, or one who achieves high test scores, or one whose IQ is over a certain number. My definition of a brainiac has nothing to do with performance, and everything to do with learning. Now, obviously these two things are likely to converge at some point in a child's academic experience. But for now—for the sake of understanding the distinction from a parenting perspective—let's keep them separate, to the extent we can.

That isn't easy. When it comes to cognitive development, "achievement America"—that segment preoccupied with results—uses every available test and measure to quantify children's capacity. From the time they're conceived, some babies are nurtured with the sounds of Mozart and Bach. They hear poetry (or maybe the *Wall Street Journal*) read aloud to them through mom's burgeoning belly for the purpose of enhancing brain function, with the ultimate goals of a perfect SAT and admission to a Tier One college (after completion of a Tier One preschool, that is).

Formal education launches with developmental child-care programs intended to enhance intellectual capacity. Throughout elementary and middle school, kids are tested and retested, not only to establish individual achievement but also to substantiate whether schools are satisfying their educational mandates. Eventually, academic competition is elevated to such extreme levels that virtually every child is "exceptional." To what end? A few years ago, a high school in my area actually graduated fourteen valedictorians with grade-point averages above a perfect 4.0 (weighted grades for AP classes, in case you wonder how that's possible).

From academic kindergarten classes where students are expected already to be reading on the first day of school, to the proliferation of tutoring businesses on nearly every suburban street corner, the focus of society's attention with respect to learning is to help children compete and excel. It's all very high pressure and, in my view, very unsatisfying. Where's the fun in learning as a competitive endeavor?

Excellence is good. It's great, in fact. I'm all for it. My four children achieve excellent grades most of the time, though admittedly Amy cannot get higher than a C in handwriting. Go figure. But I contend the reason my kids do well isn't that my husband and I emphasize the importance of getting good grades. Rather, the reason they're high achievers has more to do with their attitudes about learning—attitudes we helped them develop early in life—as well as their self-concepts of being capable and smart. In short, we convinced them they are brainiacs.

So just how are brainiacs different from other kids?

Brainiacs are the kids who read ahead in the book even if the teacher assigns only a few pages for homework because the subject matter is interesting and they want to learn more about it. They incorporate new information into daily life, mentioning something they learned about plants, for example, as they're outside weeding the yard with you. Brainiacs are good listeners, absorbing information from daily conversation as well as from the classroom and various media. They soak in knowledge like proverbial sponges, making connections in their minds between an observation about a current event and a lesson from history class.

Brainaics are interested in the world around them, and as well, they typically have a passion for a few subjects that challenge and fascinate them. Stereotypically, they like math and science, but the brainiacs in my house actually are more literary than scientific. Brainiacs are not "right"- or "left"-brained; they can be either. What they all have in common is a desire to learn something new every day because if they don't, brainiacs are easily bored.

Brainiacs and the Geek Lifestyle

Being a geek almost always suggests the stereotype of being "a brain." But the reason "Raise a Brainiac" is Rule Number One has nothing to do with advancing the stereotype and everything to do with implementing the geek lifestyle.

Consider this: A 2001 Yale University study found that teens who identified themselves as "brains" (as opposed to "popular," "jocks," "burn-outs," or "nonconformists")—kids who report doing well in school and enjoying academics—are the least likely to smoke, drink alcohol, use drugs, and have unsafe sex. One collaborator on the project said, "The findings were not entirely surprising, but they do suggest that we may be able to learn a lot about adolescents' potential for risk-taking behavior simply by knowing their reputation among their peers."

Think about that for a moment. Even if your teenage daughter does well in school, being known by her friends as being part of the popular crowd means she's statistically more likely to engage in high-risk behaviors. On the other hand, if she's known as a "brain," she's statistically less likely.

Personally, I'd prefer that my adolescent children are not out drinking doing drugs, or having sex. And better, I'd like them to enjoy learning and, yes, to do well in school. I'd also like them to find a peer group of similarly lower-risk friends. So raising a brainiac actually has merit as a safety strategy to keep kids out of trouble, as well as a tactic to help them reach their full potential.

But let's be clear—"brainiac" and "popular" are two very different social classes, for research purposes as well as in every school cafeteria across America. This is because it takes time and effort to be either smart or cool, and usually you can't effectively do both simultaneously.

SMART ENOUGH TO BE COOL

Despite the benefits of being a brain mentioned above, plus many more that are just obvious (greater opportunities, more college choices), kids still yearn to be cool and popular more than they yearn for phone calls from people asking for help on the chemistry exam. But here's an interesting observation about brainiac geeks: They're smart enough to figure out what it would take to be cool and popular, but they aren't willing to sacrifice the rewards of being smart to do it. In his book of essays entitled *Hackers and Painters,* computer guru Paul Graham comments on this paradox in a piece called "Why Nerds Are Unpopular" (he uses the word *nerds,* but try to overlook it):

> If someone had offered me the chance to be the most popular kid in school, but only at the price of being of average intelligence (humor me here), I wouldn't have taken it...Much as they suffer from their unpopularity, I don't think many nerds would. To them the thought of average intelligence is unbearable. But most kids would take that deal...who wouldn't drop thirty [IQ] points in exchange for being loved and admired by everyone?...And that, I think, is the root of the problem. Nerds serve two masters. They want to be popular, certainly, but they want even more to be smart. And popularity is not something you can do in your spare time, not in the fiercely competitive environment of an American secondary school.

Smart kids who enjoy learning and are turned on by new information like to incorporate all their interests in their social conversations. But this is one of the very reasons why they can't attain popular status. When you're gathered with your fellow seventh graders, it's just not cool to talk about what's in the news unless you're discussing the latest story about Paris Hilton or *American Idol*. Not that a brainiac wouldn't care about such things, they're just not the only things they want to talk about. A child who mentions last night's presidential candidates' debate—and not in the context of social-studies class—is just not considered cool (except by adults, but that's the subject of an upcoming chapter).

A brainiac would have to give up his true passions and only concern himself with popular culture in order to fit in. The problem is, once you're hooked on Jane Austen or www.sciencenewsforkids.org or the History Channel or *The Forsyte Saga* on DVD, you really have to think twice about giving those things up just to go to the mall.

WHY BRAINIACS ARE READERS

Something else brainiacs won't give up is the company of a good book. Studies prove kids aren't reading for pleasure as regularly as they should, but those who do, reap the rewards that only reading can offer. Consider these facts regarding reading and its relationship to and impact on learning and overall achievement:

* Kids who read well in the early grades are far more successful in later years.

* Fourth graders who reported daily reading for fun scored higher on a national reading test than peers who reported less reading for fun.

* Studies of individual families show that what they do to support literacy in the home is more important to student success than family income or education.

The folks at Scholastic Books discovered that kids believe reading is important, too. In a survey they commissioned:

* Ninety-two percent of kids enjoy reading books for fun and 90 percent say reading books for fun is important.

* Nearly two-thirds of kids surveyed agree that they have to be a strong reader to get into a good college and that being a strong reader will help them get a good job when they are older.

* High-frequency readers are more likely to describe themselves as smart, a good student, creative, and well behaved.

The evidence is compelling, if not obvious. Reading for pleasure promotes general literacy, cognitive development, and success in a variety of subjects, and also promotes the self-concept of the brainiac.

So let's say we all agree that reading is good for kids. Here are a few more statistics that ought to rattle us:

* Children spend only about one hour per week reading for pleasure, with little variation in reading time among children of different ages.

* The average time per week that the American child between the ages of two and seventeen spends watching television is nineteen hours, forty minutes. That's slightly less than three hours per day.

* Almost three-quarters of parents surveyed say they value reading as the most important skill for a child to develop—followed by critical thinking, math, and social and computer skills.

* While two-thirds of parents agree that strong reading skills are critical to future success and 80 percent say it is very important for kids to read books for fun outside of school, only 21 percent of parents identify themselves as high frequency readers.

We may say we want our kids to be readers, but America's parents aren't modeling what it means to be an avid reader and, in fact, we're not raising a generation of readers. We're raising a generation of TV watchers (and also Internet surfers, and instant messengers and electronic gamers and sports participants and even personal groomers— one study shows kids spend more time primping than reading). But readers? Not so much.

WHY BRAINIACS ARE NEWS JUNKIES

If you're a sixth-grade girl in the USA and you know who Lindsay Lohan is, you're a fairly typical sixth grader. If you know the names of both Lohan and Nancy Pelosi, chances are you're a brainiac. If you only know Pelosi...well...that's just not possible.

It's plausible to say not all juvenile news junkies are brainiacs, but I've yet to meet a young brainiac who wasn't a news junkie. And according to the research on this subject, a heightened interest in current events is yet another predictor for the geek lifestyle.

The Pew Research Center for the People and the Press learned that most school-age children are not regular news consumers. Only 29 percent of today's kids follow news about national and international issues. The vast majority don't follow the news at all. Overall, where current events are concerned, the disconcerting trend is toward a disinterested youth.

Research shows what little news kids do follow generally is about teens, celebrities, sports figures, and media. Spending as much time with media as they do, they're familiar with mega-stories that dominate the headlines (think Hurricane Katrina, Britney Spears, Brad and Angelina's family, etc.).

Topics such as world affairs, politics, economics, and science don't interest young people, but this doesn't mean these topics can't interest them. Schools where current events are taught as part of the social-studies curriculum tend to produce students who become more intrinsically interested in following the news. It stands to figure, then, that you could produce the same effect by promoting this habit in your home.

But why bother? Why encourage our children to become regular readers of newspapers, for example?

It's all part of implementing the geek lifestyle. Raising a newspaper reader promotes a brainiac outcome. Consider these findings from Dr. Edward F. DeRoche in his book *The Newspaper: A Reference for Teachers and Librarians:*

* Newspapers help teach students to be effective readers.

* Newspapers can help develop and improve student vocabulary, word-recognition skills, and comprehension.

* Newspapers are effective tools for teaching many math concepts, particularly fractions, decimals, currency, and averages.

* Students who use newspapers tend to score higher on standardized achievement tests—particularly in reading, math, and social studies—than those who don't use them.

* Students who read newspapers in school tend to continue reading them when they become adults.

Do I include this shameless plug for newspapers in my book because I happen to be a newspaper columnist? Am I trying to help children grow into geeks or am I transparently promoting my own best interest?

Don't be ridiculous. Of course I'd like all good little geeks to grow into regular readers of my weekly column. Why wouldn't I?

Nonetheless, I want to stress that children benefit from developing an interest in the world around them. We can't expect our kids to evolve into a generation of learners and leaders when their worldviews are limited to the comings and goings of a Britney Spears and the steroid-laced sports exploits of a Barry Bonds. To be effective citizens of the world—

and to take responsibility for the world—they need to know it's even out there.

WHY BRAINIACS ARE ARTISTIC

Another stereotypical image of a brainiac is the band or music geek. Our modern folklore conjures a mental picture of a mousy, if not homely, girl, settling herself into the first chair of the orchestra's cello section, pushing her glasses up her nose as she reads music through the stringy hair that hangs in her face. Poor little thing.

I don't know why our collective mental picture instead isn't a Renaissance geek—a brilliant and artistic child whose heart and soul resonates with beauty and inspiration. After all, most artists from history and even today are known for intelligence, insight, and perception.

Still, image-wise, a band geek is a band geek and that's just the way it is, and while we're at it we can lump the drama kids and the visual-arts kids into the mix. But let's all stop pitying the arts geeks because research emphatically proves that studying the arts as a child—especially music—actually makes them measurably smarter. And according to the Web site www.artsusa.org, the benefits of arts are evident elsewhere, as well. Young people who participate in the arts are:

* Four times more likely to be recognized for academic achievement
* Three times more likely to be elected to class office within their schools
* Four times more likely to participate in a math and science fair
* Three times more likely to win an award for school attendance
* Four times more likely to win an award for writing an essay or poem

Young artists, as compared with their peers, are likely to:

* Participate in youth groups nearly four times as frequently
* Read for pleasure nearly twice as often
* Perform community service more than four times as often

Not everyone lives in a school district where the arts are rigorously taught (or even taught at all, since budget shortfalls have mandated cuts in core curricula for many schools). All the more important for us to promote the arts in our homes, where children are coincidentally free to be geekily enthusiastic about surrealism or jazz or the sound track from *Wicked*—whatever artistic expression makes their boats float. As a strategy for bringing up geeks, incorporating the arts into the life of your child can't be beat.

WHY BRAINIACS ARE FUNNY

It's impossible to make sweeping generalizations about the senses of humor of all brainiacs since every person's sense of humor reflects his unique personality and experiences. But hey, it's my book, so I'm going to generalize anyway: Brainiacs, being somewhat more articulate and well versed in a variety of subjects than other children, tend also to have relatively intellectual senses of humor. Which is not to say that a brainiac child will not laugh at a fart joke. All children will laugh at a fart joke, as well they should.

However, most humor (other than physical or visual humor) involves words and wordplay. This is why children who use and appreciate a breadth of vocabulary and have knowledge of myriad subjects have access to a wider range of humor.

Moreover, having a good sense of humor is really important for a host of reasons. Research about children and humor proves that a well-developed sense of humor reveals and also feeds a well-developed intellect. In addition, a good sense of humor both fosters and promotes strong interpersonal skills and also improves the overall learning process. Plus, not for nothing, laughing kids are happy kids.

Not only have researchers discovered how a sense of humor helps a child, they also have documented the stages of a child's developing sense of humor, from initial smiling and laughing in infancy to the silliness of a preschooler's humor to an appreciation of riddles as a seven-year-old, and so on. Each stage in childhood offers opportunities to find the fun in life; as parents, we need to look for reasons to goof and giggle because it's good for our children (and good for us, too).

BRAINIACS AND ACADEMIC SUCCESS

As you'll see in the pages to follow, there are things you can do to help your child reach his full intellectual potential and, in my mind, the reason to employ these suggestions is that they're inherently good for kids—they help children to become all they are able to be. To be clear, the reason to do these things is *not* to give your child a leg up on the competition when the time comes to take standardized tests or apply to high schools or colleges. I think helping kids to be smart is a valuable goal in and of itself, since achieving it allows them to enjoy and appreciate the world through the eyes of curiosity and competence.

Having said this, I can't deny that there's a commensurate benefit in the real world to raising brainiacs: Brainy kids do well academically and kids who do well have more and better opportunities in life. That's just the way it is.

In fact, what we've discovered in our parenting journey is that we don't have to teach or tell our kids to be academically competitive. The desire to do well as compared to their peers is something they value on their own because it's a natural reflection of their particular skills and gifts. Moreover, that competitive spirit some parents work so hard to instill is very difficult to impart to another person—at least, not without creating an unhealthy emotional relationship.

Just observing my own four children has led me to conclude that the "killer instinct" in a competitive situation must be an inborn thing—some kids have it and some don't. For this reason, the notion of promoting learning as a competitive endeavor will fail in a child who doesn't care about "winning" on the academic battlefield. They're bound to give up that natural curiosity if it's all about high achievement. Talk about a lost opportunity!

Instead, throughout childhood, learning must be a pleasure for its own sake. Ideally, a brainiac child will discover that it feels good to be on the honor roll and thus his efforts to learn may be rewarded. But beware the temptation to push kids to succeed or to put too much focus on grades and test scores. When we do this, we sap all the energy out of their curious spirits.

As children get older, competition in academics becomes more evident and unavoidable. We've worked carefully with our children to broaden the focus for high school from effort to outcomes in their academic performances, since many of the choices available to them later depend on their overall school success. I say we've worked carefully because we haven't wanted to dampen their learning habits in favor of a hypercompetitive grades-are-everything point of view. Rather, we've let them know that they can look forward to a wider range of choices in the future if they're willing to work hard and do well.

In this vein, I'm not opposed to using available resources to help kids learn more effectively, especially as academic material gets more difficult and the stakes get higher, as they do in high school. Tutors, seminars, test-prep classes, and online resources all are good things and often are necessary to help kids learn effectively. Not every child needs these things to succeed, but those who do can benefit in better performance and greater self-confidence. The fine point to consider is this: Are we enrolling kids in a course or getting a tutor because they really need assistance, or because we can't bear to lose that competitive edge?

Some people might say I'm splitting hairs here. Am I saying "compete, but don't say you're competing"? No. I'm saying "learn all you can, and in doing so, enjoy the fact that you will be competitive and successful." The difference is one that keeps the focus on learning and reaping the benefits of educational pursuits.

How to Help Your Child
Become a Brainiac

A cautionary tale: I've always hated dinosaurs. I think they're boring, they're ugly, and I'm not surprised or unhappy that they became extinct. I can't spell their names—I can't pronounce most of them either—and truth be told, I can live very happily without ever visiting a dinosaur exhibit at a museum, watching another *Jurassic Park* DVD, or even seeing the opening sequence of *The Flintstones* where Dino jumps all over Fred, licking him puppy style.

So imagine my chagrin when my only son, Jimmy, at about age three, became passionately interested in dinosaurs. Beyond the typical preschool affection for Barney, the irritating yet educationally impeccable PBS dinosaur, Jimmy developed a fascination with the real thing—prehistoric beasts of every size and shape. Each evening before bed we read dinosaur books; each day he played with a growing collection of plastic dinosaur figurines. Though only a preschooler, he knew all their scientific names and could tell me which ones were herbivores, which were carnivores, and which were omnivores. He knew which dinosaurs hailed from the Mesozoic period and which from the Jurassic. He pored over the pictures in his dinosaur encyclopedia for hours on end, sharing each factoid with me again...and again...and again.

Did I mention I hate dinosaurs?

No matter. I learned to love them because of the joy they brought to Jimmy's life.

Jimmy's dino fixation is a great example of the capacity for virtually any child to learn about something that lights the fire of his imagination. For some kids the topic might be trucks and other kinds of transportation; for some it's dolphins; for some it's bugs, frogs, and turtles; some kids love planets, stars, and space; some delve into presidential history or state capitals.

Regardless of the subject that fascinates a young child, this natural curiosity is the cornerstone on which I urge parents to raise a brainiac.

FOSTER AND ENCOURAGE YOUR
CHILD'S NATURAL CURIOSITY

Remember, my definition of a brainiac is one who loves learning and indulges his natural curiosity to satisfy a need to know more. It's not about native intelligence, because let's face it, not everyone is born with exactly the same intellectual capacity. For example, some of us (not me) are blessed with exceptional memory, and of course, having a great memory is very helpful during one's school years. Without it, even a bright person might struggle to get good grades on tests.

But extraordinary native intelligence—the kind that gets you into Mensa—isn't required to become a brainiac. What is required is a thorough understanding on the part of parents of how a child's natural curiosity correlates with a desire to learn, and further—and just as importantly—an understanding of the role you play in advancing this process.

In an article entitled "Curiosity: The Fuel of Development," Dr. Bruce Perry explains:

If a child stays curious, he will continue to explore and discover. The 5-year-old finds tadpoles in a tiny pool of mud on the playground. This discovery gives him pleasure. When he experiences the joy of discovery, he will want to repeat his exploration of the pond. [Pleasure leads to repetition.] Each day, he and his classmates return. The tadpoles grow legs. [Repetition leads to mastery.] The children learn that tadpoles become frogs—a concrete example of a complex biological process. Mastery—in this case, understanding that tadpoles become frogs—leads to confidence. Confidence increases a willingness to act on curiosity—to explore, discover, and learn.

A big key to this process is confidence. As children gain confidence, they naturally reach further beyond their comfort zones to discover new and more interesting things. Confidence feeds curiosity, and curiosity "fuels development." This is where parents (and teachers) come into play, as summed up by Dr. Perry: "The most positive reinforcement—the greatest reward and the greatest pleasure—comes from the adoring and admiring gaze, comments and support from someone we love and respect... This approval causes a surge of pleasure and pride that can sustain the child through new challenges and frustrations. Approval can generalize and help build confidence and self-esteem."

In short, when our curious child shares his discoveries with us (Jimmy: "Mom, check out this Ankylosaurus."), our positive response to his exploration (Me: "Cool, dude. I didn't even know there was such a thing as an Ankylosaurus.") fosters the self-confidence needed for further exploration and discovery.

What Dr. Perry describes is simply a circular learning process:

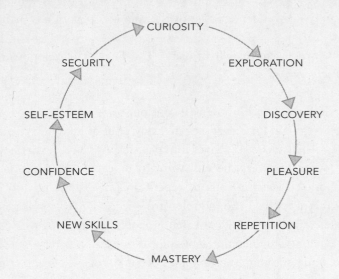

This shows how a child stays curious. But how does a child lose his curious nature? Fear, disapproval, or an absence of a supportive and enthusiastic adult.

A fearful child already is looking for a safety zone, so he's unlikely to go out on a limb to find intellectual adventure. A disapproving environment (think, "don't get dirty," "don't touch that rock," "don't ask questions") is one in which curiosity is inhibited. And the lack of an approving adult means there's no one around to cheer on that curious kid and, as well, no one with whom to share his discoveries.

It's easy to understand this concept by considering a dino-obsessed three-year-old. But what about older kids? Can they continue to be curious and, in the process, feed the self-image of a brainiac? Absolutely.

To wit: Katie's fourth-grade passion for all things *Titanic*. It was the year of the movie blockbuster by director James "King of the World" Cameron. Being geek parents, we didn't allow our ten-year-old to see the film, but Katie had heard about it from her friends and was curious about the *Titanic*, big-time. I encouraged her to find a book about it at the library. Well, in short order she read every book about the *Titanic* she could get her hands on. She read some of those books two and three times. She became a walking History Channel on the sinking of the *Titanic*. In fact, her fixation became so complete that I had to remind her that this wasn't just the plot of a hit movie, but in fact represented a human tragedy of magnificent proportions. In any case, yes, even a tween can invest herself in learning about an interesting new subject if her curiosity is piqued and her exploration is encouraged.

DISCOVER AND EXPLOIT YOUR CHILD'S SPECIAL SKILLS

Another aspect of learning that comes into play as we raise brainiacs is the idea of multiple intelligences. This is a theory developed in 1983 by Dr. Howard Gardner of Harvard University. He suggested that the traditional idea of intelligence as measured by IQ tests was too limited. Instead, he said there actually are eight kinds of intelligence:

1. Linguistic intelligence ("word smart")
2. Logical-mathematical intelligence ("number/reasoning smart")
3. Spatial intelligence ("picture smart")

4. Bodily-Kinesthetic intelligence ("body smart")
5. Musical intelligence ("music smart")
6. Interpersonal intelligence ("people smart")
7. Intrapersonal intelligence ("self smart")
8. Naturalist intelligence ("nature smart")

I remember when I first learned about Dr. Gardner's theory, I finally felt vindicated. I've never taken an IQ test, but I did take the SAT and let's just say my score would not have allowed me to be a student of Dr. Gardner up in Cambridge. Nonetheless, I always knew I was smart in many ways that weren't covered on standardized tests. Every child exhibits strengths in one or more areas of intelligence when viewed in this holistic approach. So even if a child isn't "smart" in the ways that are traditionally rewarded in the school setting, he most certainly will excel in some aspects of intelligence.

As a parent raising a brainiac, your job is to help your child discover the areas in which he exhibits the greatest facility and build on the natural tendency to do well in those. Some children are gymnasts, some are pianists, some are artists. Some exhibit such exceptional interpersonal skills that from an early age you'll swear they're meant for politics, while others are drawn to nature and flourish whenever they're able to interact with the natural world. From a parenting perspective, it's crucial to help your child discover his strong suits and give him both opportunity and encouragement to exploit those. Doing this, coincidentally, builds self-confidence, which propels a child to feel capable when approaching tasks within other areas of intelligence that may represent a greater challenge.

RAISE A READER

The benefits of regular reading outside of school having been well established, just how do we create households of young readers? As in all things, our children will develop the habit of reading as we teach them that it's something we value. To do this, imagine you are creating a three-legged stool on which your brainiac reader can sit and enjoy a good book—the first leg is to be a model reader, the second is to create opportunities for reading, and the third is to assure the availability of appropriate reading material.

Model Regular Reading Habits

All the research says kids learn to be leisure readers by example, so be an avid reader yourself! Your children should see you reading the newspaper, magazines, and books routinely. Leave a book in your car for times when you must wait in lines or sit at a sporting event. Keep a stack of books on the bedside table so your child sees that you also read before bed. Read before bed!

Equally important as setting an example is reading aloud to your children. You can start in infancy and don't stop even when they're old enough to read to themselves. (My husband used to hold a baby bottle in one hand and the sports page in the other while reading stories aloud about the Yankees. I think it was some sort of indoctrination thing.) Once your kids can read, take turns reading aloud to one another.

Let your kids hear you talking about books. Tell them about the books you're reading, and when gathered with other parents, ask what they're reading and steer the conversation toward books—let your kids hear you discussing your reading lists.

Join and occasionally host a book club. Let your children see you as a literary person whose friends are readers.

Collect books and be sure your home evidences your reading habit. Buy used books from the library and at garage sales as well as new ones from the bookstore.

Create Opportunities for Regular Reading

One of the most challenging but best ideas to raise a reader is to set aside reading time for children every day. I say challenging because simply maneuvering around the seemingly endless activities on the calendar leaves hardly enough time to brush our teeth much less read books, but all the more reason to make reading intentional. Bedtime works for most families, but consider also allowing a book at the breakfast table (or at lunch or dinner if it's especially casual or you're not sitting down as a family).

Certainly the biggest rival for reading time is the television. You've got to be the one to turn it off. And while you're at it, turn off the computer, electronic game systems, and other forms of electronic entertainment and suggest reading instead.

Use "junk time" for reading. Keep a book for every child in the car for travel time. Put kids' books in the bathroom and encourage young children to take their time and read a few pages. Help them develop the habit of having a few books going at the same time—one in the car, one next to the bed, one in the backpack. In this way, reading becomes more varied (just like watching a variety of TV shows).

Declare "reading roundups"—gather up the kids, pour a cool drink for everyone, and meet in the living room for twenty minutes of shared reading time. (I only can do this when we're on vacation or during the summer. It's totally unrealistic at any other time of the year due to hectic schedules—but it works!) Occasionally initiate a family book club—choose a book everyone can read and enjoy, take turns reading it (or read it aloud), then spend a family dinner discussing it.

Help Find Good Reading Material

The biggest complaint of kids who don't read is that they can't find anything to read that interests them. This is where we parents need to do a better job of helping our kids identify the genres that excite them. The children's librarian at your local public library, your school librarian, or the manager of the kids' section at a good bookstore can help you choose new material that isn't familiar to you. Also, think back on the books you liked as a child—my husband and I both enjoyed books by Beverly Cleary and it turns out our kids love them, too.

An alarming number of kids have TVs in their bedrooms these days (more on why that's alarming in the next chapter), but do our kids have enough books in their rooms to prove they're readers? Create a personal library for every child in your family. Put bookshelves in their bedrooms and help children collect books. Give a book to your child at every gift-giving occasion. Use a book as a reward for good behavior, achieving a special goal, or reaching a major milestone (keep a list of titles that you and your child have created so you'll know what to pick when an opportunity comes up). Pass books from older to younger kids. We make a big deal out of cleaning out the bookshelves and handing off books to the next child—I love listening to the "book talks" by the older kids as they tell their younger siblings which ones they loved best and why.

As they've grown older, I've had the fun of sharing books from my bookshelves with my older daughters. For example, they've grown to love every book by author Adriana Trigiani, whose work is written for adults but is completely appropriate for mature teens. I once hosted my book club to discuss one of her books and we even had Adri on the phone for an author conference call. *That* was a night when my girls realized how cool it is to be a reader.

To vary the reading content for your kids, in addition to hunting down good books, subscribe to age-appropriate magazines. Kids love to get mail and receive a new magazine each month. Just make sure the magazines you choose reflect your values, not only in editorial content but in advertising. I love *American Girl* magazine because there aren't any ads; *Girls' Life* and *Boys' Life*, the official magazines of the Girl Scouts and Boy Scouts, are terrific examples of wholesome, fun magazine content—and you don't have to be a scout to get them. There are tons of kids' magazines, and they make great gifts.

USE A VARIED AND RICH VOCABULARY

Truth be told, each of my children has at one time or other been accused of being weird for using unfamiliar vocabulary. In the seventh grade, Katie even endured persistent accusations that she read the dictionary for fun. Imagine reading the dictionary for fun. What kind of anomalous oddball would scan the pages of the dictionary in pursuit of entertainment? Geek? Make that freak. She denied it because no middle school girl with a modicum of self-awareness would ever admit that she finds it fascinating to learn the definitions of new words and, even more unthinkable, looks for opportunities to use them in conversation.

Not that she "dumbed down" to fit in, but she wasn't looking for a label (egghead, weirdo, bookworm, mutant—take your pick—they all mean the same thing to a twelve-year-old). Was it true she read the dictionary? Indubitably (a word Katie still loves to use).

It's hard to learn new words these days, even if a child is a reader. This is because of the trend to simplify the vocabulary of modern-day children's literature on the assumption that easier words make for more voracious reading. I suspect, however, it's only resulting in a generation of people who may never encounter so-called rare words. Watching TV and hanging out in cyberspace aren't teaching children many new terms either, other than acronyms and slang. Culturally speaking, it takes a determined parent to teach descriptive words that reach beyond the limits of *cool, stupid,* and *awesome,* rhythmically enhanced by the persistent use of the word *like.*

The best way to help our children grow a strong vocabulary is to use one when talking to them. Once you define a word for your child, start to use it more regularly in conversation, and soon enough, it simply assimilates into the known words stored in his ever-expanding brain. For example, when my children were small, I adopted the phrase *I don't negotiate with children* as an answer to the incessant begging so characteristic of kids to whom the word *no* has just been uttered.

It only took one or two times to define the word *negotiate* before they understood my meaning. By age five, any one of them might ask, "Are you open to negotiation?" when trying to get his or her way.

I'm not a linguist and I'm not going to belabor this point, but let me add that raising an articulate child doesn't begin with baby talk. Just as a foreigner is not made more able to understand the English language when it's spoken at a higher volume, a child is not made more cuddly by replacing the letter *r* with the letter *w*. Speak articulately and you will teach articulation; use a strong vocabulary and you will teach the use of a strong vocabulary.

PROMOTE THE HABIT OF FOLLOWING
CURRENT EVENTS

Even in our high-tech world of 24/7/365 news coverage, studies show that while a majority of Americans get their news from television, the best-informed people are still those who read newspapers. To help your child become a bona fide news junkie, you need to create motive and opportunity to read the paper. Here's how:

Subscribe to a Newspaper

As in all things, we parents must model the behavior we want our children to exhibit. Parents who pay the least amount of attention to issues of the day also are the least likely to encourage their children to follow current events. Conversely, the children of parents who read newspapers are the most likely to follow this example. Why not just watch the news together on TV? There's nothing like newsprint on your fingers and nothing can replace the cadence and character of the conversations you can have while sharing the pages of your daily paper.

Encourage Your Child to Read About
What Naturally Interests Him

Learning to read the newspaper and otherwise follow current events is best achieved in the same way you encourage other kinds of brainiac behaviors—gradually and naturally. Don't force a child to read a lengthy commentary about the latest congressional budget battle; instead, entice him with tidbits that attract his desire to learn about cicadas or hybrid cars or a juggling contest at the local shopping mall. Even a reluctant reader can find something of interest in a newspaper. Introduce the sports section, movie and book reviews, feature stories, and recipes. Preschoolers can read the comics; everyone can work on the crossword, word jumble, or sudoku puzzles. As children make a habit out of reaching for their favorite sections of the paper, encourage them to scan the front page and local sections for interesting stories.

Talk About News Stories

As your child grows, ask questions like, "Hey, did you see the story about the robbery on Main Street?" or "What did you think of the quote from the governor?" Treat your child like any other newspaper reader—even if he's not exactly devouring every section yet. In this way, you'll send the message "I'd like to know what you think about the stories we might both find interesting." When your child wants to read a story aloud to you that he finds fascinating (or gross or disturbing—whatever)—even if you've already read it—let him recite it and listen attentively. It's sometimes time-consuming, but in a good way, and it's extremely cool to realize your child is such a news junkie that he is becoming your own personal anchorman (or anchorwoman, as the case may be). Also, ask about how the news is presented at school and what teachers and friends are saying about big news stories.

Expose Your Newspaper Reader
to More News Sources

Age-appropriate news outlets abound, thanks to school-based news sources such as Channel One and Scholastic News and television news segments geared for kids. Find out if your school uses these or other news sources and make sure you talk to your children about what they learn through these outlets. Establish the connection between reading the daily newspaper and watching or reading school-based news outlets. Kids love to be the first ones to know and tell "the news," so capitalize on the childhood propensity to be competitive in this regard.

Finally, invite your budding news junkie to join you for a newsmagazine on TV or a documentary on a topic that interests you both (but avoid letting kids watch coverage of gory or sensational stories such as school shootings without vigilant supervision and limit their intake of video footage) and subscribe to a few newsmagazines, including specialty magazines on favorite sports or hobbies.

INCORPORATE MUSIC AND THE ARTS
INTO YOUR CHILD'S LIFE

Assuring that your child gets enough of the arts is one aspect of geek parenting that's just plain fun. Arts education is a crucial part of a well-developed school curriculum, so I'd certainly encourage participating in arts programs at your child's school (especially since volunteers often are needed to make such programs go!). But bringing the arts into your home will make all the difference in helping your child to become a brainiac, since exposing a child to the breadth of visual and performing arts nurtures his intellect while feeding his soul. Plus, the arts bridge the gap between generations, offering something your whole family can do and enjoy together. Here's how:

Bring the Arts into Your Home

Rather than just accept the notion that kids will only listen to what's currently popular on the radio, give them credit for the capacity to appreciate a wide variety of music. Especially when they're young, expose your child to all kinds of musical styles. Every so often, turn off the Saturday-morning cartoons and blast a CD of your favorite jazz artist or Broadway-musical sound track (yes, really). Introduce your kids to the rock-and-roll bands you loved when you were younger and show them that you still know all the words. Long car rides are especially good for exposing kids to different music. Having done this for years, our kids even have favorites—songs they'd never ordinarily listen to but have become our traditional travel music. So, for example, if we're driving at dusk, someone will ask for *The Best of Van Morrison,* and when we're about an hour from our vacation destination, don't be surprised to see our van rocking to the late Beau Jocque and the Zydeco Hi-Rollers.

Music surprises kids. They think they won't like something, but with exposure to new styles and a little bit of background information, they can learn to appreciate all kinds. Get CDs of choral music—especially children's choirs—as well as opera and vocal recitation. Put them on every so often in the background as you do chores or while you're cooking. Don't make a big thing out of it; just play them.

Make your home artsy not just because it adds beauty to your house, but because it's good for your kids. Hang real art on your walls. Even cheap, local art is better than a preframed print from the mall. Hang your kids' art on your walls, too, not just on the fridge. Every so often, splurge on professional custom framing of one of your child's pieces of art and place it in a prominent spot.

Find the Arts Outside Your Home

Again, it's fun to realize that exploring the arts in your community actually makes you a darn good parent. It's difficult to find the time and the money for season tickets to a local theater or for regular gallery walks on the weekends, but that doesn't mean you can't frequently work an arts event into your life. The trick is to make this a casual prospect, not a "field trip." Turning kids on to the arts—whether it's attending a play, visiting a museum, seeing a concert, or just wandering a street fair—should feel like a natural part of life, not like a chore or an academic experience.

Vacations are a great time to explore the arts. No matter where we go, we try to take advantage of a museum or gallery in the area we're visiting, and there are very cool museums everywhere. You can make these excursions fun, like the time we took our kids to the National Gallery in Washington, D.C., and brought along sketch pads and pencils for all four of them. Every so often, they'd sit on a bench and try to sketch a famous work hanging on the wall. Giving them the freedom to do this gave them an excuse to sit down every so often and eliminated the whining about being bored that we might have expected.

Your ability to immerse your family in the arts in your community is limited only by your imagination. There's a ton of free stuff from poetry readings to concerts in the downtown plaza to authors' visits at the local bookstore. Make it a priority to nurture this aspect of your child, and you'll show him that you value the arts and the beauty they bring to life.

Nurture the Artist Within Your Child

Once you bring the arts into your home and you're regularly heading out the door to enjoy the arts in your community, you'll fast discover you are raising a budding artist, in one capacity or other. To the extent you're able, offer music lessons, a dance class, or a drawing class. Encourage your child to audition for a play at school, or if there isn't one, check out the auditions in the paper for children's theater. Find a children's choir either at your church or through a community music program. And give your child the chance to try lots of short-term artistic activities so he can figure out which area suits him best.

Here's the challenging part, especially in our sports-obsessed, over programmed culture: insist that your child pursue *something* in the arts. We've made it a requirement that our children play a band instrument and join the band at school. This means in addition to the regular music class that all kids must take, ours get a few extra hours each week of music by playing in the school band.

This strategy has had varying degrees of success as far as musical development goes. Katie flourished on the flute and continues to play, anticipating joining the orchestra in college. Betsy and Jimmy, playing the clarinet and trombone respectively, probably won't pursue it beyond high school. Amy's just choosing an instrument and getting ready to join the beginner band. They've all taken at least some piano, as well, to promote their music appreciation (it's also supposed to help with math!). Do I expect to have a preferred seat someday at Carnegie Hall when one of my children debuts a new piece of original music? Um...no. But will they all appreciate the effort and intricacy of a band or orchestra whenever they hear one? Absolutely. And that's the point.

HAVE FUN AND BE FUNNY

Helping your child develop a great sense of humor even a sophisticated and intellectual one—strikes me as a hugely self-serving aspect of parenting. We shouldn't assume children will only laugh at bathroom humor and practical jokes. Kids have a capacity to appreciate irony and paradoxes. They get political humor, too, especially as they regularly follow current events.

From a geek-parenting perspective, there's a way to capitalize on the intellectual capacity your child exhibits to appreciate all kinds of humor. The best example of this I can think of is my husband's insistence that our children would enjoy certain skits from *Monty Python and the Holy Grail*. Back in 1975, when Graham Chapman and John Cleese wrote this movie, it was considered the height of bawdy British humor (or humour, depending on which side of the pond you reside). Nowadays, it enjoys a second-generation "cult" following—which is to say, children of geek parents now are discovering why *The Holy Grail* is funny (think, "bring out your dead!"—a line I use around our house when calling for dirty laundry). Some of it's not that appropriate for younger kids, and maybe there are better examples. Suffice to say, a satirical look at medieval history isn't funny to a lot of kids. For one thing, you have to know the history to get the jokes. This is what makes it funny to geeks. Geeks get the jokes.

SOCIAL STRUGGLES FOR BRAINIACS

Okay, let's review: A brainiac is a kid who's curious about all kinds of topics, who feels smart and capable of learning new things, and who is particularly intelligent in certain areas. He's well read, well informed, well rounded, and fun to be with. Jeez—it sounds like we're raising the class president!

Why is it, then, that this genuine, enthusiastic, empowered kid who is known to his friends as a brainiac may have more than his fair share of social struggles? Truth is, raising a brainiac is not usually the route to popularity and can sometimes make for a rough road.

It's important to note that brainiac kids seem different from their peers. They can't necessarily hide the fact that they're smart (not that they should); they seem to know things other kids don't know; they may, like my Amy, speak a little differently from others their age. And to be honest, there are a few pitfalls I've observed that require a sensitive parental response:

Brainiacs Can Behave... How to Put This?... Obnoxiously

Being smart and enjoying school, some brainiacs shoot their hands in the air relentlessly and somewhat obnoxiously. They may not appreciate that their constant right answers don't endear them to their peers (and sometimes, not even to their teachers). Gleaning much of their positive self-image from their intellectual capacity, they don't get that showing off is not a route to being well regarded.

Brainiacs Can Seem Intellectually Superior

Believing they're smart, brainiacs may extrapolate this to mean others are stupid. To put it bluntly, brainiacs sometimes are arrogant. It's not a good idea to raise an intellectual snob.

Brainiacs Can Act Socially Unaware

Though they're smart, brainiacs sometimes can be less socially astute than their peers. They don't always pick up on social cues, even though they may have a perfectly clear grasp of social situations. This is especially true of superbright kids with Asperger's syndrome or ADD, conditions in which intelligence is typically high but social competence is disproportionately low.

Raising a brainiac doesn't mean rearing a child who values his intellectual prowess more than he values social competence. Geeks value both in equal measure, realizing that it's fun to be "book smart" but essential to be "people smart," too. This is a lesson we've faced in our home, especially with Katie and Jimmy. Both are bright and fairly competitive, as well. Each one enjoys being the person with all the answers. But they've learned that having answers doesn't mean they'll be admired by their peers; in fact, it can be a reason for resentment. My husband and I stressed when they were young the importance of letting others give the answers in class and sometimes even "sitting on

THE GEEK ESCAPE ROUTE:
A GOOD BOOK IS ALWAYS A FRIEND

In the fifth grade, Katie's homeroom teacher figured out how to help her make new friends. Not that her social life with the other fifth-grade girls became any busier; rather, Miss Larvick introduced Katie to the kinds of friends you could count on through thick and thin—the friends you meet in books.

Katie's social life in the fifth grade simply didn't take off. It was a lonely time and preceded a decision on our part to change schools, but that's not really the point. The point is, Katie discovered that she didn't feel lonely when she dove into the pages of a story.

Moreover, being a "bookworm" became her claim to fame. That year, we even had a "bookworm birthday party" and asked guests to bring as a gift for Katie one book they had read and enjoyed (also a tactic to build new friendships). As the year progressed, her voracious reading actually helped her cope with a difficult situation and gave her a sense of accomplishment and mastery even when another important area—her social life—didn't gel.

The lesson is worth crystallizing: When children face hurdles in friendship, we seem to want to jump right in and fix things. We set up more playdates, arrange for our kids to attend camps and join clubs, and generally tackle the social dilemma as if it were a puzzle to be solved.

But Katie's fifth-grade teacher saw a girl whose temperament and personality didn't quite fit with the kids in her immediate social sphere. Rather than force a square peg into a round hole, she encouraged Katie to find the library, where shelf after shelf offered the company of new and accepting friends. It was a lonely year in most respects, but in retrospect it was wonderful. She learned a valuable reason to be a reader, and ultimately in a new school, Katie found friends who shared her love of reading (and even shared good books).

their hands" when they knew the solution just to show courtesy to their classmates.

To be clear, we didn't encourage this as a route to greater popularity, though some kids do this for the sake of fitting in. Sadly, the notion of "dumbing down" to gain social status rings too true, especially in minority communities. It's heartbreaking to imagine a bright child pretending to be less intellectual than she is just to be considered part of the popular crowd, but this really happens. In fact, if your child isn't performing to the potential you are certain she could attain, this could be part of the problem.

In our case, we knew our kids already were perceived as being smart; we wanted them to learn humility and practice kindness. Over time, we encouraged them to use their abilities as good learners to help others whenever possible.

Uncool Answers

My son is hooked on electronic games. How do I get him to read for pleasure?

Even if you do all the things the experts recommend to promote reading, you still may end up with a teenager who won't read for fun but instead literally develops calluses on his fingers from the controls of his PlayStation game. How do I know this is true? Jimmy.

The seemingly obvious answer is to chuck the gaming systems out the window, and I know some people do this (figuratively). I know others who never get a game system in the first place, and for a long time we didn't have one—I was reluctant because I feared the precise outcome we now face; that the game system would replace other, better kinds of recreation.

But it became clear when Jimmy was about eight or nine years old that his friends didn't want to play at our house, but rather wanted him to come to their homes—places where there were gaming systems.

Without a system of our own, I couldn't assure that my son was playing games of which I approved, nor could I monitor his playdates (since they weren't happening at my house). So I caved—and believe me, this was a big deal. I had always said that dogs and electronic games were things the neighbors could own and we would just enjoy by visiting their houses. (We have a dog, too. Never say never.)

Which leads me to the strategy I have launched with respect to Jimmy and reading: I simply make him. Here are some ways you can do it, too:

* Keep a game log—clock the time your son uses electronics. Sometimes just seeing the truth about his obsessive game time will illustrate the point.

* Put the game system away temporarily until you see improved habits of reading. When you reintroduce the system, do it with all new rules about how much it can be used.

* Use reading time as currency to "buy" time on the game system or computer.

* Find books that correlate to the topics of your son's favorite games.

* Ban portable games such as Game Boy and PSP for a period of time. Allow only books in the car as a way to pass the time.

* Use an upcoming trip to put the focus on books. Require your son to read a book about the location prior to the trip so he can serve as a tour guide for the family. (I did this once and it really worked. My kids all wanted to be a tour guide!)

I've done all these things, but to be honest, more often than not, my demand is just that—a maternal and authoritative insistence that he shut off whatever he's doing that plugs in and instead pick up where he left off in a book.

My goal is to help Jimmy develop the habit of reading. Somewhere in there I also hope he'll just "get it"—he'll realize that reading is just as much fun (or more!) as anything else he can choose. I'm happy to report this actually is finally happening; he's been seen reading without being prompted and even been absorbed in the plot of a book to the exclusion of other interests. So stick with it. Your effort to raise your son to be a reader will pay off!

Guaranteed Geek: Tips to Turn Your Child into a Brainiac

For Geeks of All Ages:

* Teach your child to be comfortable in a quiet house. A home where the TV isn't blaring 24/7 is a home where thinking can take place.

* Be a lifelong learner. Take a class or join a discussion group and tell your kids about it. Let them see you as a brainiac, too!

* Let your child's interests lead the family to new experiences. Reward your child's passion for baseball cards with a family visit to Cooperstown, for example.

* Go to the Web site www.familyeducation.com and check out the multiple intelligences quizzes. Use them to get to know your child's strengths and unique gifts.

For Elementary School Geeks:

* When a topic lights a fire of imagination, follow your child's lead. Learn more about it and stay interested.

* Sign up your child for a music class or instrument lessons.

* Let your child know how much you enjoy listening to her talk about things she's learned.

* When it comes to school performance, focus on the effort, not the grade. Teach kids that grades follow effort and learning is its own reward.

For Middle School Geeks:

* Make sure your child has time to explore his interests and time to read. Don't book the schedule so completely that trips to the library or bookstore are off the schedule.

* Sign up for science camp. It's a brainiac-only experience.

* Have topical debates around the kitchen table. Encourage your child to argue the opposite side of his true opinion so he learns to consider all sides of an issue.

For High School Geeks:

* Talk politics at home. Be informed about events locally, nationally, and globally and talk about them with your teen.

* Invite your child to go with you to a town council meeting or a committee meeting at your church—show her how brainiacs fit in in the real world.

* Encourage your geek to join an organization that addresses an issue he's passionate about.

* Read the books she's assigned to read for school—it's an easy route to a family book club. (I finally read *The Great Gatsby* thanks to Katie's freshman summer reading list.)

Rule #2

··

RAISE A SHELTERED KID

Ever since Glenn Close boiled a bunny over her love for Michael Douglas in *Fatal Attraction,* I don't go to scary movies with suspenseful sound tracks. It's not that I stand on moral high ground. It's that I stand in the lobby, where it's safe. I don't like to be made afraid recreationally.

On the other hand, my husband, Jim, enjoys frightening films, so he occasionally goes with a buddy. One such night found Jim and his friend sitting in the theater watching trailers for upcoming releases while waiting for the evening's feature presentation to begin. Into the theater walks the mother of one of our daughter's classmates. Behind her is a group of twelve-year-olds from Betsy's seventh grade class, giggling excitedly and taking their seats as the theater dims.

Just what film did my fortysomething husband and a row of prepubescent middle schoolers enjoy together? *Matrix Reloaded,* starring Keanu Reeves—rated R. An online review service, www.screenit.com, says the movie is "heavy" in blood, gore, frightening and tense scenes, profanity, sex, and nudity; and "extreme" in guns and weapons, violence, disrespectful or bad attitudes, and scary or tense music.

My husband's review: Uncomfortable. "I'm watching these graphic scenes, but the whole time it's really awkward knowing Betsy's friends are a few rows ahead of me. I felt like the girls should have covered their eyes," he said. "Since they didn't, I covered mine instead."

What possible benefit could there have been in taking those girls to see a movie starring sex, violence, profanity, terror, and gore?

Here's a radical thought: Parents have the power to decide what their children are exposed to through TV shows, movies, music, and Internet sites, and these decisions help to either preserve or destroy childhood innocence.

A Tough Task?

Admittedly, the mom who led the *Matrix* outing is an extreme example of a parent who seems to have had little compunction about compromising childhood innocence. Most of us do struggle to provide our children with a healthy atmosphere in which to grow, feeling that our culture is working against us in a battle that is unfocused, uncontained, and perhaps even unwinnable.

In fact, the advocacy group Common Sense Media found nine out of ten American parents believe today's media contribute to children becoming too materialistic, using more coarse and vulgar language, engaging in sexual activity at younger ages, experiencing a loss of innocence too early, and behaving in violent or antisocial ways. What's disconcerting to me is something else their survey found: "Despite concerns about media's influence, most parents provide a media-rich environment for their children, often with little supervision...the majority of parents say they could do a better job supervising their children's media use."

Why do we say one thing—that the media probably exploits our children's innocence—yet do another, that is, tolerate and even provide access to unsupervised hours of media exposure?

There may be as many answers as there are baffled parents scratching their heads, wondering how to extract the speaker "buds" from the ears of their teenagers, but I suggest many well-intentioned parents don't shelter their kids because it seems virtually impossible to find the time, the optimism, the stamina—and the clear motivation.

Who among us has as much as six hours a week to research potential media choices for our children? Yet statistics tell us that our children spend almost that much time *every day* absorbing messages through various media. Equally daunting is the fact that gadgets and gizmos— and the content they carry—operate in a state of constant change.

Since we believe we can't possibly control or assess all the content and technology our kids might encounter, we take a logical shortcut to decide what's best for them: relying on the opinions of others. Guided by the parents in our children's social spheres—especially the parents we admire and respect—we conclude if "all the kids from school" spend the afternoon online using instant messenger or downloading hip-hop tracks onto personal music players, these activities are most likely safe and acceptable for our kids, too.

Time constraints aside, some pessimistic parents figure there's no way effectively to prevent exposure, so there's no point in trying. These folks even argue it's good for kids to be exposed to "real life" themes for the supposed benefits of worldliness. Others believe since media is a fact of life in our culture, it should be permitted as long as they, the parents, are there to manage its use and put its content into a proper context.

Even when we want to say no, limiting media is a tough sell to kids who expect it to be part of their daily routine. How often do we hear that peer acceptance in childhood determines emotional health and confidence in adulthood? Many of us are uncertain about where to draw the lines that impact our children's social opportunities. We're afraid we'll make our children unhappy and risk their chances for friends and an active social life. Eager to see our kids accepted by their peers, we compromise, for example, when they insist it's more important to go along with a group of friends to a movie than to stay home because the movie doesn't meet our standards.

There's no question that these are real obstacles, but I believe we lose sight of our children's most basic needs when we focus on

time limitations, the changing and pervasive nature of media technology, or the reactions from our children and their friends. Yes, those
issues make twenty-first-century parenting a unique challenge, but such
is our dilemma. The culture of cool has changed the way we have to
approach our job as parents, demanding that we take the time, know
the media landscape, and determine what's really best for our kids.

And just what *is* best for kids when it comes to the media? We
have to step back to see the big picture, then follow our instincts and
do a better job of supervising and limiting their media consumption.
Later in the chapter, I'll discuss ways to do this—and help you find the
time, the optimism, and the methods to say no in a voice your kids will
hear and understand—but first I hope to motivate you by convincing
you why.

Incentives for Geek Media Standards

Unless and until we open our eyes to the media messages that wage a
daily assault on our children, we won't begin to confront this inescap-
able truth: *If we aren't the ones teaching our kids values about respecting themselves and others and about seeking purpose and perspective
in life, the media will do it for us.*

MEDIA MESSAGES ABOUT VIOLENCE

On September 11, 2001, my kids had the day off from school. I had
gone out at around eight-thirty in the morning to take the dog to the
vet. When I got home a short time later, Katie, then twelve, met me at
the door and told me about the first plane crashing into the World Trade
Center. I stood in front of our television with my children in stunned
disbelief as the second plane made its fiery impact.

We watched in transfixed horror as the events in New York unfolded.
When the news came on about the plane in Washington, D.C., and
about another plane whose location was unclear, I said, "no more." I

turned the television off and took my children to our church to pray. I didn't know what else to do, but it seemed to me I shouldn't let my children watch such real-life violence and suffering play out on live TV.

In the days that followed, our school administrators, along with child-development experts appearing frequently on the nightly news and on national talk shows, urged parents to limit our kids' exposure to media coverage of the terrorist attacks. American parents were advised that children are not equipped to handle the brutal reality depicted, and that children bombarded with these images were being put at risk of suffering excessive anxiety or of becoming emotionally desensitized.

Certainly, 9/11 was in a class of horror all by itself. But the lessons it brought into focus about kids and media were important ones. The simple consensus: It's better to reassure kids that they are safe than to let the media stir up fears and insecurities.

Such advice holds not only for broadcasts of traumatic world events, but for all graphic violence in all media. Whether generated by a newscast or a blockbuster movie, stress is stress. Young children can't differentiate between real life and a fantasy viewed on a screen; older children have an intellectual understanding of which is which, but they're still children and emotionally and psychologically impacted and imprinted by media violence. For these reasons, though you might say, "Don't worry, honey, that dead body you see in the woods is only pretend," your explanation probably won't suffice when the lights go out at bedtime.

If shielding them from fear and stress is one reason to shelter children, shielding them from the behavioral effects of viewing violence is another, perhaps even more compelling one. Over time, viewing violent behavior as depicted in much of current media desensitizes children, promotes aggression as acceptable behavior, and leads them to the conclusion that the world is more hostile than it really is.

The violence our children absorb is distorted as well, and, when viewed often enough, implants a twisted moral viewpoint. Research shows three crucial ways in which television (and by extension all media) misrepresents violence:

* Violence is glamorized Violent acts are frequently committed by "good" characters, and even when the characters are "bad," they go largely unpunished.

* Violence is sanitized Victims don't experience pain or suffering, nor do they or their families endure long-term consequences.

* Violence is trivialized More than half of the violent acts on TV are lethal, yet 40 percent are depicted as comedy.

When all this violence becomes interactive, as in video games, it has an even more dangerous impact on kids.

MEDIA MESSAGES ABOUT SEX

Ever worry about when is the best time to sit down with your son or daughter to discuss the "facts of life"? Don't fret. By the time you find the right book to guide your discussion, practice your speech, and screw up the courage to communicate on this topic, your child already will know the words to "My Humps" by the Black Eyed Peas and your job will be done. There's nothing ambiguous about the meaning of a song that asks the musical question "Just what are you going to do with all those breasts?"

When it comes to sex, our kids are being thoroughly educated every time they turn on the radio. And the messages they get at the Cineplex and through the tube are equally clear. The American media is the most sexually saturated media in the *western hemisphere,* and the media is one of the sources about sex kids report as the most important.

Sex in the media is a big deal. It influences our children's attitudes and their behaviors. Watching sexually explicit and suggestive material hastens adolescent sexual initiation, promotes heightened sexuality in young children, and teaches them a value system that condones casual, irresponsible sexual behavior. (These aren't just my common-sense conclusions—they were substantiated in a 2004 study published in the journal *Pediatrics*.) And let's face it—all that sexy media is darn hard to escape.

The American Academy of Pediatrics' 2001 policy statement "Sexuality, Contraception and the Media" says "the average young viewer is exposed to more than 14,000 sexual references each year, yet only a handful provide an accurate portrayal of responsible sexual behavior or accurate information about birth control, abstinence, or the risks of pregnancy and sexually transmitted disease." Kids don't have to tune in to premium cable channels to find sexy content. All they have to do is watch their favorite channel—MTV—or tune in to *Desperate Housewives,* in its heyday the most popular broadcast-network show with kids aged nine to twelve.

From seemingly innocuous reruns of *Friends* and *Everybody Loves Raymond* to edgy sitcoms like Fox's *The War at Home* and the animated *Family Guy,* references to and depictions of sex are the norm. That's not just my observation. The Kaiser Family Foundation's biennial study "Sex on TV 4," released in November 2005, found 77 percent of prime-time shows included sexual content and *68 percent of all shows* included talk about sex, with *35 percent of all shows incorporating sexual behaviors into their content* (emphasis reflects my overall frustration).

Even in children's programming, young viewers will find insidious sexual messages. Case in point: the Nickelodeon animated Barbie movie, *My Scene Goes Hollywood*. The plot finds Barbie and her "My Scene" pals Madison and Delancey in L.A. to appear as extras in a movie, where one of the girls starts "crushing" on a "hot" movie star. While solving a friendship crisis, Barbie and her buddies talk a lot about who is "hot"—but of course their skimpy outfits keep them nice and cool. "My Scene" isn't even the worst of the hypersexualized market for young girls—that distinction would go to the "Bratz" collection of dolls and the collateral media they have spawned. (I'll rant about Bratz soon. Stay tuned.)

This deluge of sexual messages is having an impact—it's shaping the attitudes and behaviors of young boys and girls in ways that can have lasting consequences.

MEDIA MESSAGES ABOUT CONSUMERISM

You don't have to look very far to find the impetus for marketing to children. Just follow the money. With an estimated $15 billion per year in child-targeted marketing alone, there are a lot of people getting rich selling cool to kids. Their tactics work because children have unprecedented personal funds and the freedom to make consumer decisions, and they have a strong influence over the way their parents spend money. Here are just a few facts from the National Institute on Media and the Family to put this issue in perspective:

* In 2001, teenagers, ages twelve to nineteen, spent $172 billion (an average of $104 per teen each week), up 11 percent from $155 billion in 2000.

* In 2002, children ages four to twelve spent an estimated $40 billion.

* In 2000, children twelve years and under, directly and indirectly, influenced the household spending of over $600 billion.

Admittedly, it's been a while since I was twelve, and memory fades. But am I the only one who didn't have $104 per week to spend however I wanted? That's $412 a month!

Looking ahead, marketers see this generation as the adult consumers of tomorrow, so they're establishing buying habits early on. By infusing virtually every media experience with consumer messages pitched by celebrity role models and familiar characters, kids learn the fads, brands, and behaviors that are cool. Of course what's cool is always something you can buy. How convenient for the folks who make all that money selling stuff to kids!

But media content generally, advertising included, sells more than just products; it sells the pop-culture lifestyle and the attitudes that are shaping the next generation. Materialism is only one aspect of these messages. Kids also are inundated with examples of self-absorption, disrespect, instant gratification, and irresponsibility. If you've ever been mowed over in a mall by a pack of middle schoolers, you don't need to read the research that substantiates this trend (more about this topic in the next chapter).

BEYOND "STRANGER DANGER"—THE RISKS OF A VIRTUAL CHILDHOOD

It's an interesting irony of modern parenting: We spend all kinds of time while they're young teaching our kids about "stranger danger." Then, at about the time they finally understand the basics of personal safety, we double-click on www.pbskids.org or www.nickjr.com or www.lego.com and show them where to find the free games. By the time they're eight or nine, they're comfortable in cyberspace—a place where "stranger danger" takes on a whole new meaning.

If parents thought they understood the perils for children on the Internet, Chris Hansen's "To Catch a Predator" series for *Dateline NBC* has proved to be a sickening wake-up call. The depth of perversion indulged in cyberspace and documented in his reports ought to be reason enough to impose strict rules for computer use in every home.

Some forty million people have seen Chris's hidden-camera investigations in which he snags evil pedophiles in the act of attempting to meet young teens for sex. The series as well as the companion best-selling book of the same name have exposed to all of us the underhanded and insidious behaviors of those who use the Internet for criminal purposes. And still—*still*—millions of kids hang out on MySpace every afternoon, millions of kids have computers in their bedrooms, where they can roam unsupervised through the uncharted territories of cyberspace, and where they are routinely and repeatedly approached by icky sickos for unthinkable exploitation.

You can decide I'm just overreacting to the potential for danger on the net, but I'm not taking any chances when the fact is, being fully engaged in an Internet social life is simply not necessary to grow up as a healthy, happy, and well-rounded person.

And it isn't just the risk of meeting a creepy stranger that should concern us (as if that's not enough!). Parents need to worry about issues from spy ware and viruses destroying their equipment to pornography popping up out of nowhere. Not to mention the nasty IMs sent by so-called friends from fourth grade.

But rather than belabor the mind-boggling trends, I'll simply note that more than 85 percent of children and teens now enjoy regular access to the Internet, *while only a quarter of the young people report that their parents have rules about how to use it.*

INSTANT MESSAGING, BLOGS, AND THE QUEST FOR FRIENDS

Most kids use the Internet for instant messaging. Parents assume since their kids are only talking to friends (and friends of friends), the time spent using IM is safe. I don't agree.

Practically speaking, instant messaging steals time. Rather than go outdoors, read, practice a musical instrument, or work on a hobby, kids as young as nine years old jump on their computers and spend hours sharing idle chat and gossip.

What concerns me more, though, is the very nature of instant messages. Children who are just beginning to develop skills in human communication, both written and spoken, are learning instead to communicate only one-way and in shorthand. Teens and tweens—already emotionally vulnerable because of their ages—engage in a form of communication that allows them to hide behind anonymity, deceive their schoolmates, spread—or be the butt of—rumors, and even trash the reputations of their peers. At the very least, instant messages are the source of "major drama"—as if growing up doesn't have enough drama already. (This is what makes it fun, I guess.) Kids say things online they would never say face-to-face or even over the phone, and they gather in groups to taunt and torment unsuspecting peers.

Stories of hurt and humiliation caused by insensitive or cruel instant messages are rampant, and school administrators struggle to harness its destructive power. Because of its negative effects, my children's elementary school sends regular reminders to parents about the damage IMing can do, and this past school year, administrators scheduled two parent seminars on "cyber-bullying" (I guess this makes playground bullying a bit outmoded).

The parents I talk to are shocked to learn that teens create multiple Internet personas, but according to the Kaiser Family Foundation's study "Generation M: Media in the Lives of 8–18 Year-Olds," 56 percent of teens have more than one screen name. Of those, 24 percent keep at least one screen name secret. Kids also say they are easily able to do things online that their parents don't know about, and the majority report that they have done things of which their parents would disapprove.

Even though these problems are ubiquitous and have been well documented in the media, my children are among the only ones in their schools who aren't permitted to use IM. They have survived.

Teen Blogs: The Risks of Telling All

Another media habit that should concern parents is the use of social-networking sites such as www.myspace.com, www.xanga.com and www.facebook.com. Such sites supposedly are limited to adults over the age of eighteen, with "closed" pages for underage users as young as fourteen who can share their secret password with "safe" visitors. Of course teenagers would never lie about their ages to get an open blog page—sheesh—so the issue of safety from predators is basically null. There is no safety.

The whole purpose of social-networking sites is to meet new people and develop relationships by revealing personal information. (Some kids use social sites to live out vivid fantasy lives—all the better if they're pretty outrageous.) A quick visit to www.myspace.com also confirms that the purpose is sexual; in fact, when browsing for people to meet, sexual orientation and relationship status are two of only five demographic questions that define your search.

Blog sites are a little different—among kids they take on the flavor of an embarrassing romp through someone's diary. Blogging may reflect the propensity in our culture toward emotional exhibitionism. If you can't tell your innermost thoughts to a studio audience on *The Jerry Springer Show,* at least you can blog them for thousands of unknown readers on the World Wide Web. Or perhaps it stems from a desire to be relevant. Whatever their roots, blogs are an important means of self-expression for millions of kids.

But I believe they're perilous, and not only because they promote unguarded sexual contact and make it very easy to track down young bloggers in the "real" world, which happens with alarming frequency. Some dangers are more subtle, as in the experience of a daughter of a friend of mine. The high school junior returned home from an extended hospital stay for treatment of an eating disorder (which she had revealed on her blog), only to find posts on her site that teased her for being fat. This is the kind of insensitive head game perpetuated by communication rooted in both anonymity and self-disclosure. Lucky thing my friend had gone online to read her daughter's blog—doing so enabled her to respond quickly to what was, for her vulnerable child, a serious setback.

But what if that mom hadn't checked her daughter's blog? A news story I read about teen blogs posed the question "Is it appropriate for parents to read their teenager's online journal?" The article said this was a "gray area" because "reading a teen's online blog might intrude on his privacy," jeopardizing the parent/child relationship.

I had to reread that part of the article a couple of times because it used the words *online blog* and *privacy* in the same sentence, which I found confusing. The expert quoted in the article, whose research was funded by the National Science Foundation, actually said reading your child's blog is "tacky and reprehensible." (I guess those are scientific terms.)

Since I'm not funded by any foundations, I'm not an expert. But I say it's neither tacky nor reprehensible to be a responsible parent. This means making it your business to know if your child is blogging or has a social-network page and deciding whether this is acceptable to you. If you allow this kind of online socializing, it means setting standards so your child knows what is appropriate to post in cyberspace. And most of all, it means eliminating any expectation of privacy if your teen chooses to share personal thoughts and feelings with the cyber world.

Online diaries are hailed as avenues of creativity and self-expression, but precisely because they encourage such openness, they're another media risk that cries out for shelter.

Our children will not remember life without the Internet. The challenge for us as parents is to incorporate the net into their lives in a way that doesn't exploit them but rather enriches them. How? Funny you should ask...

How to Build Your Geek Media Shelter

Essentially, you shelter your kids whenever you assure that their life experiences promote their well-being. To build a shelter from the media, you need four strong pillars to support your protective parental cover: The *standards* you set based on your beliefs, your parental *supervision*, your strong and clearly communicated *decisions*, and the *direction* you give to steer your kids toward positive media choices.

PILLAR #1: STANDARDS

The messages conveyed in movies, on TV, over the Internet, and even through the lyrics we sing mindlessly while driving minivans across America tell our children what we value. We have to be sure that the messages they see and hear reflect the values we want them to hold in their hearts—this is the crux of setting standards to shelter your kids from the media.

If we accept that media has the power to influence our children's attitudes and behaviors, we also must accept the responsibility to determine, as much as possible, the dominant messages their exposure will promote. No, we won't be able to erect a barrier against every possible image that bounces off a satellite dish in deep space and lands, unwelcome, into their daily experience. But we can assure them that, to the extent we're able, we will keep them from content that erodes their innocence, their optimism, and their sense that our world is a safe, secure place in which to grow. All media is educational media, after all—it's just a question of what message is being taught. Our job as parents is to choose the message.

Setting standards means making rules about the programming and Internet sites we permit, as well as about the access our kids have to media in our home. But rules alone aren't the answer, at least not for me. For one thing, I have a hard time remembering all the rules I've made, and if you can't remember them all, you can't enforce them. Not to mention, rules change as kids grow. So while there are some specific "do's" and "don'ts" in the Hicks home regarding media (see below), our children understand they need to follow the spirit of the rules, not just the letter. Even I can remember the fundamentals, and so can my kids.

Our family standards: We seek out "wholesome" media for our children (a word defined as "healthy for mind, body, and spirit"). We want them to avoid content that is sexually suggestive or explicit, gratuitously violent, profane, or that which depicts immoral or illegal activities in an attractive manner. We also restrict content that demonstrates disrespectful attitudes toward adults, authority figures, and cultural or religious beliefs or traditions. Since all of this is subjective, we reserve the right to be arbitrary in our choices. Quality is a matter of taste, after all, and as the adults in our home, we decide what constitutes quality.

To be clear, the media standards in our home are different for the children than for us! As mature adults, we enjoy the freedom to choose movies and TV shows that interest us and we're certainly not prudes or squeamish about compelling or gripping content (okay, Jim's not squeamish). The standards I'm discussing in this chapter apply to our children, and as you'll see, our policies about media are dynamic and change as our children grow and mature.

The standards you set will be unique to your family because they will stem from your beliefs and values. You may discover you're strict about some things compared with parents you know, while on other issues you're more lenient. There's no right or wrong answer when it comes to making your family's media guidelines, and **the point isn't specifically what you choose, but** *that you choose*.

Our standards don't change, but our specific policies may vary. Even within a family, every child is unique, so my husband and I try to view media content through the eyes of each child. One child might not flinch when the shot rings out that kills Bambi's mother, while another may have angst over it for days. Therefore, judgments about appropriate content will also reflect the individual growth and development of each child. You can certainly look for guidance from your pediatrician, your child's teachers, a school counselor, your best friend, your mother, or even your UPS delivery person (wisdom is all around you). But in the end, being a parent means you're responsible for creating and upholding the choices that you think are best for your kids.

PILLAR #2: SUPERVISION

The premise behind supervising media is to assert control over it, not vice versa. I know parents whose tactic to manage the media monster is to eschew it altogether, pulling the plug on television (or at least canceling their cable subscriptions) and refusing to ride the Internet wave. The people who do this swear it works and they're happy, but it's not the avenue for my family.

Instead, we view the media a lot like we do the ocean. It's enormous and beautiful and full of amazing discoveries, and when the water's right, oh, what a swim. But it also must be respected for its unspeakable power. Just like at the beach, our children may never swim those potentially dangerous waters without an adult hovering nearby to keep them safe.

So the Hicks household is pretty much like any other middle-class American home. If you look around, you'll find an array of media sources including television sets, computers, DVD and video players, radios, a PlayStation 2, four Game Boys, and an odd lot of MP3 players, personal CD players, and even some old cassette players. (I'm pretty sure the eight-track player is gone, but there's a beta machine in the storage room because my husband was certain it would be more popular than VHS.)

Exactly how do we supervise the use of all these media sources? We lean heavily on the four pillars. First, we set our standards and make rules to guide our children's media choices, and we clearly communicate our expectations. A family meeting is a great forum to do this, but know that ongoing reminders will be necessary. I've never posted written rules on the fridge, but you certainly could do this if it would help.

Next, we limit the time our kids spend using media so that it's only one of many activities they enjoy. We want kids who are well rounded, so we sometimes prohibit media just to force them to do something else with their time. (The American Academy of Pediatrics recommends no more than one to two hours of quality TV and videos a day for older children and no screen time for children under the age of two. Full disclosure: I did have *PBS Kids* on TV when my children were little. Since I had babies and preschoolers in the same house, they all watched it. They turned out fine.)

Supervising content doesn't mean I keep the TV remote under lock and key. Within the media time we allow, our kids can roam freely on TV stations and Web sites we've designated as safe. Beyond the specific stations and Web sites we permit, we add more choices as we have the time to preview them.

This kind of hands-on supervision sounds more time-intensive than it really is. Fortunately, coincident with the onslaught of inappropriate media has been the rise in a great deal of excellent children's programming, with entire networks, radio stations, and Web sites devoted to creative family fare. You don't have to watch all the programs on the stations you've already approved (or play all the games on a safe Web site).

As your children grow older, they'll naturally want more variety in their media diets and this means you'll have to pick and choose specific programs on stations up and down the dial. But when you do need to evaluate material, it doesn't take more than a few minutes to determine whether an entire series or network is off-limits; sometimes all you need to see are the commercials!

Our younger kids always have to clear any new movies, TV shows, Web sites, and gadgetry with us. (Hidden bonus: While they're waiting until you have the chance to make an informed decision, a "hot" new show or device often loses its appeal.) Detailed information about new movies is easily found online with Web sites such as www.screenit .com, allowing you to decide whether a particular film is appropriate for your kids or whether you need to preview it before letting your children see it. Song lyrics are available at www.lyrics.com. These days, you ought to read songs before you sing along. (You may need to visit www.urbandictionary.com to understand what those lyrics mean!)

Rules for Surfing the Net

Our standards for TV, movies, and music may be different from other families, but my kids will tell you that our use of the Internet is probably the biggest departure from the norm. This is because the norm is to let kids use the Internet to advance an active preteen social life, and to permit a virtual existence through the use of social-networking sites. We don't do these things at our house.

Safety on the Internet starts with technology itself. We've been able to maintain technical safety in our home by using some basic Internet security and spy-ware programs. Beyond the safeguards inside your computer, experts stress adopting basic house rules for Internet use.

Our rules reflect our belief that recreational Internet use (as opposed to educational use) should be a limited and structured activity. Here are our rules:

1. No Internet use without permission. Permission has to be granted for every usage.
2. No instant messaging.
3. Internet use is allowed only when homework, chores, or other activities are complete.
4. Only Internet sites approved by Mom or Dad may be visited. No traveling from an approved site to a link without a parental okay.
5. Internet use is for education and fun. No using the net to find information on topics of concern (sex, drugs, depression, moral issues) without supervision from Mom or Dad. (It's not that we wouldn't permit research on these topics—we just want to direct our kids to sites with values reflecting our own.)
6. No blogging. No personal Web pages except Mom's, which hopefully will one day help send all four geeks to college.
7. No two-way communication with Web sites. We allow only passive participation online—no responding to surveys or offers to join online clubs or groups. No distributing information such as e-mail addresses, phone numbers, street addresses, or other identifiers. (I made this rule after allowing Jimmy to vote online for his picks in the Major League Baseball all-star selection. His e-mail address subsequently was flooded with Viagra offers.)
8. No clicking pop-ups—ever. (We don't get many, thanks to pop-up blockers and anti-spy-ware programs, but occasionally they get through.)
9. No one except Mom or Dad may ever clear the computer's history. (This allows us to track sites visited. Tracking also can be handled with tracking software, a better tactic for families in which compliance is an issue.)

PILLAR #3: DECISIVENESS

A waffling and permissive parenting style makes it difficult, if not impossible, to shelter children from the media access they crave. As I discussed early on, without clear parental authority your kids won't respect your decisions. This is why that authority structure is so crucial. Simply put: It's hard to say no if you never say no.

But saying no is a big part of bringing up geeks, and an essential part of sheltering kids from content that corrupts. At the core of geek parenting is the willingness to take a stand and declare, "This is not good enough for my child." Yet I'd be remiss if I don't warn you that this will make your parenting different from the norm. For example, it's typical for parents to tell me, "I wish I had rules about the computer like you do." I never know how to answer. What I want to say is, "You're the grown-up, for heaven's sake! Make the rules!"

Certainly, reining in the media habit for kids who are accustomed to unfettered access might be challenging, but I believe it's entirely possible. Not to oversimplify, but it's a bit like switching to skim milk. At first, kids think it's thin and watered down, but eventually, they develop a taste for it. After a while skim milk is perfectly satisfying, while drinking 2 percent is like downing a cup of wallpaper paste. In the same way, kids will feel deprived when you begin to limit their time with various media and monitor its content, but over time, they'll realize there is plenty to enjoy within the framework of your family's media standards.

Remember, too, that both kids and media are in a constant state of change. As your children grow and mature, your mandates about media will evolve along with them. Rules can change and it's okay to be flexible. ("No TV on school days" for a young child may become "No TV until homework and chores are done" for a preteen.) It's imperative, though, that you remain inflexible on the standards behind your rules. ("Getting enough sleep on school nights is our first priority; TV and other pastimes mustn't interfere with adequate rest.")

PILLAR #4: DIRECTION

It's not enough to just say no to media, and besides, there is much to enjoy and appreciate that's good for kids. The fourth pillar, direction, means helping children find appropriate and beneficial media content.

MOM'S MESSAGE TO JIMMY: WELCOME TO E-MAIL!

I'm not out to condemn my children to a life without technology. E-mail is a great tool for school and social purposes, so when they reach fifth or sixth grade, I create an e-mail address for my children. But e-mail and instant messaging are not the same. IM communications are real-time and uncaptured (unless you use a program designed to save instant messages). On the other hand, e-mails, while presenting some similar issues, are sort of the "eight-track tapes" of teen technology. Okay, maybe that's a stretch— maybe it's more like CDs versus MP3s. In any case, having an e-mail address can be great for geeks as long as certain boundaries guard against abuse. Here's the message I send all my kids when they first get an e-mail address:

Subject: E-mail Rules
Welcome to your new e-mail box! There are some rules you need to know and observe so that you can enjoy using e-mail safely and happily:

1. You may e-mail only people we know. This includes family members and friends from school or basketball. I have set up your contacts to include family addresses; check with me before giving your e-mail address to anyone.

2. An e-mail address does not entitle you to privacy. I will always know the password for your mailbox and will have complete access to it. I don't anticipate checking your e-mails but I reserve the right to read any e-mail that comes in, past e-mails, e-mail you send to others, and e-mail you delete.

3. Nothing you write in an e-mail should be considered confidential. Your e-mails can be printed or forwarded by anyone who receives them and could easily end up in the hands of any number of people, including strangers.

Therefore, never write anything in an e-mail that you would not want posted on a school bulletin board, handed to a teacher, or shown to a friend or his parents.

4. Never respond to an e-mail from someone you don't know, even if the person introduces himself to you and says you have a mutual friend. Delete e-mail from anyone you don't know without even opening it.

5. Being on e-mail is a big step because it permits a form of communication that is easily misunderstood and misused. Don't write e-mails that "open your heart" or reveal too much about your family or other private matters. Never use e-mail to gossip, vent anger, clear up a misunderstanding, or share a secret or problem with a friend. Use the phone or speak in person to someone if the nature of the conversation is important or difficult. Use e-mail only for fun and to share information about school assignments, deadlines, sports practices, social plans, and sending (appropriate) jokes.

6. E-mail is like TV, computer games, playing basketball, or hanging with friends. It's something you can do when you aren't busy and when other chores or responsibilities have been completed. I don't want there to be any fighting over using the computer for e-mail. You won't need to check your e-mail every day.

Send me an e-mail to let me know you understand these rules. E-mail can be fun and it's always a treat to open the computer and see that you have messages. Use it responsibly and you may enjoy it. Otherwise, I'll exercise my obligation to delete your e-mail address from my account. Love and kisses, Mom.

Fortunately, this is the fun part for geek parents. Rather than accept the mediocre content that passes for cool, we can seek out material that enlightens, inspires, entertains, and educates our kids.

Media Literacy: The Essential Language for the "M Generation"

In our home, providing direction to guide our children toward good media content also means teaching them to make good choices for themselves. As we identify positive content with and for our children, we teach them skills of media literacy so that they understand why specific material may be inappropriate and how to discern the underlying messages that might influence their responses. In this way, we are helping them develop a discriminating eye for quality media that we hope will inform their choices in the future.

Media literacy is the ability to assess and evaluate media content and understand its underlying messages in the full awareness that someone owns it, produced it, and is using it to promote a particular point of view. I don't believe, as some do, that developing media literacy is the alternative to sheltering children. I think we should do both—shelter them from media that robs their innocence, and while they are still innocent, teach them to be discerning.

According to the Center for Media Literacy there are five basic principles that must be understood to analyze media messages:

* **Media messages are constructed** Kids need to learn that the messages being communicated aren't there by accident; they're deliberately constructed and intended to be understood and acted upon. Knowing that all media is educational media means kids learn to find the message.

* **Messages are representations of reality with embedded values and points of view** Even in a cartoon story, all media content stands for something. There's no such thing as

valueless media; the skill our kids need to learn is discerning the values contained within the stories, songs, ads, etc.

* Each form of media relies on unique techniques to construct messages such as sound, visual effects, lighting, point of view, and voice. These elements help convey the intended meaning of media content Kids can learn to appreciate the nuances of various forms of media content. By dissecting the production of media content, we can teach them to find the underlying meaning and values being communicated. For example, bad guys tend to wear dark colors and be unattractive, whereas good guys tend to be brighter and more appealing. Conversely, when a good-looking, appealing character does bad things, the mixed message is, "Bad behavior isn't so bad after all."

* Individuals interpret media messages and create their own meaning based on personal experience We all view media through the prism of our opinions, beliefs, and values, and kids are no different—except they have less life experience on which to assess what they see. This means they're more prone to believe whatever they're told through the media and less able to assess the validity or truth of a message.

* Media are driven by profit within economic and political contexts Kids are perfectly able to understand that someone is usually making money where media messages are concerned. They can learn to be wary of media content—especially advertising—if they learn how to "follow the money" and find who profits by shaping the consumer's behavior and opinions.

Understanding these basic tenets about media content is an important first step in helping our children to be intelligent media consumers. Even children as young as preschool can understand how to view TV

shows and commercials with an informed eye. By framing our assessment of media in simple terms like, "this show has too much fighting,"
or "I don't like the way Barbie is dressed in this movie," we begin to
teach them to notice aspects of the media beyond the simple story line.
With respect to advertising, we can separate the marketing message
from reality ("I wonder if the yo-yo in the commercial is really that easy
to use?").

As they reach school age, children can be taught to look for deeper
meaning in what they see. One important focus of media literacy is to
decipher the powerful and prevalent messages that promote consumerism. Rather than raise a generation of children who are manipulated
into becoming the compulsive shoppers of tomorrow, we can help them
see how masterfully the media creates and plays on their desires.

It's not difficult to find opportunities to evaluate media messages
and teach kids to think about what they see. For example, my son and I
have talked about ads for basketball shoes that carry the names of NBA
players. As a middle schooler, Jimmy's starting to see how shoe manu-
facturers use celebrities to sell product and command higher prices. By
teaching him what's behind the ads (profit for shoe companies and the
players who endorse them), he learned that simply putting the name
of a successful player on a shoe will not necessarily improve his game,
though advertising that connects players to products is intended to
imply such a result. ("Too bad I can't just put on some LeBron James
shoes and play like LeBron," Jimmy observed wistfully.)

Learning the language of media will empower our children to
appreciate what's good and recognize the material that simply isn't useful or beneficial to them. And, of course, empowerment is the hallmark
of a geek.

Happily Sheltered and Uncool

With all the negative language that goes with sheltering kids (prohibit,
restrict, avoid, limit, etc.), you might wonder whether I'm in a constant

battle to monitor and control their media use. Do they feel left out and awkward because their peers have the freedom to be more fully engaged in the culture than they do? Can they still have full and satisfying social lives when they're not permitted to see certain movies or chat with friends online?

These are good questions and important concerns. I don't pretend that setting or maintaining media standards for children is always an easy or pleasant task, or that they always agree with the decisions my husband and I make about media exposure.

But the truth is, our kids are both sheltered and happy. Even if they balk at a particular decision, they know our goal is to protect them. They trust us to make good choices for them and to help them learn how to make good choices for themselves. And most importantly, they respect that we have the authority to make these decisions.

Restricting access to media can have some social consequences, yet despite our rules, our kids have friends—good friends. Many of the kids they hang out with come from families who enforce similar standards. And those kids who have more access to media than mine seem to accept that our rules are just different from theirs.

The biggest media issue we have faced is the decision to prohibit instant messaging, but, as with most things that capture kids' attention, the novelty wears off, they get used to what they have or don't have, and they adapt. Not for nothing, my kids are always relieved they're not involved in the IM melodramas that frequently occur.

Several years ago, when an issue of media access caused some tears, Katie lamented that someone said to her, "You are so sheltered!" She was mortified. I remember telling her then that a "shelter" is a place that protects us, and keeps us safe and secure. It was our job as her parents to shelter her so that she would be safe from dangerous elements in our culture. I said being sheltered was a good thing.

I think this is why my kids are happily uncool. They see our shelter as an expression of our unfailing commitment to assuring that their childhoods are a time of innocence and wonder, and they know our limits are a reflection of our love.

Uncool Answers

What should I do when my geek child visits a friend's house and views a program we don't allow?

The short answer is, you're raising a geek, not a hermit. If you let your child go out into the world, eventually she will be exposed to media you would not permit. When children are little, it's best to make your preferences known to other parents up front. Most parents of young children are on the same page as far as this goes, and sharing your expectations is a natural part of getting to know the families in your social sphere.

But often your young child will play at a home where an older sibling or perhaps a babysitter is present, or where the supervision is a bit lax. You may be shocked to discover (as I was) that your six-year-old daughter has seen a good portion of *Austin Powers: The Spy Who Shagged Me*. Yea, baby.

The most important thing you can do is foster an open relationship so that if your child reports she watched *Jerry Springer* or *Law & Order* or a 50 Cent music video, she talks to you about it. An angry or punitive response may discourage her from telling you about such incidents if they occur again. Instead, realize you've been given a teachable moment. This is a chance to explain why the content she viewed is contrary to your value system. Here are some ideas to handle these situations:

Role-Play
Ask your kids to review exactly what happened—how the day unfolded in such a way that the playtime included the offending media exposure. Then pretend to be the friend and give kids a chance to redo their responses and recast the outcome.

Brainstorm for Alternatives
Kids get bored when hanging out together and that's when they look for something new—and sometimes inappropriate. Boredom can be good

for kids when it spurs them to creative play. Boredom in a house without adequate supervision can create a window of opportunity for mischief. Try to generate ideas for ways they can redirect the play to avoid media as a pastime.

Invoke the "Call Home" Policy

Create a policy that kids must call home for permission to watch a movie they're not sure about, or any television program they don't watch regularly at home. The goal is that ultimately they decline on their own to watch questionable shows rather than go through the hassle of calling. (When my kids have disobeyed this policy, I usually find out—they tend to trip up in conversation and inadvertently mention things they've seen.) It's certainly not uncommon for a child to test his limits, especially when left to his own devices. Remind them how important this rule is. If you notice a pattern of disobedience, the privilege of playing with friends at houses other than yours should be lost for a while.

Decide Some Homes Are Off-Limits

If you're not confident about the supervision at a particular home, decree that all future playtime must be spent at your house, where you can oversee media exposure. Also, realize that not every child is a positive influence. Be picky about where your kids go and with whom they play. If it's a home you simply can't avoid—say a cousin's house or your next-door neighbor—you will probably have to confront the situation head-on. Once you make your concerns known, parents tend to be more careful when your kids are around, even if they think your standards are too strict. (I'm sure I come across as overprotective and controlling. But I figure, so what? My goal isn't to be admired by other parents—it's to shelter my child from influences that we deem inappropriate.)

Guaranteed Geek: Tips to Shelter
Your Growing Geek

For Geeks of All Ages:
* Never trust ratings—learn the content of movies, television shows, music, and Web sites and decide for yourself what is appropriate for your children.

* Keep the television and computer in a central location in your home. Never let either be used without your permission and supervision.

* Block dangerous channels/Web sites; be liberal about what you designate as junk.

For Elementary School Geeks:
* Protect and prolong the innocence of younger children and explain what's off-limits without going into detail by creating code words for inappropriate content (tacky, scary, disrespectful).

* Begin habits of media literacy. Talk about the messages and lessons conveyed in cartoons, sitcoms, and commercials. Start early to use media content as a springboard for conversation.

For Middle School Geeks:
* When you declare certain media content off-limits, be frank about why you object to it. ("This song has a great beat but the words are disrespectful to women. Let's find something else.") When you are offended, make sure your kids know why!

* Continue to develop media literacy habits as your child grows more aware of the deeper meaning conveyed in movies, TV shows, lyrics, and magazines.

* Just say no to instant messaging.

* Read song lyrics online before buying music for your children.

* Use online download services rather than purchasing CDs so you can pick and choose from the offerings on a particular album. Get "radio versions" that have been sanitized for airplay.

* Encourage your child to create a "wish list" on your music download service so that you can check out songs before making a purchase. If you're okay with her choices, you can finalize the transaction.

* Occasionally listen to your child's MP3 player or iPod and check out her music collection. Reserve the right to clean out the playlist if she's downloaded inappropriate songs.

For High School Geeks:

* Turn kids on to oldies, classic rock, choral and classical music, show tunes, contemporary religious music, sound tracks, etc. Explore the classics and introduce your all-time favorites—Hitchcock, Monty Python, Doris Day, Elvis, the Beatles, Motown, Audrey Hepburn, *The Brady Bunch,* Broadway musicals, Sinatra, B.B. King, the Who, and Beethoven.

* As you expand the breadth of media content you permit, talk openly about the messages your child sees and hears. Ask questions to promote media literacy and reflect on how certain themes fit within your family's value system. Use the media as a springboard for open communication with your child. Kids who talk openly to their parents? More proof you're bringing up geeks.

RAISE AN UNCOMMON KID

One day when I picked Amy up from school, she climbed into the van, buckled her seat belt, and announced, "One of the girls said I'm cool." This was a high point of third grade.

I was more than a little surprised. "Wow. How does she know?" I asked.

"Mom, that should be obvious," Amy said, implying my ignorance. Probably, I had inadvertently armed Amy with something I didn't even know was cool, like the time I bought her a pair of Phat Farm sneakers.

As we drove out of the parking lot, she smiled and waved good-bye to a group of popular girls standing on the sidewalk. By the way she was perched on her seat—shoulders back, chin up—I could see she was feeling good about herself.

But even as we drove home chatting about the events of her day and her homework for the evening, I thought to myself, *Today is not just an average Tuesday. Today, a popular girl created the possibility that Amy might be popular, too.*

Tomorrow, I thought, *it will all be different.*

Sure enough, not the next day, but a week later, the girl who told Amy she was cool decided my daughter was, in fact, weird.

Being the coolest of all the cool girls, that child's declaration met with universal agreement and approval by the rest of the cool crowd. Suddenly, just as quickly as Amy's social status had risen, she returned to the rank of "outsider."

Amy couldn't understand why everyone thought she was weird or why they would tell her such a thing even if they believed it. She didn't get why others who previously behaved like friends would turn on her. She was confused. And hurt.

I had been down this road with daughters two times before, so I could see it coming. I knew well that by about eight or nine years of age, the egalitarian atmosphere of kindergarten coalesces instead into well-established cliques that mandate who may sit together at lunch, who may swing on the swing set during recess, who is invited to after-school playdates and weekend sleepovers.

Sure enough, there I was again with a daughter who had just discovered that there are "it" girls who had the power to decide whether she was one of them.

We all know the "it" girls. Kind and caring one day, caustic and cruel the next, "it" girls define who is cool (like them). They're natural leaders, assembling an entourage of followers whose role it is to work at continually winning their approval. Of course bestowing approval is what makes their role as "it" girls relevant, and thus their favor changes from day to day—and often from math class to music.

This is why Amy was cool one week and weird the next.

I remember tucking Amy into bed and she asked, "*Why* do they think I'm weird?" It was the question I had anticipated, just as I'd expected she would soon discover the truth about her place in the social order.

"Well, here's the thing," I began gently. "I don't think you're weird, but I think you're different. And some people think being different is weird." What followed was the first of what I knew would be countless conversations about why she doesn't fit in and how it feels to be excluded.

Back then, she concluded it was because I wouldn't buy clothes for her at Limited Too or let her have Bratz dolls or carry a purse to school. Even in the third grade she was insightful enough to understand that certain rules apply to getting close to the "it" girls, many of which clearly are about owning the right stuff and showing it off.

She's starting to realize it's more than that.

Now approaching middle school, Amy understands she is different because we're raising her to be different, an uncommon individual, free to explore her own interests, her own style, and her own self-expression. She's dealing with the hard reality that our beliefs about spending and consumerism have an impact on her social standing, but at the same time she's figuring out that it's more important to us that she *be herself* than that she be like—or liked by—the "it" girls or anyone else.

Not that this was any comfort on a Tuesday night while tears streamed down her tiny face. In the yellow glow of her night-light, she seemed so small to me that I couldn't believe we were already there, in third grade, negotiating the rough waters of female friendship as she began the crossing from childhood to adolescence to young adulthood.

Fortunately, I know our geek-parenting strategy will get her safely to shore on the other side.

Geeks Dare to Be Different

In a world where conformity is required for acceptance, raising geeks means you and your family dare to be different. In fact, I believe the geek lifestyle represents the "new nonconformist"—a counterculture mind-set that rejects the prevailing attitudes, values, fads, and trends in favor of authentic, moral choices and unpopular (some might say old-fashioned) values.

It used to be that conformity was something children were expected to achieve. Only a generation ago, conformity meant we had adopted the prevailing cultural values and norms of social behavior that transcended the uncivilized and uncouth traits of childhood. You conformed to standards of manners in the classroom, in church, in a restaurant, at a store, in the theater, at a friend's home, or even at a funeral parlor. Conforming was expected; conforming was cultivated. Conforming was good. (And if you didn't conform, you could expect some other adult would tell your mom and dad!)

I hate to be the one to tell you, but if you allow your child to conform to today's cultural values, prevailing attitudes, and standards of social behavior, you may be dismayed (or even appalled) at the way your kid turns out. This is because our culture has rewritten the rule book on behavior and social expectations, and in the new rule book there is only one rule: *It's all about me.*

There once was a name for kids who displayed this sort of self-absorbed and overly materialistic attitude: spoiled brat. It's a label that isn't even an insult anymore—it's printed on T-shirts in which children proudly parade about. It's also a label that seems to describe the vast majority of kids! The evidence is everywhere—documented, in fact, through countless surveys and studies—that prove the mind-set of selfishness and consumerism is the hallmark of today's generation of children. What's worse, several surveys indicate parents believe they spoil their own kids and that this is one reason for their children's bad attitudes, but they're not willing to change their buying habits or their responses to their kids' feverish consumerism.

It seems that time and time again, we see surveys in which parents admit their role in a parenting problem but also confess they have no intention of improving. This explains a lot, doesn't it?

The organization New American Dream put out some compelling information from a survey on kids and consumerism that quantifies what we geek parents already know (and are trying to avoid):

* **Shopping for self-esteem** A majority of American youth buy things in an attempt to improve their self-esteem. More than half of those surveyed say that buying certain products makes them feel better about themselves, with twelve- and thirteen-year-olds particularly vulnerable.

* **Peer pressure to buy new stuff** While advertisers spend billions to make young people try to feel good about spending

money and having things, kids nevertheless feel a great deal of pressure to spend to fit in. About a third admit feeling pressure to buy certain products, such as clothes, shoes, and CDs because their friends have them.

* **Manipulating parents by begging** Among the vast majority of kids (81 percent) who ask their parents for money or permission to buy a product, four in ten say they know in advance that their parents will say no. And nearly six in ten keep nagging—on average nine times—in the hopes they can get their parents to give in. More than half of kids surveyed said begging works. Eleven percent of twelve- to thirteen-year-olds admit to asking their parents more than *fifty times* for products they've seen advertised.

These statistics explain the "spoiled" part, but what about that "brat" thing? If you've ever wandered the aisle at your local toy store or stood in line at a fast-food place and listened to the way children routinely speak to their parents and other adults, you must wonder, as I do, how it has become commonplace for a whole generation of children to address their parents with the disdain and disrespect you might normally accord a cockroach.

This sort of behavior doesn't reflect just bad manners but bad attitudes. Dr. Michele Borba, author of twenty-one parenting and education books, including *Don't Give Me That Attitude*, says, "Bad attitudes are far more deadly than mere behaviors because they are more entrenched and are kids' operating beliefs for life. And there lies the danger: bad attitudes such as disrespect, bullying, arrogance, and cheating are becoming 'acceptable' to all too many kids."

I'd take that a step further—I'd say most kids. The sad reality is that good attitudes—respect for others, courtesy, humility, integrity, and a decided lack of materialism—now are the hallmarks of an uncommon child.

Especially uncommon is a child who doesn't define himself by the stuff he owns—or more accurately, by what other people think about the stuff he owns. Show me a child who doesn't give a lick that he listens to music on an off-brand MP3 player—or heaven forbid, a portable CD player—not an iPod nano—and I'll show you a geek.

There's More to Life Than Going to the Mall

Years ago, the term *mall rats* emerged to describe the packs of tweens and teens roaming the corridors of America's shopping malls. Then, taking full advantage of this cultural phenomenon, Hollywood in 1995 even made a movie called *Mallrats* starring Shannen Doherty and Ben Affleck. I heard it was awful. Anyway, we all know the term *mall rats* refers to the underground culture of young materialists who use America's shopping malls as the backdrop for their adolescent exploits. Traveling the mall in large, loud groups, they wander from the food court to the movie theater to the arcade on a quest for fun and new friends.

Going to the mall remains a primary social activity for most urban and suburban kids. But rather than provide a safe haven to lunch, laugh, and look, shopping malls serve as incubators for the growing materialism that gradually is eating away at our kids.

Thanks to the mall-rat mentality and the extreme influence of marketers through the media, being social beyond the age of eight now means hanging out in stores, spending money, and having the stuff "everybody else" has.

THE PRESSURE TO CONFORM MEANS PRESSURE TO CONSUME

Who is "everybody else"? The cool kids, of course. Cool kids glean from the media what the hottest trends and fads are, and with the help of their indulgent parents, they set out to accumulate every toy, gadget, shoe, and clothing item that marks them as cutting-edge. Forget about knockoffs—cool kids know the labels that establish them as authentically cool. Brand identity and brand loyalty begin in toddlerhood—yes, toddlerhood! By the time your child reaches kindergarten, there are kids wearing Abercrombie jeans and Happy Bunny T-shirts that say SPOILED across the chest (as if there was any doubt). With this kind of consumerism commonly established at such a young age, you can see why marketers literally salivate at the thought of the twenty-seven million tweens (that's nine- to twelve-year-olds) with fists full of disposable allowance.

Keep in mind that the most important factor in belonging to the cool crowd is conformity. You need to look like them, talk like them, act like them, dress like them, own what they own, and do what they do. And conforming in the culture of cool means you simply must spend your way into the cool crowd—it's the cover charge on participation at any level.

There's a parenting crisis in all this spending, as well, which is brilliantly discussed by Dr. Madeline Levine in her book *The Price of Privilege*. She posits that affluence in America allows adults to pacify their children with material goods rather than sustain them with emotional connection. Her practice deals largely with teens facing dangerous depression and emotional despair, though they "want" for nothing.

Dr. Levine draws an alarming connection between materialism and a lack of healthy self-development: "Materialism is both a cause and a symptom of impaired self-development. Materialism is not only about having shallow values; it is also about how easy it can be choose the simple seduction of objects over the complex substance of relationships. Materialism sucks the life out of purpose and altruism as kids become increasingly self-centered and indifferent to the needs of others."

That's an alarming reality! As a culture we're giving our kids all the stuff they think they want to be happy, but we're leaving them lacking in the stuff that constitutes true connection—and thus, true happiness. Not only is materialism inveigling itself into children's hearts and souls, but the objects that occupy their attention also are value-laden in ways that further corrupt kids' budding morality. In other words, it's not just *that* we're buying them stuff, it's *what* we're buying, too.

TOYS THAT TEACH (QUESTIONABLE) VALUES

If what I'm writing here so far suggests the image of tween girls sporting designer purses or teenage boys with an iPod in one ear and a Bluetooth receiver in the other, think again. Materialism is a value that's taught from infancy. Or at least, buying tons of stuff on behalf of infants is viewed as the first step to good parenting. But once you're past the baby stage, you have to get toys in the house, right?

Look out, because the culture of cool has permeated the aisles at your local Toys "R" Us, transforming children's playthings into tools for perpetuating the dominant values of consumerism, materialism, and self-absorption—and worse. These are the toys, games, and gadgets you *must have* to be cool. *Everyone* has them.

To wit: Bratz dolls.

You undoubtedly know about the "Bratzpack," the updated version of the fashion doll designed for a new generation. Bratz are billed as "the only girls with a passion for fashion," though the fashions they sport are best described with that classic Southern catchall word *skanky.* And the clothes aren't even the point. The fantasy world of Bratz dolls focuses on going to the mall, the prom, and the dance club—places every five-year-old girl dreams about, right?

The keyword for Bratz is *hot*—hot styles, hot makeovers, hot guys. Now maybe I'm overreacting, but then someone will have to explain to me why the holographic collector card that came with "Beach Bratz" dolls featured a picture of a Bratz character in jeans and a midriff-baring T-shirt (caption: *cool days*) and the same doll casting an unmistakably sexual expression while wearing a string bikini (new caption: *hot nights*). I think it's safe to say the creators of Bratz have ignored the statistics I mentioned a chapter ago about the dangers of hypersexualizing our children.

Another message that exudes from the Bratz collection is the fixation on materialism. Bratz are all about shopping for, buying, having, and showing off the coolest, hottest stuff. Among the fantasy scenarios most commonly portrayed by Bratz is going to the mall. (The Bratz Web site also has a strong shopping component aimed at kids.)

Bratz is one of the most successful and lucrative toy lines in toy history. Not only are the dolls' collagen-pumped lips, tattoo-liner eyes, and anorexic bodies slapped across every imaginable collateral item available to be marketed (lunch boxes, scooters, bedspreads, kids' electronic games including a Bratz laptop), but, as with all multimedia marketing strategies, Bratz have come to life on TV, in the movies, and over the Internet.

But what's the big deal? Bratz are just toys—no different from Barbie was for our generation, right? Wrong. I think the image exuded by the entire line of toys is intentionally trashy because its exaggerated sexuality is supposed to speak loudly and clearly to a generation of insecure young girls. It's all about the hair, the makeup, and the stuff that ultimately makes you popular and gets guys to notice you, and what gets noticed is being sexy. And sexy is something you can buy at the mall.

If it seems I'm on a rampage about this particular line of toys, I'm not alone. Dr. Diane Levin, professor of education at Wheelock College and coauthor of *So Sexy So Soon—the Sexualization of Childhood*, says, "The Bratz send a host of harmful messages about play, appearance, sexuality, and what it means to be a young girl. They teach girls to focus on appearance and fashion, to aspire to an eating-disordered body, and to play at being sexy before they're even capable of understanding what sexy means."

I'm thinking Dr. Levin is probably a geek mom.

Equally disconcerting are games and toys geared at boys. Believe it or not, in the culture of cool, there's a hierarchy of acceptance based on the gaming system you own. Here's how my son explained it to me: The bottom-feeders, gaming-wise, are any systems in their previous generation. "The graphics just aren't as good," Jimmy says. He should know. We have a PlayStation 2.

Nintendo Wii is "only okay" because, while the technology is cool,

the games (so far) are considered "babyish." So even though it's relatively new and expensive, it's near the bottom of the gaming food chain.
Next up the ladder is PS3, the most current (and expensive) version of
PlayStation. It's cool because it lets you play "pretty good games" and
"the graphics are sweet." Coolest of all is the Xbox 360 Elite edition.
The guys who have this system play *Halo, Doom,* and *Gears of War.*
Jimmy can't tell me much about these games because, as of this writing,
he's never played them. But he knows these are the violent games the
cool guys in his class play.

These games are rated M for mature players. Jimmy and his friends
are all around thirteen. In my opinion, thirteen is not very mature. Or
maybe that's just my provincial worldview.

Now, I'm not trying to pitch this next idea as hard science by any
stretch of the imagination, but it's interesting all the same. When I asked
Jimmy, "If I decided to do a one-eighty on all kinds of technology and
got you an Xbox 360 and a Wii and a flat-screen TV in your bedroom
and a cell phone and a laptop, would you be popular and cool?"

"I don't know," he said, "but I think there would be some guys who
would come over just to use my stuff."

I took my hypothetical question one step further. "If I let you get an
Xbox 360 but I didn't let you have the cool games like *Halo* or *Gears
of War* or other games rated for mature players, would you be cool and
popular then?"

"No," he said. "It's not just about the gaming system. It's about
which games you can play."

So it's not just about owning certain stuff. It's about having *access*
to games and other media that makes the cool people cool.

These games are worth noting. The culture of cool stokes aggression
and self-centeredness in boys by pushing electronic games that indulge
the worst elements of human nature. Researchers have documented
beyond doubt that violent video games increase hostility, aggressive
thinking, and behavior. By living vicariously through the dark and
sometimes criminal behaviors of video-game characters, our kids get
the chance to feel the "thrill" of fulfilling fantasies of violence against

others. Consider that in 2002, the video game *Grand Theft Auto: Vice City* was the number-one-selling video game among teens and preteens. It's rated M for mature players, I guess because it takes a fair amount of maturity to simulate having sex with a prostitute and then kill her. But then again, maybe not, since preteens enjoy the game, too.

Don't tell me these games aren't feeding the epidemic of bullying on school playgrounds as well as the rampant road rage we find on highways across America. I'm absolutely certain they are.

PASSING FADS PASS BY GEEKS

Geek parents just say no to Bratz dolls. Same with violent video games. Same with iPods and cell phones for preteens. Same with laptops and TVs in kids' bedrooms. Same with clothes that cost extra to reveal body parts that should be covered and are imprinted with advertisements for a chain of stores that exploit the innocence of the very children doing their insidious marketing. No, no, a thousand times no.

For a geek parent, spending money has to make sense, and spending money to gain entry into a social circle just doesn't.

Not that my geek philosophy about material consumption has been easy. We've blazed our own trail and that fact makes us different. And remember, if conformity is the key to acceptance, being different must be…bad.

Nonetheless, here's an example of how it plays out: For several years, Bratz was the most common theme for birthday parties among my daughter Amy's school friends. Bratz dolls were the number one gift requested by every little girl we knew. All Amy wanted to give her pals were Bratz dolls because that's the gift all the other girls would be giving.

Unfortunately for Amy, I simply would not conform when it came to Bratz. I felt strongly that these dolls resembled streetwalkers in Las Vegas. Not only did I refuse to give them as gifts, I wouldn't even walk through the Bratz aisle in the store because I felt like I was cruising a rope line at a nightclub. Instead, we gave her friends pajamas or a book or a board game. Amy would go to parties where all the other kids' gifts elicited squeals of delight ("Ohmygosh! I don't have this Jade doll yet!") and her gifts...well...they were different.

No matter. I stuck to my principles. Eventually, when they came out with "Lil' Bratz"—the baby doll version of the fashionista dolls—I realized our culture had reached a new low in sexualizing its children. Lil' Bratz dress like biker babies.

I said no to those, too.

WHEN MONEY MATTERS

Addressing the issue of materialism, Dr. Madeline Levine makes a profound statement: "Materialism is not the same as having money." The attitude of materialism permeates every socioeconomic class. Of course it may be easier to say no to the materialistic lifestyle when you honestly can't afford to keep up with the children of the Joneses. Our relatively large family (by today's standards, anyway) means my four kids are accustomed to being told "that's not something we can afford" when looking at a Sunday circular for electronics, for example.

But this isn't always the case. Oftentimes we're perfectly able to afford something, but buying it doesn't reflect the values we want to teach our children about spending money and owning things. When the budget isn't calling the shots, you can send an even stronger message to your children about what you believe is necessary and appropriate.

On the other hand, I know plenty of parents who clearly spend beyond their means to give their kids all the latest cool stuff. It amazes me that families who struggle to get by and work long hours to make ends meet are assuring that their kids' desires for high-end extras are met, no matter what. This sends a message, too—an equally strong one—that indulging the wants and desires of children is more important than Mom and Dad's time, the family's time, or other things the family might buy and enjoy. There's a commercial for a cell-phone carrier that plays into this phenomenon, where Dad announces to the kids, "Great news! We got a new cell-phone plan that lets you send all the text and picture messages you want." The kids say, "But we do that already." Then Dad says, "Yeah, but now Mom can quit her second job." Mom walks in wearing a taco suit while going through the day's mail. Hilarious, right? Except it's true.

I confess I would feel differently about parents working long hours to pay for violin lessons or science camp. Those things aren't necessary either, but they seem to send a strong positive message to children that you're willing to make a sacrifice so they can have a valuable life experience. In my view, that would be a worthy effort, whereas busting your tail to pay for a cell-phone line with unlimited text messaging for a twelve-year-old is not.

How to Teach Values and Spend Time the Geeky Way

As with all things, when teaching your children about consumerism and the role of materialism in your life, your values are the starting point. Are you concerned about the rampant consumerism our kids are experiencing from even their earliest days? Do you want your kids to learn to play and entertain themselves rather than rely on various media to entertain them? Do you want them to grow up with an awareness and understanding of the cost of things and to learn to appreciate what you give them as well as the things they earn on their own?

I'm guessing if you've read this far and you haven't yet put this book aside you're nodding yes to those questions. Here's the thing—you can't get to yes without saying a lot of noes.

Curbing materialism in our children takes an enormous effort because of the sheer force of the marketing machine against which we're all doing battle. Our kids see some forty thousand advertisements per year. *Forty thousand.* (Makes you wonder how many times you're saying no in response to those ads, doesn't it? I think it's best not to count.) Moreover, cross marketing means even a trip to the store for school supplies is a trip down merchandising lane (think SpongeBob folders and notebooks that cost double the price of a noncharacter item).

The biggest challenge is that marketers have access to our kids even when we're not there to shield them from consumer messages we don't want them to get. Sheltering our kids from media only goes so far when there's a commercial presence even at your school's book fair! Consider this from Josh Golin, program manager for the Campaign for a Commercial-Free Childhood in an article entitled "Marketing and Parental Responsibility":

> Even the most attentive and well-intentioned parents cannot pro-tect their kids from all child-directed marketing. For one, there is simply too much of it. Marketers spend more than $15 bil-lion a year targeting children, much of it deliberately designed to circumvent parents and undermine their authority. The absence of parents is one reason corporations like to target children in schools. Viral marketing—which provides popular children with free products to market to their unsuspecting friends—is another way marketers make an end run around parents. At the same time, advertisements frequently undermine parental authority by encouraging children to nag for products.

What this means for geek parents is that refraining from commer-cialism and materialistic attitudes is first and foremost a matter of imparting our values about consumerism to our children.

Sharing your values is a matter of explaining your choices and deci-sions as you exercise the power of your purse strings. This is an area of parenting where it's especially important to always answer the question "Why?" When my kids have wanted things that were not consistent with what I value, I'll say, "I don't like the ads for Abercrombie, so we're not shopping there," or "I don't think a ten-year-old is responsible enough to own a $199 iPod," or "I'm not buying notebooks with characters on them because they cost twice as much as plain ones."

In those three responses, I convey that I believe it's wrong for marketers to send hypersexualized messages to and about children, I believe it's foolish to give expensive "toys" to people who are likely to lose them, and I think it's wasteful to fill the coffers at Nickelodeon just so you can walk around with the same folder as everyone else.

It's not really difficult to do this, believe it or not. When you parent in this way, your values are driving the bus, not your desire to make your kids happy, or your hope that they'll fit in with their peers, or your guilt about working long hours away from home, or even your willingness to buy things because you happen to think your kids are so doggone special. (Mine are, too—that's not the point!) What makes our kids special—read: uncommon—is that we're imparting a value system about the relative importance of material things in their lives. You can say, "I love you and I want you to be happy, but I don't want to teach you that happiness is something we can buy." It works. I swear.

GEEKS AND CONSUMERISM

All of this isn't to say that you might not occasionally buy something "cool." Betsy happens to appreciate designer accessories, but she had never owned a designer bag because we don't spend our money on expensive handbags when a cheap one will just as effectively hold your wallet and keys. So, while we were shopping together during spring break, I once bought her a Coach purse (on clearance). I did it because she honestly loved the thing, she had been incredibly helpful to me throughout the vacation, she was spending her last spring break with us (future breaks already promised for Habitat for Humanity trips), and, most important, *she never asked for it.* To be clear, I didn't buy the bag because I had crafted some morally acceptable reason to do it—I did it because I wanted to. But let me reiterate—*Betsy never asked for it.*

Here's another example: For her ninth birthday, I drove Amy to Chicago for the day to visit American Girl Place, have lunch, and see their show. It was motherhood nirvana. How much better does the job get than a day when you, your little girl, and her two dolls eat lunch in a charming restaurant? Since it was her birthday, I told Amy she could get three outfits—one for each doll and one for herself. She also had birthday money to spend from her grandparents, so she was living large.

We shopped and compared prices and figured out what the best choices would be, eventually making our way to the cashier's desk to pay. As we turned and walked away from the counter, Amy looked up at me and said, "Mom, thank you so much. These outfits are wonderful and I'm so happy." Just at that moment a woman walking past us stopped in her tracks, literally gasped with surprise, and held her hand to her heart. She just stood there looking at Amy, stunned, I gathered, by a little girl expressing gratitude.

Well, naturally, I was proud of Amy. But I wasn't that surprised by her display of heartfelt appreciation. She *was* appreciative and it came straight from her heart, but the fact is, I am accustomed to hearing my kids express their thanks. They all do it virtually every time we shop for them—even if we're just buying school supplies.

These two stories about my daughters reflect the kind of response you can only give if the experience of receiving something is exceptional or at least unusual. If every day is a shopping day and your kids typically come home from school to find a purchase waiting for them, you'll have a tough time impressing them with your generosity. I know parents—moms especially—who seem frustrated that they don't feel the appreciation that their gift giving should elicit. So what do they do? Buy bigger and better stuff. This is the mentality that culminates in *My Super Sweet Sixteen,* MTV's reality show about sixteenth-birthday bashes-on-steroids. Ugh.

No child is born knowing how to shop or even how to feel about shopping. Our kids may be inundated with marketing messages—both from marketers and from their peers—but how they feel about those messages and what they believe about them comes from you and your values.

Teaching kids positive values about materialism and consumerism is part of raising an empowered child. If you teach your child that he is not the sum total of what he owns, that he can't buy his way to healthy self-esteem, and that anyone who judges him based on his material possessions isn't worth having as a friend, you'll raise an empowered kid who isn't a slave to consumerism. It *can* be done.

THE PURPOSE OF PLAY

With all the emphasis on buying and owning stuff, our kids are losing sight of what a toy is for: play. It's widely understood that play actually serves countless good purposes for child development, from promoting creativity to exploring and understanding the world to testing various emotions and behaviors. They discover problem solving, critical thinking, and physical agility through play. It's how kids learn—in fact, some educational theorists such as Montessori call play a child's "work."

The problem in our culture is that play no longer accomplishes a lot of what it should because of the way the world of marketing has eliminated so many aspects of good, positive play. If a child plays with a set of Shrek figures, for example, he's likely to simply act out the story lines he's seen in the movies. I've heard my youngest daughter and her friend do this—they don't create new situations for the characters they know from movies, they just reconstruct the dialogue from the film. Cross marketing of characters robs kids of the chance to be imaginative because every doll already has a name, a personality, and a fantasy associated with it.

Thanks to today's generation of toys and games, our kids have very few opportunities to use their imaginations and, especially, very few reasons to pretend—and parents are the ones buying the stuff that eliminates the real fun. Here's what I mean: Go to any toy department and you'll see those child-size pop-up tents with Disney princesses or Spider-Man printed on the fabric. You can set those up in the basement or a kid's bedroom or even outside and you have a nifty little fort to play in.

Personally, I think those kiddy pup tents are just a big bummer. My kids always loved building forts and tents, especially when the weather was warm and they could do it outside. Their structures involved blankets, broomsticks, chairs, and pillows. They would drape a blanket over the furniture or hang it from the branch of a tree, and magically, it became a New York City apartment. They changed their names ("I'm April" and "I'm Heather"), announced their professions ("let's say I'm a hairdresser"; "let's say I'm a flight attendant"), and the game was off and running. The fun part was in the building and creating—solving the problem of getting the blanket to stay—finally getting the environment right so the pretending could begin. They played like this for hours, since Heather the flight attendant could always get lunch for everyone, and what they learned about themselves and their capacity for invention was irreplaceable.

Toys and games should offer avenues to beneficial play. If a child gets easily bored with a toy, it's probably because the thing doesn't offer enough of what play is really all about. Here are a few ways to infuse playtime with more of what makes playing so important:

Teach Your Kids Some "Old" Games

There's a resurgence of interest in traditional games like hopscotch, jacks, checkers, and kickball. Even marbles are making a comeback, thanks to people like Michael Cohill, one of the principals of Akron Marbles and the American Toy Marble Museum. The lost game of marbles now is taught in seminars (are our grandfathers laughing about this?) and it's gaining ground along with other traditional pastimes in part because parents (I'm guessing geek parents) are deeply concerned about the way our modern toys and games promote isolation and boredom. The trend is perhaps best proven by the popularity of brothers Conn and Hal Iggulden's best seller *The Dangerous Book for Boys*, a collection of games and stories that weave history and tradition back into playtime.

Let Your Kids Get Bored

Necessity being the mother of invention, kids will necessarily find creative ways to play if we let them get a little bored now and then. Our kids are so accustomed to being entertained at every moment—if it's not a sports practice or a lesson of some kind, they jump on a computer or plop down on the couch and zone out in front of a TV. There's very little effort expended to entertain themselves—downtime is time when someone else—generally a TV producer—takes over to fill a child's brain with thoughts and responses to those thoughts. I concede it's hard to find the time for boredom, programmed as we are throughout the year, but a child who never is bored is a child who never needs to think for himself what to do for fun. The trick to making this work is when a child complains of being bored, we need to resist the temptation to fill that moment with suggestions. Instead, we need to say, "Well, you can find something fun to do that doesn't involve electronics or TV, or you can unload the dishwasher." You'd be amazed at how many kids will choose emptying the dishwasher. (Just kidding.)

Tolerate a Mess

I'm not going to lie—I'm a neatnik. I admit it and I'm certain it's a form of neurosis, but there it is. So this next piece of geek-parenting advice is actually a tough one for me, but the fact that I give it is indicative of how important it is: Kids need to make a mess when they play. Making a mess with mud, soap, flour, paint, permanent marker, Play-Doh, Lite-Brite bulbs, poker chips—whatever the medium—is a huge way to learn while playing and having fun. I think we parents have grown to put so much value on our houses and our stuff that we want everything "just so" all the time. But kids' playing is messy business. Consider that it's much neater and more convenient to let Junior sit in a chair and use his Game Boy than it is to watch him dump out a box of LEGOS on the floor, spilling pieces under the furniture only to be lost until the carpet gets cleaned. But which is better for Junior's growth and development? Which toy gets him thinking, creating, problem solving? Messy projects and toys with small parts are the bane of every neat-freak mom's existence, but they're the best way to play the parenting game.

HOBBIES AND PASSIONS

As children get older, their recreation time changes for obvious reasons. You can't build forts in the backyard forever, but if you don't hang out at the mall and you don't own the very latest, hippest gadgets (and you certainly don't have freewheeling access to the Internet—not to mention a TV in your bedroom), what the heck are you supposed to do for fun?

Kids who grow up as geeks have time to pursue hobbies. The idea of being a hobbyist pretty much has gone out of fashion, but recently it's started making a comeback perhaps as backlash to the overly structured life today's children lead. A hobby isn't like the extracurricular programs kids do—structured, adult-supervised activities such as team sports. It's usually creative or involves collecting and is pursued simply for the sheer joy of thinking and learning about a particular topic or activity.

Over time, a child who engages in a hobby may develop a passion for his activity or interest, and this is just incredibly cool (in the way a geek mom thinks things are cool!). For example, I know a young man whose music hobby—playing the violin—turned into a passion for playing the Irish fiddle. By age thirteen he was playing reels and winning competitions all over the country. Another young man I know turned his digital photography hobby into a small business making personal DVDs for special occasions. Very cool.

Just how do we encourage our kids to find and cultivate a hobby?

Leave Some Time Unstructured

Hobbies take time. In children, they're often born of boredom and it takes time to get bored! Keep a close eye on your child's calendar and accept that a kid who is overprogrammed is actually not able to experience a well-rounded life. Consider cutting back if your child doesn't routinely get at least one free day on the weekend and one or two nights per week when there's nothing going on.

Expose Kids to the Possibilities

Visit a local museum of interest or peruse the local library shelves for topics your child enjoys, then head to the hobby shop to find a corresponding activity. Consider a community education class such as photography, drawing, painting, or scrapbooking (a class may sound contrary to the advice above about unstructured time, but I'm talking about an introductory class that's a few hours in duration and designed to present the basic "how-tos" of an activity). It's fun to find a hobby for kids that allows them to make things they can give as gifts, such as knitting or woodworking.

Make Room

Find a spot in your child's bedroom or elsewhere in the house where he can work on his hobby without having to always put it away. Leaving the materials out allows him to work on a modeling project or pick up a paintbrush even when there's not a lot of time. Hobbyists like to look at their projects while in progress—it helps the creative process.

Join in the Fun

Kids of hobbyists tend to pick up a hobby. Once again, we parents find ourselves in a win/win situation—by pursuing a hobby, you teach your child the merits of doing so. You may or may not share the same hobby as your child, but just seeing that hobbies are something people enjoy sends an important message.

ELECTRONICS FOR GROWING GEEKS

I'm not writing this book in a bubble. Electronics for children as a way to play and pass the time are here to stay. This is the media generation that will never recall life without computers and digital technology and toys that do big things but fit in the palm of their hands.

Moreover, electronics can be fun. I can't help myself—whenever I wander into the playroom where we keep the PlayStation 2 and Jimmy is lounging on the beanbag chair playing a game of *NBA Live,* I get sucked in as if I'm watching the real thing—only it's better because he creates a player on the team named Jimmy Hicks who has an incredible three-point jumper and some serious hops to dunk the basketball. It's easy to see why he loves to play this game.

It's worth repeating, however, that many of the most popular games, especially those marketed to tween and teen boys, are simply bad for a kid's heart and soul. Games that promote fantasies of gratuitous violence, misogyny, crime, horror, and gore are known to feed the dark and dangerous side of human behavior. Geek parents don't allow them in their homes and make a big fuss if their kids are exposed to them elsewhere.

Similarly, I have major concerns about online gaming communities as a place for kids to play. With all the information we have about the rapidly growing incidence of predators using the Internet to find and exploit children, I can't see the utility in allowing a child to "go play" in a virtual-game room with a bunch of strangers. All the warnings and common sense in the world don't work against a shrewd and conniving person who is intent on finding a naive child. Therefore, at our home we simply don't permit online gaming, even with friends.

This issue is important only to my son, a young teenager. For a few years now, he's been asking me if he could go online to play *Age of Empires* with a buddy of his, who also plays this game on his home computer. The boys have tried to convince me it's safe to play remotely from their own homes in a virtual-game room because they would only be communicating with each other. They say it would be more fun than sharing the mouse and taking turns on our computer because there apparently are features in the online version that don't come in the home edition.

I've listened to this very reasoned and well-articulated argument from Jimmy and I understand why he'd like to do this, but the answer is still no. I only needed to read the first few pages of my friend Chris Hansen's book *To Catch a Predator* to be convinced that online communities may be "virtual" but they're still gatherings of strangers taking place in your living room. And remember: Strangers are people you don't know.

Games come and go and new ones are introduced almost daily. The games you allow for your kids will reflect their tastes and interests. Rather than make a list of the specific ones we permit for our kids, I think it's more useful to consider the guidelines I use when choosing or approving an electronic game:

The Goal of the Game Has to Be Wholesome and Fun
Note that I didn't say the goal of the game has to be educational. I think every experience has educational value in some form or other, even if all you're learning is that extreme skateboarding tricks aren't as easy as they look. I'm fine with games that have competition built into them, as most do. For the PlayStation, we favor sports games and strategy games such as *Kingdom Hearts,* in which Disney characters must conquer a variety of levels to win. My favorite use of the PlayStation is for *Dance Dance Revolution,* the game where you bounce on a dance pad and try to keep up with steps on the screen. It's aerobic, competitive, and fun. Jimmy and his pals love *Guitar Hero,* which explains his newfound interest in the late Jimi Hendrix. What goes around comes around.

When they were younger, my kids all enjoyed point-and-click games for the computer. Amy, in particular, still can be found putting outfits together for a computerized Barbie fashion show. For a while Betsy played a computer game in which she built her own restaurant—it turned out to be harder than it looked because she had to follow a business plan and if her café went broke she had to start over.

All four kids play Texas Hold-Em on Game Boys, which means they can also play a real hand of poker with my husband around a game table, and this makes him happy.

The Concept of the Game Has to Jibe with Our Values
Just as in choosing TV shows, movies, and music, if you choose electronic games that reflect your values, you set some very concrete parameters. At the risk of repetition, we don't permit gratuitous violence, sexual themes, vulgar or profane language, crime themes, terrorism, gore, and horror, so right away a whole bunch of games don't make it through my front door.

I've mentioned that my son plays *Age of Empires* and *Age of Mythology,* two games that pit armies against each other to do battle for territory. You might think since these strategy games include wars that I'm not being consistent regarding violence. The difference to me is in the graphics and in the intent of the game. Not all war games are strategy games like the ones my son plays; in his games, he must first build a village, grow crops, add people and armies, build forts and weapons such as trebuchets, and then when he feels he's able, he does battle with his enemy. The actual scenes of war look like small splashes of color and tiny flames. Contrarily, war games that glorify violence focus on the adventure of hunting and being hunted in the field of battle (which these days is an urban setting). The graphics are "realistic" and the violence is gratuitous, bloody, and gross.

Unlike other kinds of media ratings, electronic games are rated based on content as well as age-appropriateness. This means you can get some information about a game from its packaging. The Entertainment Software Rating Board uses a universal system to warn parents and kids about graphic and mature content—their Web site at www.esrb.org has a good search engine in it that lets you find games by rating, platform, and content. But be warned: the ESRB doesn't actually play all the games it rates. It relies on the information provided to it by the games' publishers with respect to content. ESRB claims its stringent self-regulatory rules create strong disincentives for publishers to hide a game's true content. If you're like me, though, you're surprised and dismayed to learn the game rating system isn't based on a review by an independent evaluator.

The Use of the Game Has to Be Measured
Electronics may be here to stay, but they ought not to dominate the recreational time our kids enjoy. I don't want my kids playing only electronics, just as I don't want them playing only one sport year-round, or playing the piano to the exclusion of all else, or reading and never riding a bike. Childhood should be full of a variety of activities. An hour of gaming on a rainy day is fine. Six hours of gaming after dinner until 2 A.M. is not healthy.

CHESS: THE GEEK TRADEMARK

When I was about twelve years old, I played chess with my cousin Audrey and she beat me in something like five minutes. Audrey was nine. She was brilliant then, as she is now. That experience—humbling as it was—helped me realize that people who play chess can have a lot of fun doing something smart.

My husband has taught all four of our children how to play chess—thank goodness, because if I taught them they'd never win a game. In middle school, Katie and Betsy joined the chess club, and along with Katie's pal Meredith, the three of them constituted the female contingency in the organization. So, in addition to winning chess games, they were in charge of the food. Chess club was a small group—a geeky group—but among their favorite activities for a while.

Playing chess remains a hallmark of the geek lifestyle, but even so it's surging in popularity, especially in Harlem. There, the world's first black grand master, Maurice Ashley, and the Harlem Chess Center are teaching hundreds of kids the benefits of this ancient game: problem solving, patience, perseverance, focus, and concentration. Playing chess increases self-esteem and self-confidence and gives kids a sense of their own potential, which is why it is also used as part of the core curriculum for fourth to sixth graders in a Harlem school for gifted students. Chess also fosters maturity and teaches kids you can have fun doing something that's inherently challenging.

Though it's gaining ground on some fronts, chess remains the antithesis of all that is cool in our culture. It's not electronic, it's not fast, and it's not sexy. This explains why there's a chess set on our coffee table all the time, just in case anyone wants to play.

Uncommon Self-Confidence

Envision a child who is taught to resist the lure of materialism. She grows up playing wholesome, fun games and enjoying activities that feed her curiosity and enrich her existence. She isn't concerned about whether her hobbies or her interests are considered cool by her peers. She's not encumbered by the constraints of conformity.

This child has freedom to be herself. She's not a slave to trends or fads. She's not burdened with anxiety in her effort to fit in or be just like everyone else. She never worries what people think about her.

This child has uncommon self-confidence.

Geek parenting hinges on getting comfortable with the notion that our kids are uncommon. By daring to be different—daring to teach our kids that being different is good—we're empowering them with real self-esteem, not the artificial kind kids feel when they gain peer acceptance based on the wrong things.

Not that geeks don't experience self-doubts from time to time—that's a natural part of growing up for every child, cool or uncool. But I would argue that a geek has a greater chance of developing the kind of self-awareness and self-acceptance that come with mastery and achievement and, especially, with knowing that you aren't what you own.

Uncool Answers

My parents seem to think the way to establish a relationship with my kids is to buy lots of "cool" stuff for them. How do I curb this?

Grandparenting in America seems to have evolved into a financial arrangement for many families, which seems sad to me. It's one thing to spoil the grandkids with treats and indulgences, but showing up with an electric scooter or a stack of new DVDs seems more typical these days.

The tricky thing here is to be both grateful for their generosity and firm in your request that they back off on some of their cool shopping expeditions. And the really important thing to do is to facilitate a healthier, more genuine relationship between your folks and your kids.

Here's a place where developing a hobby could serve a useful purpose. As long as your parents want to spend money on your kids, how about they pay for a photography class at the Y or a knitting class at the yarn store? They could even do this together with your child and, in the process, establish a friendship that doesn't revolve around things but around an activity or shared interest. The point is, where spending is concerned, you can try to redirect your folks to things you feel good about.

I'd make it clear to your children, though, that asking for specific items is a no-no. Gifts are supposed to be freely given and graciously received, not ordered from friends and family like online purchases. (The trend of registering for birthday and Christmas gifts makes me physically ill, in fact.) If your folks are only responding to your child's repeated requests for things, the problem isn't really your parents, is it?

On the other hand, if your children are really not asking for stuff and you've politely gushed that their gifts are unnecessary—and if your hints about giving something more appropriate aren't heeded—I'd say a conversation on the topic is in order.

We need to share with our families how important it is to raise our kids with a healthy appreciation for the cost of things, and with a grateful heart when receiving things. If you explain your concerns about materialism and tell your parents how important it is to you that your kids grow up differently from the cultural norm in this regard, they probably will join you in the effort.

Most of all, no matter how you feel about a gift your parents give your kids, insist that every gift is acknowledged with a thank-you note. In the end, your job is to teach your kids gratitude and an appreciation for the generosity of others.

Oh, and no one says the kids must have access to every item that lands in the house. You're still the parent, and it's your job to call the shots about what is and isn't an appropriate toy or gadget.

Guaranteed Geek: Tips That Dare to Be Different

For Geeks of All Ages:

* Teach kids the cost of things. When shopping, show them how you compare prices as well as how you make choices about what you can afford.

* Help kids learn to save for things they desire.

* Focus on the character and personality of your child's friend, not on what she owns—even if your child would rather tell you about her stuff.

* To curb materialism, keep gifts reasonable, even at Christmas. (We're fond of recalling that even Jesus got just three gifts.)

* Teach your kids to compare items with high-end labels to comparable off-brand items and discuss whether it's worth it to spend extra for a name brand.

For Elementary School Geeks:

* Use shopping trips for birthday parties as a time to teach your values about possessions. No matter what "everyone else" is giving, make your gifts a reflection of your values.

* Keep your own birthday parties simple and small so that your child doesn't equate birthdays with an onslaught of presents.

* Limit your purchases of merchandising for products you use (macaroni and cheese shaped like cartoon characters, for example). Explain to your kids that character merchandising makes products unnecessarily expensive.

* Find a hobby that can grow with your child.

For Middle School Geeks:

* Find ways to help kids earn the things they want (babysitting, chores, bottle returns).

* Think long and hard about how necessary it is that your middle schooler gets a cell phone or pager. Then think again.

* Build adventure into your geek's life and at the same time demonstrate that materialism isn't as much fun as sharing a cool experience (think water rafting, a night at the theater, a session of horseback-riding lessons).

* If you choose to buy something considered "cool," expect uncommon gratitude in return.

* Talk about consumerism and reinforce your values about its impact on people's behavior.

For High School Geeks:

* Talk about materialism and the commercialization in our culture. Keep the conversations going about your values as your kids exercise more choices about what to own.

* Don't forget you're still the authority figure in your home. If stuff starts to own your kids rather than your kids owning their stuff, remind them they can live without it (i.e., take some things away for a while if you must).

* Turn your teen on to the fun of resale shopping, yard sales, and outlet malls. Help her develop an uncommon sense of style and make sure she knows you admire her for it.

Rule #4

RAISE A KID ADULTS LIKE

One summer day, Betsy invited a girl she knew from school to spend the afternoon at our house. We drove to her home to pick her up, and when she climbed into the car, Betsy initiated a friendly conversation. "How's your summer going?"

"Fine." (Not, "Fine, how about yours?" Just "fine.")

"What have you been doing?" Betsy tried again.

"Nothing." (Not, "Nothing. What about you?" Just "nothing.")

"Do you have anything fun planned?" I had to give Betsy credit. She wasn't giving up.

"No." (Not, "No, but stop asking me so many stupid questions," though that's what it sounded like from the driver's seat.)

Look up the word *awkward* in the dictionary and you'll find the transcript from that car ride. It was excruciating.

I did what I always do at awkward moments—I started talking. Attempting to bridge the gap in conversation, I talked *at* this child as though she were interested. Betsy joined in, and within a block or two, my daughter and I were engaged in a lovely conversation about the various considerations a family must make when planning a trip.

I remember thinking how nice it was, enjoying the company of such a well-mannered and polite child—my own daughter! But despite our efforts to engage the friend in our conversation, she sat in the backseat like a stone.

Clearly, it was going to be a long day for Betsy.

If conversational skills among young peers are on the decline, getting children to talk to an adult is like cracking a bank vault.

I remember Jimmy once invited a new boy at school to play at our house for the first time. Since I didn't know him, I tried to visit with him while making the boys' lunch. Note I said I *tried* to visit with him. I asked how he liked school, inquired about his favorite subjects and what sports he liked best—just the usual banter that grown-ups attempt with kids.

To every question, the boy gave me a sullen "I don't know" while staring blankly at my kitchen floor.

Now, I realize it's not always comfortable for a twelve-year-old boy to chat amiably with the mother of his friend, but I wasn't asking deeply personal questions that would put him in the conversational hot seat. "Do you like math or science better?" is hardly a delicate inquiry.

The sad fact is no one ever taught that boy how to engage in polite conversation. Jimmy said he talked when they were alone, as I know most kids are willing to do with their peers, but even between the two of them, Jimmy found the conversation stilted (my word, not Jimmy's). Unfortunately, his rude behavior left me unimpressed. He hasn't been back since.

Kids can be shy around adults they don't know well, and I'm not one to judge a child's pleasant quietness too harshly. Often—especially when I'm driving kids places, it seems—if I'm transporting a particularly reserved child, I'll look over my shoulder and say, "Listen, Susie, I've had enough of this jabbering. You're dominating the conversation and we'd all like to get a word in edgewise." If they're not completely confused by my oddball sense of humor, this will generally elicit some giggles.

By comparison, I'm certainly willing to concede that my own kids are unusually talkative; a fact that has been well documented at many a parent–teacher conference. But still.

The unwillingness on the part of most kids to engage in polite conversation with adults is just one issue reflecting the woefully dismal expectations on the part of our culture of children's social behavior. Beyond poor conversational skills, the overall lack of training in manners and etiquette is leaving us with a generation of rude and thoughtless people headed into adolescence and beyond. Look out.

On the other hand, kids who *are* raised to practice the conventions of polite society and trained to exhibit good manners are bound to be geeks. And geeks are kids adults like.

Rude Is the New Normal

Being concerned about manners is a hallmark of the geek lifestyle, but not a big factor in the culture of cool. In fact, cool kids sometimes seem to relish the chance to deliberately demonstrate their rudeness. They're aloof and unresponsive to teachers (especially substitutes—I know; I was one), they roll their eyes at school administrators, they grunt in reply to questions from other adults. They aren't likely to take their headphones off if you initiate a conversation with them. They *are* likely to abruptly walk away, leaving even a self-confident and mature adult feeling awkward and abandoned. (All the better if a cool friend is nearby—then the posturing and boorish behavior is even more pronounced.)

Apparently, it's cool to be rude.

In our culture, it's also expected. Somehow, we've twisted our understanding of adolescence to mean a period when self-centeredness and bad manners correlate with growing maturity. Tweens and teens, we're warned by parenting experts, must necessarily assert themselves in this way as part of the process of achieving their individuality. This belief is rampant among child-development "experts," as best exemplified by this quote I found online from a social worker at a major children's hospital:

Independence is another reason for children talking back. As children grow and become more independent, they have a need to assert more control over their own lives. Talking back can be a way for children to separate themselves from their parents...Kids need to talk back, but they need ways to do it that aren't disruptive to your relationship.

Kids *need* to talk back? *Really?* And we need to *help them do it* in ways that aren't disruptive to our relationships? Man, there sure is a lot I don't know. Quick. Someone, sign me up for a degree in child development.

I'd call that opinion a bunch of hooey, but I have to say it's a theory that has inexplicable traction. Back when Katie's thirteenth birthday approached, I heard endless warnings about what my future would hold with a teenager in my home. Because she is my oldest, I had no experience with teens, so parents offered this new conventional wisdom: "She'll turn into a monster," and "Get ready to find out just how stupid you are," and "Don't worry. It'll get better by the time she's twenty-three."

If I had a nickel for every time someone told me to get ready for the change in my daughter, I would have—well, I would have a big, honking pile of nickels.

I couldn't imagine or believe that my delightful teenager was destined to become a holy terror for ten years or that there was nothing I could do about it. More than that, I wouldn't accept an assumption I simply didn't buy.

Why should I believe that my daughter couldn't help but talk back and otherwise treat me like a necessary encumbrance, causing me to wish away her growing years because of excessive obnoxiousness? Who says?

I decided the whole "rude is normal" thing is just a big fat myth. Rude is not normal unless we accept it. I vowed I wouldn't indulge the immature and impolite urges of any adolescent child—least of all my own—nor would I allow my kids to believe that it was permissible to act rudely to anyone. Especially to adults.

Well, guess what? Three of my four children are teenagers, and none of them need to be rude. Neither does their tween sister. It's not because they *aren't* growing and maturing. It's not because they *aren't* individuating, whatever that's supposed to mean. It's because they've been taught that behaving respectfully toward others is how mature people behave. It's also not optional. The result? My kids are known for their exceptional manners and they are highly regarded by adults as comfortable, easy to talk to, and pleasant to be around.

Sadly, for our culture and more so for our kids, too many parents have bought into that stupid myth. Of course we start out okay—we all work with our kids in their early years to learn "the magic words" and "use your manners," but by about age eleven or twelve—the age when hormones start to evince themselves in an unwelcome tone of voice—we don't hold them to standards of polite behavior. We just say, "That's a preteen for ya!" and throw our hands in the air. In doing this, we shortchange them from living up to their potential to be well mannered and well regarded.

WE'RE RUDE AND WE KNOW IT

Now hang on for another shocking revelation (not): An Associated Press annual "rudeness poll" found that almost 70 percent of Americans believe that as a society, we are ruder than we were twenty or thirty years ago. When asked who was to blame for this trend, the number one response—get ready, folks—was "parents not teaching good manners to children." Once again, parents are able to see and admit a problem and realize that they are at least partly to blame for it (in this case, mostly to blame), yet they aren't changing their parenting styles or their expectations of their kids. (Except you—you're becoming a geek parent!)

You can probably guess what the poll's respondents said were other factors in our ruder nation: not enough time to be polite, bad celebrity role models, and TV shows that portray rudeness—all of these excuses garnered a fair share of blame. But really, they're just excuses in my book, just like the myth that rudeness is normal and appropriate teen-age behavior. Because even if we're busy beyond reason, even if we're inundated with news footage of celebrities flipping off photographers and TV shows of ignorant boobs behaving like ignorant boobs—even with *all that,* most of us know what good manners are and that we can choose to practice them. Some people do.

Of course teens aren't the only ones behaving rudely—kids of all ages are commonly ill-mannered. The "rudeness poll" found 85 per-cent of respondents encounter children behaving rudely in public at least occasionally (half of those said they see it frequently). Is it any wonder we're resigned to the notion that bad manners are the norm where kids are concerned? Or that a child who practices good manners is uncommon?

The culture of cool doesn't value manners except as a tactic to manip-ulate adults. Among the cool crowd, there often are some kids who use the training they've received at home to sweet-talk other parents and teachers. In classic "Eddie Haskell" style, they say "Hello, Mrs. Hicks" and "How are you, Mrs. Hicks?" and "I'm fine, thank you for asking." (If you don't know who Eddie Haskell is, you were too young for *Leave It to Beaver.*) Their facility in demonstrating great manners means they can fool some of the adults some of the time, but this doesn't mean they're expressing genuine respect. Mostly, when hanging with the A-list, it's cool to be sarcastic, outspoken, and disrespectful. A kid who earnestly believes and behaves otherwise is a geek.

TECHNO-RUDE

More from the "rudeness poll": Eighty-five percent of those surveyed observe people talking rudely on their cell phones at least occasionally. I'm going to assume the other 15 percent are the ones on the phone, so they haven't noticed this trend. Offensive cell-phone usage is so chronic that restaurants now display the universal "no cell" symbol in their windows, akin to signs in truck stops that say NO SHOES, NO SHIRT, NO SERVICE. It's come to this.

The generation of children growing up in America today hardly knows a parent without a cell phone, and we parents are the ones teaching kids what is customary and proper when it comes to cell-phone manners. I confess I used to be much more of a cell-phone junkie than I am now, in part because I was working in a job that had me communicating more by phone. But I realized at some point that I often would pick my kids up from school while talking on the phone and still be talking when we pulled into our garage. We'd go into the house and I'd keep my call going, motioning to my kids about a snack and mouthing "What homework do you have?" It might be an hour before I actually hung up and spoke to them! How rude was I!?

When I left that job, I decided it was time to improve my manners as I reordered my priorities. My new policy was never to be on the phone when my kids got in the van at the end of the school day, and I think I honor it about 95 percent of the time. This sends a huge message to my children about what it means to exhibit good manners toward them (and as well, if I happen to be on the phone, they understand that it's an unusually important call).

At some point, we all (or at least 85 percent of us) have been subjected to personal information about strangers that we really shouldn't have heard. When our kids are with us, they're hearing it, too. Thanks to a buffoon nearby, they get to hear all about someone's bladder-control problem and their boss's BO. I once sat in a crowded college admissions office while my daughter was being interviewed in the next room. I had to pull out my laptop so I could try to ignore the man on the sofa nearby discussing by cell phone with his mortgage broker why he was denied a loan for a condo. This information was not anyone's business, yet this guy didn't seem to mind that a room full of strangers learned the details of his personal finances. (Begging the question "Why call finances 'personal'?")

Every time our kids see and hear someone on a cell phone, they learn about cell-phone manners. Is it any wonder, then, that when kids get phones of their own, they use them incessantly and without regard for the sensitivities of others?

Of course talking on the cell phone is pretty much last century. Kids use phones for texting almost as much as talking, which means there's one more way for them to be distracted and rude to the people in their presence, adults and kids alike. And with PDAs becoming more affordable, we now find kids accessing the Internet to IM and surf the net no matter what else is going on around them.

All of this technology is designed for communication. But as Betsy was reminded on that summer day with the uncommunicative friend, the real skill of communicating with others—the art of conversation—often is nonexistent.

Techno-rude goes beyond phones and PDAs, especially when it comes to kids. This is because Generation M is perpetually plugged in with earbuds. What once was a novelty that allowed folks to listen to music while running in the park or enjoy a book on tape while sitting on an airplane (remember the original Walkman cassette player with AM/FM radio?) now is a sleek, steadily shrinking iPod or its less-than-cool MP3 equivalent. Living near a college campus, I can tell you it's customary to see young adults walking around with a wire hanging from one ear and a cell phone affixed to the other. They do this in groups, but they don't talk to the people they're actually with. And sorry to say, by age twenty or twenty-one, their manners (or lack thereof) are pretty much written in stone.

Wandering the world while listening to personal music players is so commonplace that the idea that it might be bad manners never even occurs to kids. I recall once looking in my rearview mirror while driving my van and seeing a thin gray wire hanging in Katie's hair. I asked her what it was (though we both knew perfectly well) and she said, "Oh, I can hear you just fine, Mom." She could see where I was going.

Whether she could hear me was not my issue. This was not a long car trip like those on which I permit my children to plug into their personal music devices to pass the time. It was a ten-minute drive to the doctor's office for flu shots, offering us a chance to catch up about the busy school day and get a handle on the homework load for the evening.

I said, "I may not have mentioned this before, but wandering around the planet with an earbud in your head is rude. It tells people you don't want to give them your full attention."

The trend created by all our technology is a growing sense of isolation and the feeling of a social void. It's less effort to just tune out with our own music choices than to give our time and attention to others. Never mind the lost art of small talk with strangers such as store clerks and taxi drivers; the generation we're raising will be hard-pressed to communicate effectively with friends and loved ones because they're not practicing as they grow. If you ask me, techno-rude will have long-term consequences.

HAPPY BIRTHDAY TO ME

Sadly, while birthdays and other social events should offer regular opportunities for kids to learn and practice good manners, they seem to be times when bad manners are even more evident. With the materialistic mind-set from the last chapter in full force, children view birthdays through the lens of acquisition—they're all about the presents. In addition to getting a lot of new and cool stuff, the culture of cool views birthdays and other kinds of gatherings where invitations are issued as excuses to demonstrate that some kids are cool, while others are not.

It should go without saying that exclusive invitations are meant to be kept exclusive—meaning, they're supposed to be just for those who are invited. But these days it's common for kids to announce not only that they are hosting an invite-only gathering, but who is and isn't invited. We geek moms have done our fair share of consoling children about being left off an invitation list. There's nothing you can do but agree that it's rude to make a point of leaving people out. After that, I just remind my children that they, too, may choose their birthday guests (though I expect them to refrain from talking about whom they invite).

You'd think this particular form of rude behavior would get better as kids get older and become more aware of what is hurtful to others. What I've found troubling is that rather than diminishing as kids get older, purposely excluding others continues well into high school. It's

IS THE MANNERS THING JUST ME?

It was parent observation day in the dance studio. The dozen girls in Amy's musical-theater class were set to show off their newfound skills, acting out emotions and belting out show tunes at the top of their little lungs. It's one reason why Amy may become a drama geek—and well worth the money!

Unfortunately, I couldn't concentrate on Amy and her fellow thespians-in-training. All I could focus on were the two children behind me whose abominable behavior was multiplied by the fact that they were reflected in the mirror on the opposite wall.

With just enough space between the last row of chairs and the wall behind us to run back and forth from one end of the room to the other, a five-year-old sister of one of the girls in the class engaged the interest of someone else's nine-year-old brother, and together they went about entertaining each other.

The problem was, the entertainment was supposed to be out on the dance floor. I turned my head just enough to look over my right shoulder and sent a look to no one in particular that said, "If those are your kids, you might want to settle them down." Then I turned back to watch Amy and her classmates.

The behavior behind me didn't stop. Instead, it turned into a stage-whispered ruckus. Again I turned back. Again I looked generally over the group of parents. Again I sent a glance to say, "Hey, folks, if those are your kids, you might want to think about a lasso."

A few more bars of music, and still the rowdy pair behind me continued their antics. With plywood flooring beneath their feet, their running sounded like an army battalion marching through the room. I'm exaggerating only a little here.

I decided a dirty look was in order, but this time, when I turned my head, I realized I couldn't glare at the parents of these two children because I couldn't figure out which of the adults in the chairs around me were their parents. All the adults in the room were facing forward, intently watching the girls perform their dance steps. Nobody else seemed to even notice or be distracted by the rude kids running behind us.

I asked myself, "Is it just me?" Perhaps I was the only person who expected children to sit quietly and watch their siblings during a performance.

The fact that kids misbehave is nothing new. But what I'm seeing more and more are parents doing nothing to correct their kids. No "shushing" or whispered admonitions to sit still. No warning glances or shoulder taps. Not even a wry smile as if to say, "Just because you're adorable doesn't mean it's okay to be disruptive." There seems to be a pervasive attitude that rude behavior in children is not only to be expected but tolerated, which brings me back to the question "Is it just me?"

I don't want to get used to rude children. I don't tolerate it when my own children behave thoughtlessly in public, and I don't see why I should put up with it when other people's children run amok.

I just haven't figured out yet what to do other than send a series of progressively more irritated glances toward the adults whose job it is to react—which obviously doesn't work.

After that performance I remember saying to Amy, "You did such a good job staying focused even though those rude kids were disrupting things."

"What kids?" she said.

Sigh. Maybe it is just me.

common for middle school and high school kids to gather in conversation circles, loudly talking about how much fun the sleepover is going to be, or what time the movie starts, or who is riding with whom to the big game. It makes no difference that two or three kids in the circle aren't included in the social plans—as everyone knows! There's virtually no compunction to hold the chatter until the uninvited kids are gone.

No child expects to be invited to every party or sleepover or pre-game gathering. My kids will tell you there are groups they just don't mix with and this doesn't bother them. But neither do they want to be confronted at every turn with the fact that they're left out. For some reason, the rule about not talking about an event in front of people who aren't included has gone the way of the dodo.

Why Manners Matter to Geeks (and Should Matter to Everyone)

A truism about manners is: They're contagious. Just watch the way you react when someone cuts you off in the Target parking lot and steals the space you were waiting for. You may have been patiently biding your time while some woman loaded her bags into the trunk of her car; you may even have cheerfully endured the extra moment or two it took for her to get settled in her seat and make a cell call. You're practically a saint, right? But then somebody jumps in front of you and snags the space for which you waited patiently, and suddenly you're laying on the horn and using vocabulary that would get you kicked out of your own living room. Why? Because the bad manners of the other driver provoked your rude response. (If this sounds autobiographical, it's just a coincidence. Really.)

This is the cycle our kids are learning. So the answer to the question "Why do *our* manners matter?" is, in addition to either adding to or detracting from the civility of the world in which we live, we're teaching at every moment what it means to be mannerly.

GOOD MANNERS GET NOTICED

Raising well-mannered children—children adults like—matters because our children will be judged throughout their lives on the ways in which they present themselves to the world and the ways in which they treat others. Teaching good manners is one way to give kids a leg up in the adult world. Simple habits such as looking at the person to whom they're speaking, using people's names in conversation ("I'm fine, Mrs. Smith. How are you?"), saying "please" and "thank you," or holding a door for an elder are valued and appreciated by adults such as teachers, coaches, and employers.

Good manners also help promote positive self-esteem. This is because kids who demonstrate social skills receive compliments regu larly on their mannerly behavior. People are very quick to let a child know when they see manners that impress them, so kids who are taught to exhibit good manners also receive a lot of positive feedback, and not just from their parents.

One area where good manners are noticed is over the telephone. From the time they were old enough to answer the phone, which we deemed to be about age four, our children have said, "Hicks residence, [name] speaking." Our kids have never been allowed to simply say, "Hello," though that's the way my husband and I answer our home phone. The difference? We're the adults; they are the children. We're confident that our "hello" won't sound disrespectful or flip, whereas kids can easily sound sloppy if they don't have a structured script. At least, that's our view.

I cannot tell you how many compliments we receive on the telephone manners of our children. I am not exaggerating when I say that almost every single time I am handed the phone by one of my kids, the person on the other end remarks, "That was the most polite child I have ever heard on the phone," or "Wow. You got yourself some little secretary there," or "How do you get 'em to do that?"

Go back to the introduction of this book for how we get them to do it—the answer has to do with parental authority in the home. The policy is: This is how kids answer the phone at our house. If you can't follow that rule, you can't answer the phone.

It strikes me as culturally significant that something so simple—something I think is so basic to respectful behavior on the part of a child—is apparently so remarkable that people need to remark on it. Yes, I'm proud that my kids are noticed for their excellent telephone skills. But honestly, it just shouldn't be so rare.

Similarly, my husband and I often hear from friends—and more so from the parents of their peers—that our children are wonderful conversationalists. It's typical for us to hear, "I'm so impressed that Katie handles herself so well," and "Betsy seems really comfortable talking to adults." Jimmy, too, is noticed as a polite talker, and Amy...well...I actually got an e-mail once from a friend in which he simply had to recount for me the details of a conversation he had with Amy. That's how impressed he was (and how funny she was).

Again, are Jim and I proud of our kids? Naturally. But we're not surprised by their skills. We've worked on them! We spend time coaching them about how to converse politely, we correct them when we see rude behavior, and we engage them in social chatter so they can learn to chat socially. Heck, we even practice handshaking and getting them to look us in the eye when they say hello. (Not anymore, as they all have nice, firm handshakes—but we did when they were little.)

You can learn good manners by having them modeled for you (just as you can learn how to be rude), but if you want to really teach how to behave in polite society, you have to do some skill drills. (Don't panic—this is as simple as starting a pleasant conversation at your own dinner table.) Practice may not make perfect, as we all slip sometimes where manners are concerned, but practice will promote good habits, and this is what you're out to achieve.

The snag for kids is that children in the culture of cool don't really care about good manners. This isn't a yardstick against which they measure one another for popularity and social status. When was the last time you walked past a group of trendy-looking teens at the mall and overheard them saying, "Oh, I just love Brad. He's so polite!" In fact, Brad's probably only going to get the attention of those girls if he behaves like a self-absorbed jerk.

But manners *are* valued in the adult world, which is why a mother might say to her daughter, "Brad is so polite. You should invite him to go with you and your friends to the movies." Yeah, right. Like that's gonna happen. Brad, by impressing this mother with his exceptional manners, has sealed the deal on his geek status. What's better from my point of view, Brad is now guaranteed to stay at a safe, risk-free distance from the popular crowd, as will any child a parent recommends to a cool kid.

GOOD MANNERS SHOW RESPECT

Promoting good manners in our children isn't something we do just because it's self-serving or because it makes parents proud. Will a polite teen do better in that college interview than a kid who lacks basic manners and conversational skills? Absolutely. But that's not the point.

The point is, manners are the expression of respect, and teaching our children to respect everyone, all the time, is the character trait that exudes from their social skills. This means manners aren't something you accord only to adults; to be authentically well mannered, children must treat their peers politely, too. But be warned: Kids who do this are geeks.

In our kids' world, it's cool to swear, especially if you do it loud enough for an adult to hear you (thus making you look tough). It's cool to talk back to adults, especially your parents, and especially if you do it in front of a peer. It's cool to whisper and snicker in class, write and pass notes, and do things to deliberately embarrass others—even your friends. It's cool to blurt things out to get attention, and most of all, it's cool to look bored and roll your eyes to express disdain when an adult is talking.

All of this brash behavior communicates children's profound disrespect. Now, you might think I'm stretching this description to make a point, but I am not. Consider my visit to Jimmy's seventh-grade English class, where I was invited to be a guest speaker. The teacher, Mr. Murphy, asked me to tell the students about my life as a writer so that they could learn ways in which people use writing in various professions. He's trying to connect the dots so that they see that they will use writing later (unlike algebra, which I have yet to use, but I digress).

You'd think I would have an advantage in this setting since I knew the parents of nearly all the boys and many, if not most, of the girls. Not so. Not even my threat to walk out if they didn't stop their rude behavior deterred a group of cool kids from acting arrogantly disinterested. I could hear them talking and snickering about me as I presented the lecture, and when it was time to work quietly on the assignment I gave them, they just socialized among themselves, ignoring my prompts to participate in the exercise. They were way too cool to be interested in what I presented.

Mr. Murphy was mortified, while I was just appalled.

You're probably thinking, how the heck do kids get away with that in a classroom? I wondered the same thing. The teacher told me it's not uncommon to get that kind of behavior from kids these days, and that his efforts to reprimand them and to get parents involved in correcting and disciplining them are mostly met with defensiveness. The only parents who would respond with concern were the ones whose kids were behaving appropriately in the first place.

Suffice it to say, I reminded Mr. Murphy that if my son ever behaved in such a fashion, I would most certainly respond. He said I needn't worry.

But wait. Maybe it's not the parents' fault. Aren't all seventh graders naturally self-centered? There's nothing we can do about it, right? We parents just have to accept that this kind of rude behavior is a part of growing up. We have to wait for kids to outgrow it.

Only guess what? Kids don't outgrow rudeness; they simply become rude adults!

GOOD MANNERS BUILD RELATIONSHIPS

Another benefit of behaving in a mannerly fashion is the positive impact manners have on relationships. People who practice good manners are known as kind, considerate, caring, and thoughtful. They're well liked and highly regarded. Well-mannered people make good friends, and a well-mannered child is one who has the potential to develop strong bonds with his geeky peers.

Note: Manners won't boost a kid's popularity or social status in middle school, but of course that's not our agenda, is it? Remember we're looking way down the road, toward real life and adulthood. Our job as parents, and our goal with respect to manners, is to prepare our kids to succeed in life. To do this we need to arm them with a lifetime of practice in appropriate social behavior.

The reason well-mannered kids make good friends is that manners inherently are other-directed. This is really uncommon in a culture where child-centric parenting and self-absorption in children set the stage for collecting a cadre of self-centered friends. Conversely, a polite kid is one who knows how to share, how to take turns, and how to make concessions and compromises for the sake of a pleasant and cordial friendship. The topic of friendship is a big one, so it gets an entire chapter yet to come.

Geek Manners and Etiquette 101

All manners stem from respect. Good manners demonstrate a good measure of respect; while poor manners exhibit disrespect. This is why it's crucial to expect and command that our children treat us—their parents—politely, and thus respectfully.

Unfortunately, too many parents aren't demanding respectful behavior from their children and the ramifications go beyond disobedience to displays of outright contempt. I recall an episode several years ago when Katie was starting high school. She and I were in the school bookstore, checking her class list and collecting the books we needed to buy for the coming year, when we overheard a mom and daughter a few feet away. Mom sheepishly asked a question about whether a particular book was needed and her daughter snapped back as rudely as could be,

"I *told* you I don't need that book!" And so it went, back and forth, Mom tiptoeing around her daughter's bossy and brash tone of voice, until at last they left the stacks of books and headed to the checkout.

When Katie and I left the bookstore, I asked what she thought about the dialogue we had overheard (volume control also being an issue for the rude teenager in question). Katie's conclusion: The girl was obnoxious. "I would never want someone to hear me speaking to you that way," she said. "Aside from the fact that it's rude, it would just be really embarrassing."

I agreed that the girl was rude, of course, but I actually didn't hold the daughter completely culpable. "That mom is doing herself and her daughter a huge disservice by putting up with such a lack of respect," I told her. "It takes two for that sort of attitude to be displayed."

This is why whenever my kids have slipped and spoken to my husband or me impatiently or curtly, we let them know it's not okay. Of course they may be annoyed about something, they may feel edgy or irritable—we all do from time to time—but they may not speak to us in a tone of voice that feels disrespectful to us. They have to apologize and adopt a courteous tone of voice. We also require other displays of respect, such as giving up a chair to a parent, fetching things for us, and listening quietly when we're speaking to other adults.

Once children learn that Mom and Dad must be treated with respect, they naturally extend this behavior to other adults. The key here is that children have to be taught that *any* elder must be respected just because they're older. Period. No caveats, no exceptions. Elders don't have to do anything special to earn a child's respect. In fact, a kid may decide some adults are as dumb as a box of rocks (some are!), but they still are owed respect just because they're adults. Age has its privileges and this is one of them.

The media undermines this notion in a big way. Just watch an hour or two of the current sitcoms aimed at kids and you'll see adults behaving like clueless morons while the child stars are the all-knowing, all-insightful fonts of wisdom. Invariably there'll be some pivotal scene in which the goofball mom, dad, or teacher says something like, "Gee, I should have known better. You're really growing up, honey." (This is the stuff that makes *me* roll *my* eyes.)

In particular, we need to pay special attention to the way in which our children treat the adults in their lives with whom they have regular contact, such as teachers, school administrators, coaches, and caregivers. In a world where excellent manners are increasingly uncommon, adults in these roles are literally taken aback by a geeky "Good morning, Miss Mitchell" before class or "Thanks, Coach" after practice. A child brought up in the geek lifestyle does these things out of genuine respect but also out of habit, proving not all habits are bad. This is one habit that may also turn your well-mannered geek into a "teacher's pet," since teachers appreciate receiving the respect they so justly deserve. (Several years ago, a few states actually legislated that children treat teachers with respect by using courtesy titles such as Mr. and Mrs. or by answering "yes, ma'am" and "no, sir." Without getting political here, I think it's laughable that anyone thinks we could solve this problem by putting a law on the books, though it sure does illustrate how desperate our culture is to uphold courteous behavior.)

We also teach kids to behave respectfully when we teach them empathy. Thinking about the feelings of others is crucial to good manners since all behavior demonstrates whether or not a person is truly considerate. So, while I don't think considering the feelings of others is the cornerstone of a moral code of right and wrong (more on that in Rule Number Nine), empathy for others is imperative in teaching how to act respectfully and thoughtfully. As far as this goes, the most important rule of geek etiquette is the Golden Rule.

RULES OF ETIQUETTE MAKE LIFE EASIER (AND GEEKIER)

There is almost no end of resources for parents to teach manners and etiquette. You could take the advice of Letitia Baldrige or Emily Post, or just jot down a bunch of Proverbs from the Bible; the rules are out there in one form or another. Whole books and Web sites are devoted to the topic, and given the dearth of manners generally in our culture, I think it's worth doing a bit of research on the subject, especially if your kids are still very young. The bottom line is rules of etiquette are intended to make life easier. We have fewer questions and concerns about what's proper if we learn the traditional rules of social grace.

What follows, then, isn't an exhaustive list of rules of etiquette but rather a geek's list—manners that seem to be associated with our geek lifestyle.

Conversational Skills

Even very young children are capable of learning the art of polite conversation. All we have to do to teach it is to converse with them. Remember there's a difference between talking at our kids and conversing with them. A conversation requires both talking and listening, so one thing we need to model and teach is a listening ear. If we speak with our children in the same way that we would speak to their teachers or to our pastor or our neighbor up the street, they learn patterns of social conversation. When we're talking to other adults, we need to require our kids to listen patiently, but also we must include them in conversations when it's appropriate. In this way we can coach them a bit and help them gain confidence when speaking to adults. At our house, we have talked about talking (we're talkers, I admit it), which is to say, we help our kids learn this skill by discussing what makes a good conversation. Consequently, they've picked up on conversation starters such as "So, have you been to your cottage yet this summer?" and "I was noticing you got a new bike. How do you like it?" When they get really confident, a geek is likely to be heard asking his social-studies teacher, "So, what's your take on this election cycle?" This is why grown-ups love geeks.

Telephone Manners

Instead of letting kids say hello, employ a script for the children in your home when they begin answering the phone. "Smith residence" or "Susie Smith speaking" sounds polite and courteous, even when spoken by the smallest family members. In a geeky household, answering the telephone is a rite of passage when other manners have been mastered, so if you can't get to the phone, don't let your geeky toddler pick up. You teach your kids that answering the phone is important when you reserve that task for children who are old enough to do it right. When the time does come to allow a child to answer the phone, practice all parts of the phone call—"may I ask who is calling, please?" and "may I take a message?" are just as crucial as a polite pickup. Finally, while you may believe it's as cute as can be to let your child leave the voice-mail message at your house, I'm here to tell you the rest of the world does not think so.

Cell-Phone Manners

My kids don't get cell phones until the summer before high school, which I used to think was early, believe it or not! It's totally typical these days for the makers of school backpacks to put a cell-phone zipper pocket on a Hello Kitty backpack. (They do this because they know parents are looking for a safe place to keep little Jessica's cell while she goes to fourth grade.) Whenever your kid gets a cell phone, make some rules about how and when to use it properly: Never leave the ringer on when it could disrupt a gathering such as a team meeting or a church service. Always remove yourself from a group to take or make a call. Silence the ringer and ignore calls when you should be paying attention to something else (babysitting, doing homework, reading). Most schools, like ours, prohibit the use of cell phones during the school day. If yours doesn't, you should make that a family rule. Perhaps more insidious and harder to control is incessant text messaging. I have a child who types faster on her phone than she does on our computer keyboard, and yes, I'm aware this is pathetic. We're working on it. For starters, we've indicated it's not polite to text someone while you're talking to someone else (unless the reason is logistical and/or obvious). Incidentally, when my kids answer my cell phone for me, they say, "Marybeth Hicks's cell phone, [name] speaking." This is important because anyone calling my cell is expecting to hear my voice, and getting one of my kids would be confusing without such a script.

Techno-Manners

Personal music players are great, but an iPod should not be used to communicate the message "iRude." Remembering that manners are other-directed, we restrict iPod use to times when our kids are doing something on their own and don't expect to be conversing with others. It also makes me crazy when I call for a child in my home and they don't answer because they're doing homework with earbuds in their heads, so I've mandated that the volume can't be louder than the sound of me calling from the kitchen. We use personal devices with headphones on long trips. In the van it's easy to get someone's attention to talk to them, though if we're traveling together on a family vacation, we'll ask the kids to unplug for stretches of the trip so we can chat or listen to something together on the car stereo. Nobody minds.

Invitations, Gifts, and Social Graces

This is an area where all the old rules worked and should still apply. We stress that party invitations be kept on the down low since we don't want to hurt the feelings of anyone who might not be invited. We always send invitations to the home address rather than give them out at school. We never originate a party from school, where it would be obvious we were hosting a social function for only a few kids (and as if you can't guess, we don't hire limos for kids' functions). We try to give gifts that are reasonable and appropriate. We teach our kids to receive any gift with gratitude, paying attention to the gift giver as they open a present and commenting on how nice it is. Thank-you notes are a must—I require that my kids write them before they can use a gift. This tends to get those suckers written quickly! As for the "magic words," the only thing you can do is harp, harp, harp. They do become habit over time.

Table Manners

For obvious reasons, I'm not going to use a name as I write this section, but one of my children has a friend—a great, nice, smart, and otherwise polite child—whom I cannot be with while consuming food. This child

literally spews food while chomping, openmouthed, and perching a full
fork at the ready for another bite. It's truly the grossest eating experience you could possibly imagine. So when this child visits us, I always
suggest the kids take their plates to the basement and eat together there.
Perhaps the only upside to having this child over once for a meal was
that my own kids were as grossed out as I was; it was appalling but
instructive. Table manners are crucial for success in life, but the good
thing is we don't have to figure out what's appropriate—it's all the same
stuff our parents taught us: Close your mouth when you chew, elbows
off the table, hold the fork properly, wait to eat until everyone is served,
rest your utensils occasionally, don't talk with a full mouth. The basics
haven't changed—and neither has the requirement that we repeat these
rules to our children at virtually every meal. No one ever said the job
wasn't relentless. At our house, we often spend a few minutes at the end
of a family meal talking about a particular aspect of table manners. I'm
fond of reminding my kids that poor manners won't keep them from
getting a first date with someone, but they will most certainly preclude
them from a second date. They're getting old enough to care about this,
so their cooperation has improved over time.

Everyone Grows Up Eventually

Just as it's true that impeccable manners are not exactly what the culture of cool values in adolescence, it's equally true that adolescence
doesn't last forever. Everyone grows up. Adulthood is our destiny and
this is good news for a geek. As certainly as a geeky seventh grader will
be teased for using the phrase *How do you do?* when meeting a new kid
(and no, I'm not really suggesting that any child would say that), that
child will one day wait in a receiving line at the White House, where
uttering the question *How do you do, Mr. President?* is the most appropriate thing you can say.

As geek parents, we need to keep our focus on the future, when fitting in means behaving with manners and even refinement. Just as we

train up our kids to save money, make meals, do laundry, or drive a car, teaching them to know and practice good manners is a life skill that will either promote their opportunities or keep them from experiencing their full potential. For certainly, a rude person doesn't go quite as far in life as one who is caring and thoughtful.

My geeky old friend Fred and I have taken it upon ourselves to organize several of our high school class reunions. The last one celebrated our twenty-fifth year since graduating—a quarter century for folks to go their own ways and make something of their lives. When it was over, I came home and told my children what I discovered: The geeks from high school are hands down the coolest, most accomplished, most interesting, and best-mannered adults in our class. They may not have been considered cool or popular back then, but there's no getting around their elevated social status now.

Raising kids adults like is my litmus test for geeky manners. I figure if you can hold your own and behave appropriately when you're only nine or thirteen or sixteen, there's a good chance you'll be one very cool adult.

Uncool Answers

Frequently when dropping one of my kids' friends off after a playdate at our home or an event we have hosted, I'm stunned by the poor manners I observe on the part of their pals. It seems they can't get out of the car quickly enough and a word of thanks is rare! Should I ask for a thank-you from their friends when I pull in the drive? And should I worry that the bad manners they exhibit will rub off on my kids?

Sometimes it definitely feels like you're the only adult teaching your kids to say "thank you," much less to use other forms of polite behavior. Parenting is a thankless job as it is—who among us needs that point driven home by a rude and ungrateful child? I've reminded myself more than once that an adult ought not to be offended by an eight-year-old, but still. After repeated incidents of poor manners, you can tell who's being well trained at home and who isn't.

Which brings me to your first question—should you speak up and ask for a word of thanks? My rule of thumb is if a child seems otherwise consistently polite but occasionally forgets to say "thank you" on the way out of the car, I let it pass on the assumption it was just a slip. On the other hand, if I notice it repeatedly, or if my child's friend seems not to practice general habits of mannerly behavior (one-word answers, no magic words, no eye contact), I feel it's in his best interest for me to prompt him. Of course kids are people, too, and you won't help the child if you embarrass him. So I do it by paying his folks a compliment, like this: "I know your mom and dad have taught you well to say 'thanks,' Bobby, so don't let them down!" I'll always get a wry "thank you" in reply. The younger the child, the more freedom you can feel to correct kindly. I won't hand over so much as a slice of cheese to a little one who doesn't say "please"—I just say, "What's the magic word?" Small children frankly expect this sort of thing out of adults.

As to the second concern, it's something to discuss with your child. I've gone so far as to comment, "Boy, it sure disappoints me that your friend doesn't say 'thank you' when I drop her off." I want my kids to understand that parents notice this behavior and that it matters to adults. I don't think the poor manners on the part of my kids' friends have rubbed off—in fact, I think it's the reverse. When my children thank me for whatever it is I've done, their friends chime in. Don't fume and fuss about a kid's poor manners in front of your own child, but do mention that you expect him to always use his best manners no matter what.

Guaranteed Geek: Tips to Impress Adults

For Geeks of All Ages:
* Start early to teach good manners to toddlers with books for children such as *Excuse Me! A Little Book of Manners* by Karen Katz.

* Teach and practice the triad of excellent social skills: eye contact, a firm handshake, and use of a person's name in conversation. Really practice!

* Use mealtime as manners time. Regularly (but not every night!) choose an aspect of table manners to teach or review.

* *Always* tell your kids when you receive a compliment on their manners! They deserve to know they're getting it right.

* When an adult addresses your child, never answer for him. Let him speak for himself and only offer a prompt if he's genuinely stuck.

For Elementary School Geeks:

* Get a copy of the American Girl book *A Smart Girl's Guide to Manners* for your daughter. It makes manners fun and relevant.

* Read the classic American poem "Boy Wanted" to your son (I used to read it to Jimmy every night before bed). Don't be surprised if your son asks you what a "prig" is—the language is just a tad old-fashioned. Nonetheless, if we raise boys like the ideal in that poem, we're doing all right. Find it in William Bennett's *The Book of Virtues for Children*.

* Use Web sites such as www.emilypost.com for ideas and advice for parents as well as etiquette information just for kids. (In my book, Emily Post is still the hallmark of good taste.)

* When you decide it's time to have kids answer the phone, practice! Ask grandparents and other relatives to call in throughout a specified evening to give your child the chance to test her phone skills. Don't let kids answer the phone unless you're sure they won't put it down and forget about the caller.

For Middle School Geeks:

* Talk about talking! Teach the art of good conversation and talk about what makes an interesting conversationalist. Practice con-

versation skills at dinner or in the car by inviting your child to choose a topic for a family chat.

* Don't let kids wear headphones when the atmosphere should be social. Politely ask your child to take them off, and instead talk about the music he likes and ask what's on his favorite playlist.

* Get a book on manners your middle schooler will actually read, such as Dr. Alex Packer's *How Rude! The Teenagers' Guide to Good Manners, Proper Behavior, and Not Grossing People Out*. It uses humor and doesn't preach while answering questions about social behavior that young teens really want to know.

For High School Geeks:
* Send an occasional text message reminding your teen to use her best cell-phone manners. Make it funny and friendly, not nagging.

* Spring for dinner in a fancy restaurant. Plan ahead and review table manners beforehand, including what all that silverware is for and how to order from a high-end menu. Exposure to a fine dining experience is the only way to really learn the social skills needed in life, especially in the professional world. (Can't afford this idea? Do it at home and use the good dishes! Invite a special guest such as your pastor or your boss.)

* Demand polite speech. Kids are free to disagree, hold strong opinions, and even be angry with you. They shouldn't be free to be rude.

Rule #5

RAISE A LATE BLOOMER

Katie and Betsy were only seven and five when they learned what it meant to be a tramp. My mother told them.

It was our first "girls' getaway"—a weekend of intergenerational bonding. I had packed a few fashion magazines and a copy of *People*—the annual best- and worst-dressed edition—to peruse during the four-hour drive.

I did the driving, so my mother did the perusing. She perched her bright red reading glasses on the end of her nose and opened the slick pages of *People* to take in the full-color photos. On page after page, the magazine offered its take on celebrity style statements—the daring, the delightful, the dazzling, and the disastrous dresses that turned heads on red carpets from New York to L.A. and beyond.

My mom isn't one to hold back when she feels strongly about something. Suffice to say, the pages of *People* generated a visceral response as she expertly licked her fingers and flipped the flimsy paper of the special double issue.

"Look at this woman," she shrieked, holding up the magazine so I could glance over and see the photo without endangering us or the other folks on the expressway. "What a tramp!"

"What's a tramp?" Betsy asked.

"A tramp is someone who dresses like this," my mom said in a roundabout explanation, slapping the photo for effect. "She's practically naked."

"Icks-nay on the amp-tray," I said in pig latin. "We've never actually defined that term at home."

"Well, it's never too soon to know what a tramp is and how to avoid dressing like one," my mother declared. That's the weekend my girls learned my mother's definition of "tacky" and what modesty means. At an early age, they understood that their clothing choices can tell the world who they are and what they stand for.

Grow Up, Already!

I've read that modesty is making a fashion comeback, but you wouldn't know it by looking at what's on the racks in the department store. Paper-thin fabrics, belly-baring halter tops with sayings like READY OR NOT and WILD CHILD, skirts slit to here, animal prints—all designed to exude hypersexuality in the female who wears them. And those are just the choices in the girls' department! The attire in the juniors' department is so explicit it belongs in a catalog with a heavy brown paper wrapper.

Apparently, the folks on Seventh Avenue haven't heard about the modesty trend. Neither are they concerned about maintaining a wholesome, youthful image for today's children and teens through the clothing they produce. In their relentless pursuit of "fashion" (a word that here means "money"), they offer season after season of tacky togs intended to cover as little of the human anatomy as possible. In fact, it sometimes seems the skimpier the outfit, the higher the price tag.

But designers of kids' clothes don't create these fashions in a vacuum. They're responding to what the marketing department demands. And, of course, the marketing folks are just responding to the data, which says...what?

Well, back in 1998, the *Wall Street Journal* ran an article entitled "Kids Today Grow Up Way Too Fast" in which author Kay Hymowitz chronicled the emergence of "tweens" as an age group—formerly a group known simply as "children." The article cited a study of tweens (a study sponsored by Nickelodeon...hmm) that found that by the time they were twelve, kids described themselves as "flirtatious, sexy, trendy, athletic and cool."

Hymowitz noted ten years ago that marketers were introducing bikini undies for preteenagers (time flies—now they can get thongs), among other fashion surprises. "But the tweening of childhood is more than just a matter of fashion," she said. "Tweens are demonstrating many of the deviant behaviors we usually associate with adolescence."

She referred to statistics that showed criminal behavior, drinking, drug use, depression, and even suicide were growing trends among young teens and preteens. She also warned of the early onset of sexual activity among kids who grow up as "tweens" and not simply as children.

And of course we all remember Oprah's 2002 revelation that middle schoolers were engaging in oral sex on the back of the school bus. The actual prevalence of this supposed "epidemic" is still debated, but the fact remains: Oral sex at eleven or twelve years old is just plain wrong, no matter how many kids are doing it.

I agree with the general conclusion among child-development "experts" (remember, I'm not one of them) that kids today are growing up too soon. By this I mean they're engaging in the adult world at a younger age than we did only a generation ago.

But this conclusion is more than just a sense on the part of those who observe children and trends. The age of physical maturity, especially among girls, has gradually crept downward for the past several decades. Consider this research finding: A few generations ago the average onset of breast development and menses was thirteen and sixteen respectively; now these come at around nine and a half and twelve and a half. Science has come up with reasons for this trend, but it has resulted in a whole bunch of children walking around in the bodies of miniature adults. What this means is that young children—especially young girls—face a confusing dilemma: hanging on to a sense of childhood innocence while watching their bodies grow uncontrollably into adulthood.

But is the onset of precocious puberty the only culprit in the societal manifestation of early adolescence?

In her article, Hymowitz questioned, "What change in our social ecology has led to the emergence of tweens? In my conversations with educators and child psychologists who work primarily with middle-class kids nationwide, two major and fairly predictable themes emerged: absentee parents and a sexualized and glitzy media-driven marketplace. What has been less commonly recognized is the way these two influences combine to augment the authority of the peer group."

Okay, think about that for a minute. Absent parents means kids leave for school and return again to an empty house. Empty house equals ample opportunity.

Opportunity for what? Well, how about for the "sexualized and glitzy media-driven marketplace" Hymowitz mentioned—chiefly MTV, the single most important media influence for Americans under the age of twenty-four. Comfortably ensconced in that empty house, tweens arrive home from school, flip on the tube, and sink into the sofa for an afternoon of Doritos and soft-porn hip-hop music videos. Actually, they hardly ever play music videos. Instead, MTV runs reality shows of young adults hooking up. What better way to learn how to use those inexplicable and bothersome new hormones?

Now add the peer group. Equally isolated and on their own, the kids from school also sit at home absorbing the values offered through the media. What next? Well, heck, let's all jump on the laptop and trade sexual innuendos on MySpace and in instant messages! Fun on a bun! Don't forget, belonging to the group means doing what they do—conforming. This is why the peer group has so much authority.

Remember we're talking tweens here—nine- to twelve-year-olds, and in some researchers' views, that bottom number is eight. That's right—your little darling has roughly eight years of "childhood" until the folks on Madison Avenue shift her into a new and powerful demographic group.

So let's review that recipe for growing up too fast: isolation and a lack of parental oversight, access to media and media values, and a dominating peer group. We can sometimes add premature physical development, but of course we all know skinny, flat-chested cool girls who rule their cliques. The fact is you don't actually have to have breasts to wear a bra from the Pink Collection at Victoria's Secret.

WHO'S BUYING THOSE BRAS, ANYWAY?

Bras and other "adult" clothing don't just magically appear in the dresser drawers. Someone has to put them there—or at least, put the money in the hands of our tween shoppers. Clothing choices are perhaps one of the most outwardly obvious aspects of the culture of cool, and that culture promotes extreme sexuality as its prevailing fashion statement.

Now, kids' wanting to look and act older than they are is not new. We all did this to some degree as children and young teens—heck, I used to change out of my red leather oxford shoes, hide them in the bushes, and put on my older sister's patent-leather dress shoes—with heels! This was not a speedy way to walk to kindergarten, but a girl had to do what a girl had to do.

Today, however, looking older and more grown up means one thing only: looking and acting sexy. Before a child even knows what sexy means, she is wearing a T-shirt emblazoned with the words YES, BUT NOT WITH YOU. Boys, of course, aren't left out of this trend. Shirts for guys have phrases like TELL YOUR GIRLFRIEND I SAID THANKS and I'VE LOST MY NUMBER. CAN I HAVE YOURS? Crude shirts are more popular among guys, too, with those featuring the F-word a favorite of the most bold and jaded.

Revealing tops, low-slung jeans, lots of exposed underwear, stilettos, tight-fitting tanks, and the ever-present exposed midriff all have become fashion fixtures in the closets of teens and tweens alike.

Yet I can't think of a time when I talked to a parent who said, "Gee, I sure like the way kids dress these days. They sure look wholesome and healthy."

In fact, the hypersexual appearance of today's kids makes parents uncomfortable, but too many are not engaging in the battle of the exposed belly button. Most parents will tell you it's a fight they can't win; they choose their battles and they generally save arguments over clothing choices for special occasions when they need greater parental clout.

Not that parents are receiving much support to get into the fray on clothing issues. For example, the Web site www.familyeducation.com offers pages of advice and insight for parents from experts—generally family therapists and psychologists—who answer questions posed by moms and dads. I found three interesting answers came from one Carleton Kendrick, a private practitioner and media regular.

When asked what he thought about a seventeen-year-old boy who wears pants with sixty-inch diameter bell bottoms as well as multiple piercings, Kendrick said, "Parents need to get out of the way of their own egos and roll with the fashion fads that their kids adopt." Another parent expressed concern about a fourteen-year-old daughter who dresses in revealing clothes that make her look seventeen or eighteen. Kendrick said, "At 14, what she wears brings her a sense of power in creating an identity for herself during this very intense, confusing, hormonally charged time of her life...My advice is not to express concern about her physical presentation of self unless you believe her appearance is deteriorating health-wise." (Huh? I guess this means only speak up if her skimpy top is causing her to get a cold.) A third letter posed a question about a fourteen-year-old girl who wants a pierced navel. Mom says no, but now the teen won't speak to her. Kendrick's advice: "If your daughter agrees to have her navel pierced under the hygienic conditions insisted upon by her doctor, and she understands what she must do to prevent that area from becoming infected, you should give her permission to pierce her navel...Allowing her to pierce her navel does not mean that you are a permissive parent or that you gave in—or will give in in the future because she stopped talking to you. It means that you gave careful consideration to a wish of hers and agreed to grant it after much thought and discussion with her regarding her responsibility in the matter."

Sorry, Mr. Kendrick. Allowing a fourteen-year-old to pierce her navel after you have already forbidden such an act is what we non-experts call "caving in."

I need to make a point here—strenuously, in fact: I'm not suggesting that we parents should lay out our kids' clothes every night. And I'm certainly not saying we should mandate exactly what they wear. On the contrary! As you'll see shortly, I believe children need power over their appearance and input into decisions about their clothing from a very early age. The more we involve kids in this process, the more we can help them explore their tastes and establish their own comfortable, confident styles within the context of the values we're teaching them.

But honestly. A child's self-expression doesn't mean you have to permit just anything. Any parent who purchases sexually explicit T-shirts, or who allows kids to wear revealing tops and bottoms, or who buys thongs for a preteen is not assuring a normal, healthy sense of self in a child; you're assuring your child will look like a skank.

There. I said it.

What's the big deal, though? Didn't we all go through periods of rebellion when we wore styles that appalled and confounded our parents? And somehow, we managed to understand the relationship between a blue interview suit and gainful employment.

Yes, a little apparel-induced rebellion may be typical and even healthy. But that assumes that proper values are already formed that lay the foundation for healthy self-expression. When it comes to clothing, styles may change but one thing that never changes is this fact: Our clothes speak volumes about who we are, what we value, and how we wish to comport ourselves in the world. We must teach our children that their appearance says something about them, and more importantly, that their appearance creates expectations on the part of others. Not to teach this lesson shortchanges kids and very well might put them at risk.

Believe it or not, some so-called experts think there is nothing problematic about sexual expression in kids. To wit: An ABC News story entitled "Some Say It's OK for Girls to Go Wild" according to which "Jaana Juvonen, who studies at UCLA the development of middle and high school students, said that because girls hit puberty earlier now than they did decades ago, they're tempted to mimic the appearance of their older peers. That doesn't mean they're engaging in acts that ought to be beyond their years. 'Many girls might look very differently from how they act,' she said. 'We should not judge them based on what they look like.' Nor should adults assume that teenagers are having sex because their style of dancing or taste in music suggests it."

This woman is either naive or else... well, there is nothing else. She's naive. Personally, I think she should expand her research and include high school and middle school *guys,* who will most certainly attest to the fact that the girls who dress provocatively are the ones they hit on most frequently, for obvious reasons.

And anyway, what's really absurd, in my mind at least, is that this trend isn't the result of some natural change in the way children grow and discover their sexual selves. This is the direct result of a marketing culture that preys on kids' desire to feel cool and be included.

Here's an important excerpt from an April 2007 *USA Today* article:

Chalk it up to "age compression," which many marketers call "kids getting older younger" or KGOY. Retail consultant Ken Nisch says it shouldn't be a surprise or an outrage that kids are tired of toys and kid clothes by 8, considering that they are exposed to outside influences so much earlier. They are in preschool at 3 and on computers at 6. That's why marketers now target 9-year-olds with apparel and accessories once considered only for teens, says Nisch, chairman of the retail consulting and design firm JGA. Generation Y, those between about 8 and 26, are considered the most important generation for retailers and marketers because of their spending power and the influence they have over what their parents buy...

This marketing guru goes on to explain the delicate strategic balancing act of appealing to tween girls while still getting the cooperation of their parents—who, after all, have the money and the car keys to drive to the mall. Is it just me or is the truth about marketing conveyed in this article as arrogantly manipulative as it seems?

TALK ABOUT YOUR MIXED MESSAGES

There's no question that marketers and other media promote the notion of "age compression" and, with it, the sexual awareness we see among children. But if I were a kid, I think I would be really confused. This is because adults send some seriously mixed messages about sex and sexuality. Let me explain.

If you put this book down for a few minutes and pick up today's newspaper, you're sure to find at least one or two stories about horrific sexual exploitation of children. Perhaps there's been a discovery of an Internet predator in your town. Maybe there's been a well-publicized case of sexual abuse of a child, or tragically, there might recently have been a kidnapping and murder of a child that included a sex crime. All of those stories were in the news this weekend as I worked on this chapter.

The disturbing stories of abuse directed at children—cases that more and more frequently include criminal sexual behavior—seem almost to be exploding in the media. We read about child-porn rings or bizarre family situations involving incest and we're outraged—and rightly so. Beyond these felonious episodes, we shake our heads and wonder about the twisted values that force girls as young as thirteen or fourteen into polygamist marriages, perpetrated under the guise of religious freedom.

And then we put down the paper and take our kids shopping *at Abercrombie & Fitch.*

Am I the only one who sees this as incongruous?

Again, imagine you're a child. Your parents are appropriately aghast at the abuse and exploitation of children. They respond by teaching you all about "good" and "bad" touching and how to keep safe from strangers and perverts. They make a big point to warn you about creepy people who could talk to you online about naughty, inappropriate things. *But then Mom takes you shopping at a store whose owners are determined to teach you how to be sexy! And she spends a fortune buying you sexy clothes!*

Let's look at Abercrombie & Fitch, for example. This store is the favorite retailer of America's teens and tweens. When you shop there, you have to walk right past the billboard-size photo of a male torso wearing unzipped blue jeans, strongly suggesting sexual arousal just below the belt. (To be fair, the photos rotate. Sometimes the partially nude bodies are women.) Once inside, you can hunt down a bargain *(not)* on slim-fitting pants, short shorts, and skimpy tops for young people. To top off the retail experience, you can bag it all up in a paper sack adorned with—that's right!—more seminude models—and then hand that bag to your thirteen-year-old daughter while you meander through the mall.

Partial nudity apparently is what sells best for this "lifestyle retailer."

Not to lose out on the buying power of tweens, the retail giant offers a separate shop for this demographic group (in fact, there are three other storefronts aside from the original Abercrombie & Fitch). The clothes at Abercrombie are about the same as those at A&F. There's slightly less nudity in the displays at the tween shop, though shirtless guys abound and the models employed are *way* older than twelve.

Sexual marketing directed at children ought to repel parents from shopping at Abercrombie, but based on the company's success, not many of us are taking a stand. I guess they figure, what's the point? And I guess my own experience bears out that sentiment. I once waged my own little culture war with this company after I attempted to complain about the strong sexual messages it uses to sell to youngsters. I was told by "Ryan," the only person from the company I could get on the phone, that they believed any attention for the store was helpful—good or bad—which was why, despite numerous complaints that their marketing campaigns were offensive, they weren't going to change. They don't lose money on sex-laden window displays, even if they offend community standards in towns like mine.

Mind you, it's not just clothing retailers that sexualize children. It's everywhere, including in sexually infused toys for girls as young as five and six. I already permitted myself a rant on Bratz dolls in a previous chapter, but there's so much more. For example, girls can play the Bratz version of Girl Talk, an update on the classic board game for teens from the late eighties. This one is for girls *eight and up*. Here's the product description from Amazon:

> *Product Description* Sure you've played truth or dare before, but have you ever played the Bratz way? Now you can express your passion for fashion while you reveal yourself to your friends. Whether it's the crazy questions ("name three things you wish you were old enough to do") or the silly stunts ("make up a song and sing it to the group"), you'll get lots of laughs every time you play.

Lest you decide I simply have it in for the makers of Bratz, there's also a "That's So Raven" version of Girl Talk that asks, "Will I go to the prom with someone geeky?" (My answer: If you're lucky!) That question also is posed to girls age eight and up.

Here's the product description for the "Bratz: Passion for Fashion Game":

> *Product Description* Tonight is Bratz Nite Out, and you've gotta look good. But when you check your closet, you find that someone has borrowed your clothes. That means you'll have to figure out whose closet they're in and get them back before the big night. Be careful: if somebody borrows an item you already

have or messes up your hair, you'll be in a fashion funk. Only an emergency visit to the local beauty salon can help you then. Will you be the first to mix 'n match the hottest fashion looks and make it home to win the fashion game? It's all up to you.

Of course, if you're not into board games, you could always get the "Girl Crush—Airbrush Tattoo Washable Body Art Designer," the perfect gift for a future star of TV's *Miami Ink*.

When you put it all together—clothes, toys, games, movies, TV, music, and advertising—the impact on children, and especially on girls, is significant. Not surprisingly, this was the conclusion in 2007 of the American Psychological Association Task Force on the Sexualization of Girls. They defined sexualization as "a person's value coming only from his or her sexual appeal or behavior to the exclusion of other characteristics. The analysis of all the available research on the subject showed evidence that this sort of sexualization can negatively impact a girl's self-confidence, body image, self-esteem, sexual development and mental health."

CONNECTING THE DOTS CREATES AN UNHEALTHY PICTURE

Do you see a familiar pattern? There it is again—*we know what's wrong in our culture and we know how it's hurting our kids, but we're doing it anyway and we're not going to change.*

Why is that? I believe it's because it's just too unbearable for most parents to contemplate being uncool or to impose an uncool lifestyle on their kids. The conflict with kids is too exhausting, and the outcome, for many parents, is simply not worth the effort. And besides, didn't that expert say kids are dressing one way and acting another?

The problem is, the statistics on sexual behavior don't bear out the notion that kids' sexual identity is all smoke and mirrors. It's real, and it has consequences.

In an earlier chapter, I mentioned a 2004 study in which researchers found a direct correlation between watching sex on TV and a precocious sex life. What's noteworthy in my mind is something else the study says—that "early sexual initiation is an important social and health issue...most sexually experienced teens wish they had waited longer to have intercourse; other data indicate that unplanned pregnancies and sexually transmitted diseases are more common among those who begin sexual activity earlier."

Other than some dangerous folks on society's fringes, there just isn't anyone who believes it's good for kids to engage in active sex lives. In fact, we know it's manifestly bad—children suffer physically, emotionally, mentally, and spiritually when they become sexual beings before they are truly mature.

And yet we see news stories such as the one that appeared in 2006 on MSNBC, "Ten is the new 15 as kids grow up faster: From dating to cellphones, music to makeup, behavior shifting earlier"—an article that describes the cool culture's impact on younger children. Visit any of the biggest parenting-advice Web sites and you'll find all sorts of questions about when it's appropriate for children to begin dating—questions like "Is eleven too soon for my son to have a girlfriend?"

Eleven? Um...yes, that's too soon. But why does mom have to write to someone online to ask? I guess because all around her are parents who allow their eleven-year-olds to hook up. No wonder parents struggle to protect the innocence of their children.

That retailers and media send strong sexual content to children is generally understood. That a hypersexualized childhood is bad for kids also is understood. That our culture is providing both is something I, for one, don't get.

The Geek Alternative: Late Blooming

If growing up too quickly is what's cool, late blooming is the geek alternative.

Just what does it mean to be a late bloomer? If, as studies prove, children (especially girls) as young as nine years old undergo what is now considered a normal onset of puberty, one definition of a late bloomer in our culture obviously must be a child who doesn't begin physical maturity until thirteen or fourteen (and recall that this used to be the norm).

Certainly, the onset of physical maturity and the implications of it on childlike behavior are important. More on this in a moment.

In my geek vernacular, however, late blooming has less to do with actual physical maturity than it does with innocence and an extended period of childhood, beyond the cultural definitions of the "tween" years. (As we saw, that's just a marketing label anyway, though I concede it's one that's here to stay.)

Late bloomers are geeks—genuine, enthusiastic, empowered kids—appreciating and enjoying their childhood years by ignoring the media and marketing pressure to grow up too quickly.

When it comes to dress, late-blooming geeks can own closets full of fashionable outfits. Mine do—and I have the laundry to prove it. Recall that in the introduction I set out the parameters of the geek lifestyle and one of those is: no too-short pants or pocket protectors! Geeks who are late bloomers can dress stylishly within the confines of modesty and as a bonus they don't ever have to worry if their pants are falling off.

When the focus is off looking and acting older, kids are free to enjoy innocent childhoods. They spend more time pretending and using their imaginations, indulging their creativity, and learning about their world and the environment. Late bloomers are the kids you see playing in the driveway with their geeky friends, pursuing hobbies and playing with toys (imagine that!). When a late bloomer talks about "going out," he means he's heading outside, not getting a girlfriend.

Notice I didn't say late bloomers are immature. In fact, I've observed that children who grow up in a way that focuses on accumulated age and experience rather than cultural standards for how to act "older" actually seem more mature, poised, and composed than their peers. There's nothing quite as refreshing as a nine-year-old girl acting appropriately like a nine-year-old, as opposed to one trying to pull off the demeanor and aura of one who is fourteen.

The late-blooming strategy works really well when your child actually is a late bloomer. Which is to say, kids whose hormones don't kick in until thirteen or fourteen tend naturally to evolve through stages of development at a slower pace. Of course slow growing can present its own set of issues (recalling the line often uttered to me in middle school, "Hey, Marybeth, where's your buried treasure? You know...your sunken chest!" Sigh). When everyone around you is changing and you're still waiting for that ever-elusive "growth spurt" to begin, it's challenging, to say the least. Still, while we've endured this process with all of our children, I wouldn't trade a moment of a difficult day in middle school for a speedier trek toward adulthood.

WHEN HORMONES RAGE

Given that physical maturity might now normally start anywhere from ages nine to fourteen, a child who follows the urges of her hormones and responds to the encouragement of today's sexually drenched media could unleash her sexual self somewhere around the fifth or sixth grade.

You might say, well, heck, she has no choice. Mother Nature strikes when she strikes. If your pituitary gland flips the switch at the age of ten, you have no alternative but to get a MySpace page and a boyfriend and kiss your childhood good-bye.

You won't be surprised when I say that's just nonsense.

Physical maturity and the resultant chemical changes to the brain and emotions most certainly affect a person's thoughts, desires, fantasies, and interests. This is true and I'm not trying to argue otherwise.

But just as true is this: Mastery over one's thoughts, desires, fantasies, and interests is not only possible but crucial, in puberty as well as in adult life, in order to develop self-control and a positive, healthy lifestyle. Fortunately for children whose bodies jump the gun on puberty, this means they get to continue enjoying and appreciating childhood even though they experience some natural—if somewhat unwelcome—changes.

It's worth repeating—kids can continue to be kids even if they launch full bore into puberty. *Living as late bloomers, innocence is maintained because it doesn't equate with ignorance about the body. It equates with wholesomeness.*

How exactly does this play out in real life? With positive, open dialogue about the difference between physical maturity and emotional maturity. For example, when your daughter starts her period in the fourth grade, you say, "Honey, everyone grows and changes at her own pace and your body has decided to begin its journey to adulthood a little early. But this doesn't mean you're an adult! You still get to play with your toys and hang out with your friends just as you are doing. You don't need to think about the things that older kids do, like boyfriends and dating, because even though your body is growing quickly, your heart and your mind need time to catch up. So relax and enjoy life. There's no rush to grow up."

Believe me, this is really good news to a menstruating ten-year-old! Life is confusing enough—excruciating, in fact. Who needs to worry about dating when you're busy hiding your sanitary pads from the rest of the girls? Nothing is more reassuring to a young developer than the knowledge that she may still play with her American Girl dolls, she can hang out with friends being silly and having fun, and there's no hurry to become someone different; someone older.

I'm going to go one step further—I think we ought to hold back our fully developed, physically mature teens from jumping too vigorously into the adult world—especially the dating game. Hormones are tricky things, as I've often warned my daughters. They can make a dangerous person look appealing and cause you to lose control of your emotions and your actions. Just because you're aware of your emerging sexuality doesn't mean you have to act on it. In fact, as the participants in those studies I cited readily admitted, there's more to life than teen sex.

LOVE IS THE IN THE AIR

Let's assume you've finished kindergarten and moved all the way through the sixth grade. The Bratz have helped you identify your true fashion sense and Raven has even answered the question about the geeky prom date. Now what?

Well, if it's seventh grade in the culture of cool, it must be time to *fall in love*. Mind you, this is different from the casual "going out" that already occurs as early as the third grade (I kid you not). That was just the "who likes who" banter that causes girls to giggle and boys to run the other way.

No, I'm talking about the real deal—*l-u-v*—the kind that can last all the way to ninth grade and beyond.

These days, love begins online or in a text message. But even though electronic media are used, there still are some old-fashioned devices in the mix, such as the best friend, the note passed in class, and the locker photo. (Some things, it seems, never change.) There still are teddy bears, gifts of candy and soda, teasing and taunts. It's still as embarrassing and eye rolling as it was in 1972.

Then again, some things have changed—pretty significantly, in fact. When we parents were seventh graders, the cool kids went to the movies or to someone's house for a party and "made out" in the dark. Now seventh graders go to the movies or to someone's house for a party and have oral sex in the dark. Importantly, they think this is making out—which is to say, they don't think it's really sex.

I've already made a good case, I think, for why this is not healthy behavior for seventh graders or even for older teens. The point isn't that it's bad but that it's preventable.

The kids who behave in this way are the miniature adults, enjoying what they think are the benefits of adult relationships (with none of the responsibilities—yeah!). On the other hand, late bloomers aren't living pseudo-adult lives. They're living like kids. So they go to movies to see the movie, not to have (non) sex.

If you grow up as a late bloomer, your high school dating life also is unlike your cool peers'. First off, there's less of it. Late-blooming geeks tend to go to sanctioned high school functions such as homecoming, the winter ball, and prom but don't tend to pair off for exclusive dating. I've mentioned previously that geeks have good social lives, and they also have fun with nonexclusive dating. When it comes to socializing, geeks focus on friendships with guys and girls—relationships that support, rather than erode, confidence and self-esteem.

There's a big upside to raising a child for a late-blooming love life: when a teen doesn't expect to get into an exclusive relationship or focus on it as a goal, she's free to simply be herself and enjoy the process of growing up. When we make it clear to our teens that we support their growing interest in romance, but that we want them to hold off on pairing up, we send them the message that their feelings are normal, natural, and appropriate—but also that they can choose to wait until they're older and more ready for an exclusive relationship.

Pairing off in high school can lead to some difficult experiences, and I'm not just talking about prematurely engaging in an adult sex life, though the whole "hooking up" mentality assumes this is part of the deal. I'm thinking here about the distraction of getting involved in real romance—the time, attention, and emotional energy it takes to maintain a relationship—all of which cut into other wholesome and healthful endeavors.

True enough, there are plenty of high schoolers involved in romantic friendships—sort of a "lite" boy- or girlfriend relationship. Without a sexual component, these relationships can be delightful and lovely. But the reality is that high schoolers generally need maturity, insight, and self-control in order to handle such a relationship.

A reminder: The ultimate goal of geek parenting is to raise kids for success in life, not for popularity in middle school or high school. Keeping this goal in mind, when it comes to *l-u-v,* a slow pace wins the race.

How to Help Your Child to Blossom Naturally

Obviously, you can't do anything to affect the age at which your child begins puberty, except possibly promote a healthful lifestyle and avoid childhood obesity (yet another good reason to avoid obesity). Much of puberty depends on heredity, and while the apple doesn't always fall directly under the tree, it usually does. So your child may very well have a growth experience similar to one parent or the other.

What you can do is articulate that you value innocence in childhood and that you want your child to be a kid and not a mini-grown-up. Infusing your values about childhood into all aspects of your family life sends a strong, consistent message that you're not jumping on the train headed for precociousness. This means in all the ways you influence your child's life you should promote what is wholesome and appropriate, and use your parental authority to discourage or even prohibit things that could corrupt your child's innocence.

ENCOURAGE MODESTY IN DRESS

Clothing is important to almost everyone, including most children. Kids want to be comfortable (for this reason, Jimmy adamantly preferred sweatpants over jeans, even as a toddler), but they also want to wear things they like. From their earliest ages, I tried to consider my children's individual tastes about clothes. I also taught them that their clothing choices showed how much they respected themselves and others. Later, as I shared, they learned that the way they dress can convey their values and even their intentions. Ultimately, if clothes "make the man" (and woman!), they also make the boy and girl.

But what parent wants to go nose to nose with a child in the fitting room at the Gap or duke it out over clothes a half hour before the family leaves for church? Not me, that's for sure.

To avoid clothing battles and also offer the greatest amount of freedom to express their tastes and personalities, I established some policies for our children that promoted our values about dress.

Innocence Is the New Black

With the exception of black velvet dresses at Christmas, I always believed dressing a baby in black was a bad idea. It seemed to me that there was only so long I could get away with dressing my kids in pink or blue clothes with bunnies on them and I thought, heck, there's a lifetime ahead to wear black. With that edict, a policy was born that turned out to be a general guiding principle—not about a specific color, but about the philosophy of how I would dress my children. I didn't want them to look sassy, sexy, or sloppy; I wanted them to look young, innocent, and whenever possible, clean. Clean was the tricky part.

Absolute Veto Power for All

Shopping together for clothes can be fun or it can be a frustrating power struggle. For us, it's pretty fun. This is because I took some brilliant advice from my sister long ago: Give everyone absolute veto power. As early as you can give your child input (for us it was around six), you and your child both may nix any clothing item for any reason. You both must agree on whatever you buy. This means you won't put down good money for a T-shirt that says I'M SPOILED. SO WHAT. But you also can't buy an adorable plaid skirt for a daughter who simply prefers pants. Absolute veto power in shopping takes a lot longer than regular shopping; you have to negotiate, search out the racks, listen to your child's wishes, and explain your limits. But in the end I have found the investment in time is worth it because I never buy something my kids won't wear. Very cost-effective, indeed.

Usually They Pick; Sometimes I Pick

Because of the policy above, I grant my kids the freedom to choose their outfits for most events, but I have always reserved the right to set a dress code if the function is especially important to me. Knowing that there are times when I can mandate a clothing choice makes for fewer arguments about clothes. And remember, they don't own anything they won't wear. Obviously, as they get older I play this card less and less—I certainly don't tell my college student what to wear! But to be honest, even when they're in high school, I reserve the right to say, "No shorts to church."

There *Is* Such a Thing as "Appropriate Attire"

There used to be rules about clothes—no white before Memorial Day or after Labor Day—that sort of thing. I can't think of a single rule that anyone takes seriously anymore except my husband's stalwart adherence to the one about khaki suits for summer only. Still, there are standards about what's appropriate for various events, and in our effort to raise kids for success in life, it's crucial to impart some parental wisdom about appropriateness. You could say this notion is fussy and old-fashioned, but then you might end up being the proud parent of a daughter who visits the White House in flip-flops (à la the Northwestern University women's lacrosse team). Kids need to learn that there are times when it's essential to dress up to reflect the importance or solemnity of an event. Family gatherings such as anniversaries and religious events such as baptisms can be good practice to teach about dressing nicely. My personal pet peeve is the whole "kick your shoes off" trend, especially among girls at dances, and since this is my parenting book, I'm just going to come out with it: Tell your daughter this is tacky.

Timing *Is* Everything

As I've emphasized, late bloomers aren't sexy dressers. But this doesn't mean older teens won't gradually exude their natural, healthy sexuality through their clothing choices. The trick is to teach them the old adage: Less is more. Less skin, that is. Girls who look flirtatious without looking trashy send out a wholesome, fresh, and yes—sexy—vibe, but they do it without advertising their availability. Teaching girls and guys to leave something to the imagination tells them we accept and respect their sexual selves, but want them to treat that aspect of their personas

MOMS OF GIRLS NEED HELP FROM
MOMS OF BOYS

This chapter deals heavily with issues that concern parents of girls. But from a cultural perspective, moms of daughters can only do so much. Our struggle to send our girls into the world appropriately attired would be easier if we had support from mothers of sons, like my girlfriend Mary Pat.

When her boys were teens, Mary Pat liked it when they gathered with friends at her house because she could keep tabs on them, but she had rules, and one of those had to do with attire.

Once, when a female friend of her high schoolers showed up scantily clad in short shorts and a shirt that barely covered her chest, Mary Pat said to her, "Honey, you're welcome at my house, but you need to go home and put some clothes on. You may not visit my home dressed like this."

Okay, so her boys didn't speak to her for two weeks. Such is the life of a geek mom.

Eventually, they got over it, and when they did, they learned that their mother expected them to treat women with dignity and respect, even if a woman doesn't extend dignity or respect to herself.

Moms of daughters need the help of moms like Mary Pat. It's not enough for us to tell our girls, "Your outfit isn't appropriate." If a girl shows up at your home to hang out with your teenage son, consider the message she sends by what she's wearing. If it's not a message you want directed at your boy, say so!

Will this make you a geek parent? Of course, but you knew that.

with dignity. Not to mention, we reduce the embarrassment of seeing a boy's backside.

"LET'S PLAY VEGAS STREETWALKER!"

Play is how kids grow and learn, but inappropriate play is how they zoom through childhood and move into the culture of cool. Raising late bloomers means keeping the focus on wholesome recreation and offering toys, games, and activities that fit an innocent childhood.

Buy Only Toys That Reflect Your Values

When you buy only the toys you really believe are good for your child, it's very possible you will not be buying some things that your child really, *really* wants. I won't bore you with yet another Bratz example (but *please,* stop buying Bratz!), because to be honest, Bratz wasn't really that big a deal around my house. What was a big deal were Webkinz, the plush toys that send kids to a Web site for games and social networking. I have two value-based objections to Webkinz: One is the unbelievable focus on shopping and spending with "KinzCash." Acquisition of "KinzCash" is the major goal of the games and promotes materialism and a consumer mind-set in very young children. My second objection is that merely playing with a stuffed animal creates the habit of engaging in a virtual social life (albeit one that is supposedly well controlled). I can't fathom why kids as young as five or six should engage in "KinzChat" no matter how safe they say it is. It smacks of playing "MySpace." If you have played with Webkinz from the time you're in kindergarten, you will naturally evolve into a tween who uses the computer as a "toy" for social networking.

Encourage Open-Ended Pretending

If you give a girl a baby doll and a doll stroller, she'll create her own fantasy game with a structure and circumstances of her own design. If you give her a doll with a story line such as Barbie's "My Scene" characters, she's less likely to create her own story and more likely to adopt the "totally hot" vocabulary and themes put out by the toymaker. Look for toys, dress-ups, and activities that encourage open-ended imagination, not prefab pretending. The same goes for boys, though the issues related to the sexualization of children affect them to a lesser degree.

Set Limits, Even in Play

We once knew a little girl who liked to play pretend, but her fantasy play focused inappropriately on sexual themes. She always wanted to be the girlfriend (never the wife) waiting at home for my son, who was supposed to arrive there to find her waiting on the couch. Her game was "pretend I'm sleeping on the couch and you come in from work and lie on top of me and give me a kiss." Suffice to say, Jimmy would have none of it. Thankfully, my older girls overheard this scenario and came to me with it. I immediately called a meeting of everyone in the house and laid down my rules about what constituted appropriate play. I directed my edict at everyone—my kids as well as the other child—because I didn't want her to feel singled out and I wanted to make sure my own children understood my limits. Plus, this gave them the geek's way out of any situation: "My mom says I can't play this game." Sometimes that's what it takes!

GEEKS AT THE PROM

Like many parents, my husband and I made a rule that our children couldn't date until they turned sixteen. Over the years, however, I have come to realize that setting a specific age isn't the point. More valuable—and value-driven—is to set some specific parameters about socializing. Obviously, those expand as kids grow and mature, recognizing that each child matures at his own pace. The goal is to foster self-confidence and self-discipline in our kids in order to equip them for any social situation.

Boyfriends and Girlfriends Are All Just Friends
Keep kids focused on friendships of all varieties and don't push child-hood romance. I'm stunned at the parents who think it's "cute" that their children have a boy- or girlfriend in middle school or younger, and actually acknowledge these relationships with attention and support. No matter what they say (or what you hear from other parents) about your child's supposed romance, treat it as a friendship no different from other friends your child enjoys. Enthusing about a sixth-grade romance is the fast track to a very serious relationship by sophomore year.

Talk Openly About Dating Before It's a Possibility
Long before you believe it's appropriate, your child's peers will begin pair-ing off and engaging in the melodramatic world of adolescent romance. Keep an ear to the ground and be sure to talk to your child about what's going on, even as early as fifth or sixth grade. He needs your insight and perspective to put into context all he's seeing and hearing. By seventh grade, I'd say to Jimmy, "So, it looks like your buddy has a girlfriend." He generally shrugged his shoulders, but he also made comments that told me what he was thinking (i.e., "Yeah, he never wants to hang out anymore"). Talking about the dating behavior he saw among his peers gave me the chance to let him know my values on this subject, such as, "One reason I think it's best not to get into dating yet is that it takes time away from your friends." I didn't hand down judgments about the behavior of others; I just used them to share my values with my son.

Encourage Mixed Socializing
Since it was clear we weren't assuming anyone would "hook up," we always encouraged our kids to socialize in mixed company if they wanted to. Our basement became a frequent site for parties in Katie's sophomore year, when almost none of the kids were paired off, but all enjoyed hanging out in a mixed group. While our children haven't dated much at all in high school, they have maintained strong friendships with kids of the opposite gender that make for a fun social life.

Dances Don't Require Dates

With all the hype, it's virtually impossible for any school dance to live up to a teen's expectations, but you can't tell that to most fifteen-year-olds. School dances are fun and exciting and they also give teens the chance to practice important social skills. Beginning as early as seventh grade, middle school dances can offer limited opportunities to test out a young teen's social competence, if not his dancing abilities. High school dances, especially the big ones like homecoming and prom, can offer excitement and lifelong memories. On the other hand, dances can be a big drag. I think it's crucial to infuse values into kids' expectation about school dances so they remain in a geek perspective. As far as that goes, we've stressed that dances don't require a date (obviously, for middle school this goes without saying). Thankfully, girls and guys now feel generally comfortable about going to dances with groups of friends even if they don't have a partner for the evening. Everyone can be included and this is a good thing. On the other hand, there are worse things in life than missing a dance. Choosing to sit out the prom rather than feel awkwardly dateless is a great choice when made in self-confidence. Our kids have done dances all ways—without a date, with a date, and skipping them entirely in favor of a movie night with friends. The healthiest attitude is one that stresses social comfort and not insecure desperation.

Dating When the Time Is Right

As a geek parent promoting late blooming in children and teens, I believe it's perfectly normal and appropriate to hold off on an exclusive relationship until late into high school or even in college or young adulthood. Watching my children sort out their social selves has convinced me they would not be as complete or as mature if they were focused on establishing and maintaining a love life in their teens. Instead, they've all developed strong, healthy friendships with guys and girls and those friendships have helped them gain poise and confidence. I know they all dream of finding romance, but it's not a fixation or even a priority. Geek parents need to reassure our kids that there's no need to go out looking for love. It will surely come to find them when the time is right.

Innocence and Ignorance
Are Not the Same

With all the focus on maintaining our children's innocence, you may assume I'm overprotecting my children or shrouding in secrecy the "facts of life." Nothing could be further from the truth.

Geek kids, because they're intelligent and curious, need information. I don't believe innocence and ignorance are one and the same; I'm just not willing to allow the American media and the culture of cool to be my children's primary sources of information about topics they ought to learn from their parents.

Recall that my children read the newspaper, so their news-junkie habits get us talking about such issues as war, crime, accidents, the environment, civil rights, politics and government, the economy and health care. These conversations afford us opportunities to educate them about "grown-up" issues that frequently have raw edges as well as reassure them when they feel worried about events of the day.

We take the same approach to our communication about behavior choices that will face our children in the future. Sheltering kids doesn't mean you dodge conversations about sex, drugs, alcohol, or experimental behaviors; it means when you do talk about these things, you seek to maintain your child's innocence.

For example, teaching children early about natural, healthy sexuality helps them to feel secure about themselves, especially as they mature. But what they learn through the media isn't the same as being well educated about the biology of reproduction or the emotional bonds of physical relationships. We start early to teach our children about sexuality and we revisit the subject frequently to add more age-appropriate information as time passes.

When they're old enough, usually around age thirteen, I even do a whole talk on sexual slang, since I don't ever want my kids laughing along with a joke or making a comment without knowing what the words mean. Understanding the terminology of the day is crucial to avoiding situations in which their dignity—if not their safety—is compromised.

But knowing the facts alone does not corrupt innocence. Context is everything. When we talk about sex, we answer every question, but we reiterate the moral framework and the importance of loving relationships in which we believe sexual behavior is appropriate and wonderful.

Similarly, when we talk about drug or alcohol use, we convey the information along with our values about resisting substance abuse. We talk about situations they could encounter and how to avoid dangerous people and destructive choices. Our conversations are frank, fact-filled, and are intended to teach our children what to expect down the road. ("This may seem hard to believe when you're only eleven, but soon enough you'll be at a party and someone may offer you alcohol or drugs. Here's how to get out of that situation…")

Life being what it is, we need to discuss reality. People die and divorce, they get arrested or abused; they have road rage and temper tantrums and cancer. We talk about all of it. We answer their questions because we respect our children's right and need to know what's going on.

There's a balance between innocence and information, though. I'm not suggesting we rear our children to be naive or gullible, but we can give kids the information they need without succumbing to a standard of media exposure that reveals more than is necessary and appropriate. By respecting their intelligence as well as their innocence, we can arm kids with information and, at the same time, foster close relationships that keep them talking about things like sex, alcohol, drugs, friendships, and the choices they must make about how to behave. By establishing an open, communicative relationship when they're young, we create habits of communication for the teen years.

Teens who talk to their parents about sex, drugs, and drinking? These teens are called "geeks."

Uncool Answers

My twelve-year-old daughter bought a skimpy top with her own money but never showed it to me. She took it to a friend's house and changed into it there before they went to the movies. Should I take the top away?

Tweens and their newfound freedom at the mall present new parenting concerns, and this episode is a good example. When a young shopper is free to make her own choices, she may choose something that would not pass your "absolute veto," as described above. And besides, as kids grow they naturally want to shop with friends and make choices on their own. The fact that your daughter bought a top you wouldn't have approved isn't my concern, nor is the issue of whose money was used to pay for it. Rebelling against your taste and asserting her independence are normal in preteens. What bothers me is that she never showed it to you, but instead changed into it at a friend's house. This tells you she absolutely knew you would not have approved of her purchase and that she understands a skimpy top isn't appropriate attire. A twelve-year-old is still young, at least in my book. I think you should let her know that skimpy clothes don't fit the values you're teaching in your home or the image of wholesomeness you want her to project. If there's a way to salvage the purchase by wearing something under or over it, I'd work out a compromise, but I wouldn't focus on ownership of the top. (Chalk it up to a poor choice and talk about donating it next time you gather up items for the needy.) Focus instead on helping your daughter to feel and look lovely by finding modest tops that prove she needn't be skimpy to feel she's growing up.

Guaranteed Geek: Style Do's and Don'ts for Uncool Kids

For Geeks of All Ages:
* Dress neatly. Be clean. Be comfortable.

* Find out what attire is appropriate for every event. Teach kids the habit of asking about attire when they're invited somewhere so they always feel comfortable and confident.

* Dress for your age—your *real* age, not the age the marketing folks think you want to be!

* Focus on the fun things you can do as a child and only as a child.

For Elementary School Geeks:
* Don't dress in miniature versions of teen clothes. Avoid stores like Abercrombie and Limited Too that mimic the styles sold for young adults.

* Don't wear T-shirts with sarcastic, sassy, or materialistic messages on them.

* Do play dress-up when you want to experiment with looking and feeling older. This is what pretend is for!

For Middle School Geeks:
* Do notice what others wear and think about how they are perceived by peers. Become aware that people are judged on their appearance.

* Do send an older cousin or college friend out shopping with a middle schooler if trips to the mall lead to stress and struggles. Give specific instructions on styles you can't allow, but otherwise, let an admired young adult help reinforce your values about modesty.

* Do give middle schoolers opportunities to shop on their own and choose their own clothes, starting with a budget and an agreement about what styles are appropriate.

For High School Geeks:

* Body piercing and tattoos aren't geeky. Don't pierce or tattoo your body without fully considering the risks and ramifications. From infections to first impressions, permanently adorning the body can be a deeply regrettable lifetime choice.

* Do wear makeup tastefully and sparingly—young women don't need much to be beautiful!

* Do wear clothes that really fit. Too small, too short, too tight, or too big are neither geeky nor sexy!

* Do find a hairstyle that works for you and don't hide behind hair that says you're insecure. Stay well groomed and remember people notice when you're not!

Rule #6

RAISE A TEAM PLAYER

The *crack* of the starter's gun sent Katie sprinting down lane number two, roughly three hundred meters from where I sat in the stands on the other side of the track. Only some fifty-odd seconds and ten hurdles stood between my lanky runner and the finish line.

Katie was incredibly nervous, but she was also thrilled to be running in the regional track meet. Throughout the season, her performance in the hurdles had been spotty; she showed potential, but seemed to need the perfect confluence of calories, sleep, disposition, and divine intervention to get her time under about 57 seconds. She wanted to run it in 52.2 that night. More than that, she wanted to prove to her coach that he'd made the right choice when he asked a sophomore to run at regionals. She was one of just a few underclassmen on the team who made the roster.

The staggered starting gate made Katie's position on the track appear bleak. She wouldn't catch the racers in the other lanes until about the second curve, and even then, she would need to be moving faster than usual. As she made the second turn, her face came into view and I could see she was struggling to catch the runner ahead of her and stay in the hunt.

Unfortunately, the hurdles kept getting in the way.

And then, as she jumped the fifth one, her trail leg dropped and she caught the bar. She was down.

Katie's face registered immediate shock, as if she was thinking, *Why am I on the ground? Am I hurt? I have to get up!*

In the flash of just a few seconds she was moving again, but not well, and though she jumped the remaining hurdles, she was already so disappointed it was all she could do to hold back her tears as she crossed the finish line. Last. By a lot.

Jim and I walked down from the stands to comfort our runner. Katie melted into my arms and cried—heavy, wet sobs. Her arm was scraped a little, but mostly her pride was wounded and her dreams were dashed. She had envisioned pulling it out—beating her previous best time and maybe even qualifying for States. She envisioned feeling like a winner. Instead she felt humiliated.

I told her I was proud of the athlete who got up off the track and finished the race. I said hurdles aren't easy and she was still learning. I reminded her she had two more years to develop her skills. And of course I acknowledged the whole thing stunk and there wasn't much I could say to make it better. I wiped her tears, offered her food, got her to laugh.

I hated that her heart was broken and all I could do was dust her off after a failed effort, knowing how much she wanted to succeed.

Then again, success has many measures. Later, after a hot dog, she strolled over to the stands and snuggled up with me against the night air. We cheered for her friends and she was ecstatic when they won their races. She had put her disappointment behind her and focused instead on supporting her teammates.

"Shouldn't you be hanging with the team?" I asked.

"No." She smiled, dropping her head on my shoulder. "I'm good."

What It Takes to Be a Winner

That night on the track, Katie showed just what kind of athlete she really was. She started out with a goal, and a challenging one, at that.

She had prepared with diligent practice. Her hard work had earned the notice of her coach, who gave her the chance to compete not because he felt assured she would be successful but because he knew she would do her best. When she fell on the track and faced a moment of defeat, she got up and showed she was a true competitor, finishing the race with dignity and effort despite a discouraging loss. By athletic standards, for Katie that regional meet was a bust.

By geek standards, the meet was a huge victory.

GETTING IN THE GAME

Sports play an important role in children's lives. My kids are typical in this regard, having started out in organized sports programs as early as the first grade. (All four participate in various sports that have included basketball, soccer, baseball, softball, cross-country running, volleyball, and track. Amy is quick to point out she also attends cheerleading camp at the high school every summer.)

Note, however, I said my kids started in "organized" sports, not "competitive" sports. There's a crucial difference. Organized sports programs—those that are child-centered and focus on teaching the fundamentals of a game and on having fun—can be some of the most positive experiences in a child's young life.

In such programs, the goal is to teach the rules and skills needed to play a game for enjoyment and fitness. With an emphasis on learning, all kids—whether or not they're particularly athletic—grow in confidence about their physical abilities. In a quality sports program, children feel successful even if they can tell that other kids are better at the sport than they are. A big benefit of these programs is social interaction.

Some people argue it's unrealistic and even wrong to introduce sports into a child's life without the element of competition. They argue we're just coddling our kids by sending them onto a playing field with the expectation that they can always come off feeling like winners. Sports are about winning *and losing,* these parents contend, so kids must learn to be competitive.

I couldn't disagree more. Now, I'll readily admit I love a good, competitive sports contest, and anyone who has ever seen me cheer for my kids at a sporting event will tell you this is true. But I honestly don't think we have to teach kids to *be competitive*.

Recalling the chapter on raising a brainiac, people, by their nature, are more or less competitive. Some enjoy it, some don't. By offering the opportunity to engage in sports, you'll see pretty quickly whether your child exhibits a pronounced competitive spirit. Over time, with maturity and self-confidence, some kids grow in this area. But I'm one who believes it's a personality trait that comes in our original packaging.

We do, however, have to teach kids *how to compete,* and therein lies the difference. Having a competitive spirit may come naturally. But competing in a game or contest requires skills, knowledge of the game, an understanding of team play, and a sense of mastery. This is why instructional leagues focus on learning *the game,* not on learning to *win the game.*

Learning how to compete also means learning about one's essential character. Tapping into physical strength and ability isn't enough—athletes often must dig deeper to what are commonly called the "intangibles": determination, courage, heart, and commitment. In the end, those usually are the keys to athletic success.

WINNING CHARACTER

Athletes of all levels who exhibit strong character feel like winners even in the face of discouraging losses. This is because the first character trait of a winner is integrity. Players who consistently work hard and deliver their best effort tend to feel good about their performances even if the team's efforts fall short. Kids learn to play with integrity when they receive positive feedback for their genuine effort. This is why it's crucial to put the focus on our child's individual effort rather than on the outcome of a game—win or lose. "Did you do your best?" and "Did you feel like you worked hard?" are great questions for the ride home. Sometimes a child will answer truthfully, "I probably could have given it more effort." This is the opening for a great conversation about playing with integrity and living up to a commitment to the coach and the team to do your best.

Integrity also is the foundation on which all even playing fields are built. Through sports, kids learn the essentials of fair play, following rules, and respecting their opponents. Integrity is the trait that defines sportsmanship.

Another vital character trait in sports is poise—maturity and composure in the face of stress. By creating an atmosphere of adversity or pressure, sports offer a healthy avenue to practice poise. Some kids naturally display poise even from a young age; some struggle to learn this trait into their teens. We've all seen kids lose their tempers on a basketball court or in the hockey rink. Poise is the trait that keeps a child focused on the game and on his role on behalf of the team.

Perhaps no other trait is learned as well through sports as the trait of perseverance. Unlike most activities a child may pursue, sports require that one push himself beyond his perceived personal limits. With a rewinding tape running through his head saying, "I can't, I can't, I can't," perseverance is the element of good character that says, "Want to bet?" and keeps an athlete going. Since my children participate in the sport of distance running, I've watched time and again how this trait propels a child to succeed. Giving up is always more appealing than going hard to the end of a long race, but through the sport of cross-country running, my kids have discovered the willpower to persevere.

Team sports also teach the trait of humility. Whether they're gifted athletes or they struggle to keep up, all kids on a sports team can contribute to the effort of the whole. When they experience the power of a unified, cooperative team, kids discover that they can contribute to something larger than themselves—an outcome they could not have achieved on their own. This is how they develop genuine humility. At the same time kids who are particularly talented can learn to be humble. Talent being a gift from God, most kids take for granted that they're perhaps more coordinated or have more agility than others. But because in team sports the success of the whole rests on the effort of each person, a talented child learns to be humble when he discovers his raw abilities aren't enough without the support of his team. (If he's a quarterback and he gets sacked a lot, this point is very clear!)

Team sports also teach the character trait of grace. This point was perhaps best articulated by a poster made by my daughter Amy before a basketball game: WE PLAY TO WIN, BUT WE LOSE WITH HONOR. (They lost, but they were honorable.) From an early age, we tell kids not to be sore losers or boastful winners, but in our culture, it's typical to see both. Exhibiting grace—win or lose—is the sign of sportsmanlike conduct.

Sports clichés often sum up the character lessons that can be learned through athletics. Coaches are quick to communicate using platitudes like "there's no 'I' in team" and "quitters never win and winners never quit" and "it's all about the intangibles." In fact, Tom Izzo, the renowned coach of the Michigan State University men's basketball team, told me he worked hard to avoid sports clichés since they seem to trivialize such important messages. "The thing is," he said, "the longer I'm in coaching, the more I realize the reason those clichés hang on is because they're all true. It really comes down to how hard a person is willing to work and the character he brings to the team. That's what makes all the difference."

A METAPHOR FOR LIFE

Another reason sports clichés hang on is that they truly resonate in all aspects of life. This is because sports are a metaphor for life—they mimic in the course of an athletic contest the many trials, tribulations, and triumphs everyone faces from time to time. Whether it's hanging on to a lead in a game or pushing hard to come back from a looming defeat, overcoming a seemingly unbeatable challenge, or trying harder than you've ever tried to do something really difficult, sports create moments of personal decision.

To a geek parent, this is the whole crux of getting kids into athletics. Whether or not a team wins a championship trophy or makes it to the final round of a particular tournament or even wins the state title ultimately is *never the point*. Only by experiencing firsthand the emotions of pride and disappointment and the role of their determination in every circumstance can kids internalize the lessons that will serve them in life.

Moreover, the lessons they learn in competitive sports apply to their current lives as children, not just some distant adult future. Especially in the challenges that geeks face, traits of integrity, poise, perseverance, and grace allow them to forge ahead through some trying social situations on their way to and through adolescence. (See the next chapter for lots of examples.) Of course, when they finally do reach adulthood, these same traits, learned while sprinting down a soccer field or humbly cheering from the bench, also are needed in their professional lives and personal relationships.

In all honesty, there are times when I've felt like maybe my kids didn't need quite so many life lessons. Sometimes, couldn't it just be about playing, winning, smiling, and going out for ice cream? But that's almost never the case.

Consider that night on the track in Katie's sophomore year. In a single race—an event that lasted roughly sixty seconds—she exuded all the character of a hardworking, dedicated, and graceful young woman. She ran courageously even after she fell. She showed poise at the finish line even though she felt horribly embarrassed. And she demonstrated her sportsmanship by supporting others even though she had failed to run as she'd hoped.

I wouldn't wish that night on her again in a million years, but I know it taught her some lessons that will last forever.

WHAT'S HEALTHY ABOUT COMPETITION?

Most folks understand that healthy competition is a good thing, but of course the cultural conundrum is: What constitutes healthy competition? I think one of the reasons why some folks try to water down the competitive environment in sports is that kids begin competing too soon. Until about age ten, kids should enjoy sports on an instructional level with almost no emphasis on the outcome of a game. That's not just my opinion—it's the consensus of nearly everyone associated with youth sports.

When it's time to move from instructional to competitive play, I believe it has to be authentic. You can't fool kids—they understand full well that sports contests leave one team on top and one team falling short. Someone has to win and someone has to lose.

A healthy competitive environment, then, is one where winning and losing are viewed honorably. You face your opponent respectfully and you give them a good fight. Even if you're outmatched, you play with grit. A healthy environment stresses teamwork and cooperation, and puts the focus on executing with skill rather than winning at all costs.

Competing in a healthy environment is FUN! Kids compete because it's fun to play games with friends and work together toward a shared goal. Even when they fall short of their vision, kids love teams because they offer a social activity with a purpose. Fun is the "health meter" in competition. If there's no fun, it's not healthy.

It's worth noting that one study says kids would rather play on a losing team than sit on the bench for a team that wins. Does this come as a surprise? I think kids naturally understand that they'll win some and lose some. What matters most to them is participation and fairness, both for themselves personally and for their teams.

My son's no-cut basketball club once competed against a team that supposedly was composed of boys of the same age. Imagine our surprise, then, when one of the incoming eighth graders on the other team nearly dunked a basketball on a regulation ten-foot hoop. The whole team was similarly talented and equally physically mature. By comparison, Jimmy and his teammates looked like pipsqueaks. Turns out when that team signed up for the tournament, their coach described them as "average" ability, placing them in Jimmy's competitive bracket. Fair? Obviously not. Worse, what exactly was anyone to gain by playing such a lopsided game of basketball? (For our team, the answer was *good character*. I don't know what the other team gained.)

For competition to be healthy, adults need to assure that everyone follows the rules. These days this means providing copies of birth certificates and school records to assure that kids aren't "playing down" to catch a competitive advantage. It also means assuring that the programs in which younger children participate have guidelines to assure fair playing time.

By the time they reach high school, kids are accustomed to some pretty challenging competition and this is great. There's nothing more exciting than a sporting event where kids are giving their all while representing their schools. At the high school level, there's a greater focus on winning, but this geek mom's observation is that coaches who win the most are the ones who demand that players exhibit the greatest character. In the end, it really does come down to the intangibles.

How the Culture Corrupts Youth Sports

With so much to be gained by participating in sports, why are our children stuck in a culture that woefully corrupts their athletic experiences? It's not like we don't know what constitutes a great program, what the attributes are of a good and helpful coach, how parents ought to behave in order to support the purpose of sports, or what the ultimate benefits are to participation. I can't find a survey to substantiate this claim (go figure—there are surveys on everything else!), but I'm going to make a bold assertion: I think *just about everyone* knows how children's sports *should* be conducted!

Parents are told directly what constitutes appropriate behavior on their part. Schools and sports programs now routinely distribute rules of conduct for athletes *and their parents,* and often a participation contract must be signed that states the adults understand their proper role and promise to uphold standards of good sportsmanship. That's the parents, not the kids! Even the most boorish, over-competitive boob of a parent will tell you, "I just want my daughter to participate, get some regular exercise, and have fun." I would bet the college fund that this is the same father who leaves voice mails for the coach demanding his child get more playing time.

The problem isn't just the parents, though. Coaches routinely exhibit attitudes about winning that leave hardworking, enthusiastic children sitting on the bench. They talk the talk of effort and team play, but even when their teams are up by insurmountable numbers, they leave the best players on the floor or the playing field and run up the score to prove their dominance.

Citizenship Through Sports Alliance (CTSA) is the largest coalition of both professional and amateur sports organizations in America and works to promote positive sports experiences for kids. (Interesting name for the organization, isn't it? Note their name isn't "Alliance to Promote Gifted and Highly Competitive Young Athletes.") CTSA in 2005 issued a report card on the state of youth sports based on input from coaches, parents, officials, and program directors. Here's the result:

Areas of Review/Grade
  * Child-centered philosophy/D
  * Coaching/C–
  * Health and safety/C+
  * Officiating/B–
  * Parental behavior/involvement/D

This is a dismal portrait of youth sports! And what it reveals is the same pattern we've seen in every chapter of this book and in every aspect of parenting in our culture—*parents know how youth sports programs ought to operate to serve the best interests of their kids, but they're unwilling to change their bad habits and poor behavior.*

This is how kids' sports inappropriately become the focal point of family life. Though, as I mentioned, it's recommended that kids play a variety of sports in a noncompetitive atmosphere until about age ten, it's common for children as young as five years old to home in on a specialty sport and compete year-round. How is it possible for a first or second grader to know that he loves hockey more than soccer? Why would a third-grade girl choose skating lessons in the early morning hours before school over after-school basketball with her friends? There's no doubt that kids can genuinely enjoy a sport from an early age, but participation in it needn't preclude a healthy variety of activities.

Starting earlier and earlier is another trend in youth sports. New to the marketplace are private-membership gyms especially for children that teach the fundamentals of sports to kids as young as sixteen months old. (I'm seriously not making this up.) A Canadian company called Sportsball is establishing itself in the United States through franchises where children ages sixteen months to seven years may learn the fundamentals of seven different sports.

It's been a while since my kids were that small, but I seem to recall when they were sixteen months old, they were still trying to master the fundamentals of walking.

As ridiculous as Sportsball sounds, there are parents who earnestly believe these sorts of programs are good for their children and will give them a head start to become better athletes.

If private kiddie gyms seem uncommon, what's not unusual is for parents to direct children to specialize in a sport at an elite level. This is the mentality that leads to the culture of the "child-pro."

GOING "PRO"

Here are some compelling news stories that don't come from the sports section:

* *"Soccer Mom Alert: More May Not Be Better"* (MSNBC.com, June 2007): In this story, parents were warned that kids risk injury if they aren't allowed time to take healthy breaks from sports. Playing year-round on travel and club teams stresses growing bodies and can hinder normal development.

* *"A New Competitive Sport: Grooming the Child Athlete"* (New York Times, June 2006): This story profiles a family that spent more than $30,000 promoting one son's baseball career in the

hope that he will ultimately play in the major leagues. As a young-
ster, he attended elite camps to increase his odds for a college
scholarship.

* *"Pushing Too Hard, Too Young" (MSNBC, April 2004):* This
piece, part of a series called *Going for the Pros,* discussed doc-
tors' concerns about the intensity, purpose, and dangers of competitive youth sports. One doctor says pushing kids into sports is
a "national obsession."

Each of these articles—and thousands more—chronicle the extreme
ways in which kids engage in sports as "child-pros." Organized way
beyond the community level, programs for hockey, soccer, basketball,
and baseball operate just like professional leagues. This isn't something
I've just read about in news stories—I've actually watched such teams
play in tournaments. It's not uncommon for my kids' no-cut developmental summer basketball teams to be clobbered in games by clubs that
have recently completed a season modeled after the NBA. These organizations recruit players from all across their regions and train year-
round. Their participation requirements preclude a child from playing
any other sports, and they expect families to travel along with the team
around the state and across the country.

Spending inordinate amounts of money to participate in all sorts of
programs, parents essentially turn over their family life to coaches and
subject themselves to daily practice, game, and tournament schedules.
The parents in the stories cited above readily admitted they have no personal pursuits beyond driving their kids to play sports.

Importantly, every news story I've ever seen about the "child-
pro" culture warns of the risks to kids of overinvolvement: emotional
burnout, physical injury including those that could pose lifelong consequences, and psychological problems such as depression and drug
abuse. I've never read a single article or watched a TV news report on
the topic that didn't caution parents about being hypercompetitive and
pushing kids too hard in the name of athletic excellence. They all say

to be careful since the wrong approach can sour kids on their sport or even on athletics entirely.

The culture of the "child-pro" most certainly is the extreme, but the hypercompetitive mind-set permeates youth sports at every level. Eventually all the stress of team sports causes a full 70 percent of children who play in organized sports programs as children to quit league athletics by age thirteen and never play again. The number one reason they give it up? *It's not fun anymore!*

THE PARENT FACTOR

Sadly, one big reason kids lose their enthusiasm is poor sportsmanship on the part of their own parents. Parents who gripe about and undermine coaches, criticize their kids' performance, complain about a losing record, or harp on kids to train harder often say they are trying to improve their children's sports experience.

The issue of poor sportsmanship among parents is so commonplace that folks don't think their behavior is wrong unless it's violent or illegal. Only the most outlandish stories are newsworthy anymore: parent-coach brawls, criminal conduct such as stalking, and disclosures of corruption in youth leagues. The folks in these stories are clearly kooky, which means most parents dismiss them as rarities.

Maybe so, but bad parenting on the sidelines is not rare. Any sane parent who has ever attended a youth sports event will tell you there is someone at virtually every game yelling at the referees and coaches, making snide comments about players, screaming at their own kid, and generally making the event uncomfortable for everyone.

What drives all this competitive fury? Experts suggest a host of causes such as personal insecurity on the part of parents, the desire to live vicariously through their kids, and the need to relive their youthful successes or correct their past sports failures.

I have another theory. Back at the beginning of this book, I talked about parents who view their children as personal "accomplishments"— appendages, if you will—to the long and illustrious legacies they hope

BASKETBALL ON ANOTHER PLANET

So far in my parenting journey, I figure I have attended more than 350 youth basketball games, a tally that includes recreational-league games, school matches, and summer tournaments. I've sat through hand-wringing victories as well as hard-fought defeats. I've watched my children and their teammates evolve from enthusiastic third graders to determined middle schoolers. My son hopes to play in high school, so I may have a spot in the bleachers for a few more years. Lucky for me, I absolutely love the game of basketball, so supporting my kids' participation in the sport is fun for me.

With so much basketball in my life, the games, and even the seasons, run together in a bouncing blur. In all honesty, there's only one game I have attended that I'm certain I will never forget...Amy's last game in the fourth-grade rec league.

Amy was eager to play in the rec league, as it meant there finally would be games on our family calendar for her that her siblings would be required to attend, at least occasionally. (Amy feels strongly about equity in this regard, having been schlepped to countless sporting events.) Recreational basketball in my town, as in most, is an instructional league that offers children the chance to learn the game in weekly practice sessions, and then play scrimmages against comparable new players. In the first year, these games are unscored. Thereafter, they keep score so kids can learn sportsmanship along with the sport.

To be clear, rec-league basketball for nine-year-olds doesn't look much like basketball. In fact, it looks a lot like soccer, which is to say there are a bunch of kids running in a pack chasing after a ball. Sometimes they dribble the thing, sometimes they just pick it up and start moving. Traveling calls are appropriately few and far between.

Given that this is beginner basketball—and as well that it is played at an ungodly hour on Saturday mornings—I tend to sit with a friend on the sidelines drinking coffee and shouting out occasional encouragements to my daughter. Most folks yell "good job" and "way to hustle!" I usually shout things like, "Amy, honey, you're on offense now" and "Sweetie, tie your shoe!" The parents on my daughter's team—all friends from her school—exhibit a similar level of enthusiasm, which is to say, enough to prove we're watching the game while we're chatting among ourselves. This is what I expected to be doing at my most memorable game of youth basketball. But right from the tip-off, the screaming began.

It was the screaming that seared this game into my consciousness; the overwhelming and unrelenting volume projected by the voices of some thirty adults on the sidelines. No matter what happened on the basketball court, this group of parents went stark raving wild.

Jump ball? Shrieks of "Get it! Get it!"

Inbound the ball? Roars of "Way to go! All the way!"

Pass to a teammate? "That's it! You did it! Great pass!"

The praise for simple execution of elementary skills was ridiculous. Could the girls really believe they were doing something so extraordinary?

As you can imagine, whenever one of their daughters tossed the ball anywhere in the direction of the basket, these parents reacted as if they'd just been told they won the Mega Million lottery. They actually made yipping sounds as they slapped high fives and jumped up and down. I'm not even kidding—grown adults, both men and women, jumped up and down at a rec-league basketball game for fourth-grade girls.

The more they squealed and yelled and carried on, the more I felt I had been transported to some distant, oddball planet. The Planet of Lunatic Parents.

Their team won the game, which mattered deeply to them. Afterward, they hurried onto the court to make a human, parental "spirit tunnel," through which their players gleefully walked before collecting more hugs and hollers from their parents. Then their team had a meeting with the coach while the parents stood around the huddle.

Amy's team ate doughnuts. I swear I'll never forget it.

one day to leave behind. Through sports, these parents have a perfect opportunity to demonstrate to the world what spectacular specimens they have produced. These are the folks who cannot accept that their kids are average athletes, just like most other people's kids. Instead, they blather on about how underappreciated their children are or how much more talented they would be if only... (fill in the excuse). It's sad to see because kids realize they can never really live up to these parents' expectations when it comes to athletic prowess.

Worse, parents who display poor sportsmanship essentially negate everything important that can come from youth athletics. If sports serve as a metaphor for life, what are these parents teaching their kids? Traits of perseverance, self-discipline, and cooperation? More likely, traits of self-centeredness and even ruthlessness in the pursuit of victory. When the season of life for team sports finally does reach its end, will these parents have helped their kids to use sports as an avenue to good character, maturity, and solid citizenship? Or will all that effort come down to a meaningless win/loss record?

THE CORRUPTION OF HEALTHY COMPETITION

After years of hearing their parents yelling from the bleachers and heaping on pressure to excel, some kids adopt the mantle of the "über-jock," dominating with an arrogant attitude and predictably unsportsmanlike behavior. They hog the ball, they don't pass to certain kids even if they're open, they throw temper tantrums and talk trash. They talk back to the coach and yell at their teammates. They play with an edge that's part effort, part assumption. Whether or not these kids are among the best athletes, they act as if the team owes them something.

Sadly, any geek parent can attest to the fact that the kids who become ultracompetitive (even toward their own teammates) display those same attitudes within the social circles in which they operate off the playing field. Coincidence? I think not.

I'm not a sociological researcher and I wouldn't be a good one anyway (there is math involved), but I'm going to make a bold assertion based on common sense and personal observation: Parents who push sports success as the primary goal of their kids' participation tend also to push their child's overall popularity and social status. Therefore, the parents who contribute to the hypercompetitive climate in kids' sports also perpetuate the culture of cool.

No, I don't have research on that correlation. But you can draw plenty of valid conclusions while watching more than 350 youth basketball games.

The point is, if youth sports can be used as an avenue to develop good character, they also can be the route to poor character. When kids are taught that winning is everything, they will figure out how to win at all costs. Playing in a corrupt competitive environment, kids learn to cheat, blame others for the team's poor performance, and avoid responsibility or accountability to others.

How to Raise a Geekalete

Sports are a terrific avenue to employ and enjoy your geek lifestyle, and reassuringly, I can promise you'll find plenty of other geek parents promoting the same positive aspects that you want for your child. Unfortunately, I can also guarantee that there will be "über-jocks" and their obnoxious parents in the stands and on your teams. I urge you to ignore them and don't let them ruin the fun for your geeky family. Here are the fundamentals for raising your child to be a geekalete:

Focus on the Purpose of Youth Sports
No matter how spectacular or how inept an athlete your child seems to be, the purpose of youth sports is not to develop a superior athlete. *Rather, their purpose is to develop a superior human being. Organized team sports for children are meant to promote health and fitness, teach teamwork, create social opportunities and foster friendships, be fun, and most of all to build good character.* When you incorporate the

values you are teaching in your home into your child's sports life, you'll help him develop excellent character and grow into a solid citizen.

Expose Kids to a Variety of Sports

Sports are games and kids love all kinds of games. Even if your young child shows a particular aptitude or interest in one sport, be sure to give him opportunities to learn a variety of sports. Use common sense—an overscheduled third grader running from basketball to soccer to swimming isn't going to get much out of any of those drills. But be sure to sign up for a few different things especially when he's young and everyone is learning the game together. If you can afford it, consider martial arts, especially for kids who need help staying focused and learning self-discipline.

Be Appropriately Involved

Parent coaches are the lifeblood of youth sports programs and the best ones make it an awesome experience. If you know a sport or want to learn it and otherwise have the temperament to work with kids, go for it. But don't coach with a plan to develop your own child more than others or to assure he gets preferential treatment. Also, don't coach if your tendency is to push your child to excel. A parent who can't remain objective does not belong on the bench with the team. If you're not the coaching type, be involved appropriately by providing snacks and encouragement. Whatever you do, don't take it upon yourself to offer advice and insight to the coach from your perch in the bleachers. Either attend practices and help him out, or smile and say, "Great job, Coach!" If, by chance, you end up with a genuinely stinky coach, monitor the situation and keep your child's focus on learning the game and having fun with his friends. Seasons end. Don't make the same mistake twice.

Value Failure as Well as Success

Parents of geeks understand that losing is an important part of participating in sports. No one likes to lose, but it's valuable nonetheless. You can't learn to be gracious in defeat if you never lose. Winning is valuable also and kids need to know the feeling of victory and attaining their goals through hard work. The trick from a parenting perspective is to take each game as it comes (cliché!). Every game offers a life lesson, even if it's simply, "you win some, you lose some" (another cliché!).

Keep Competition in Perspective

Parents who heap on a lot of pressure before a big game, even without intending to do so, can distort the element of competition beyond its proper place. I know. I've done this. Out of my own jitters for my kids—especially when they compete as runners—I've offered "Coach Mom" advice that probably made the jitters worse for all of us. (If you're reading this, kids, I'm sorry.) Keeping competition in perspective sometimes means taking our cues from our kids, especially older kids. The more know-how our kids gain in sports, the more we must respect their styles as they approach a high pressure contest. When I've caught myself feeling too invested in the outcome of a meet or match, I make myself watch but not cheer. It's one way to keep overcompetitive behavior in check.

SPORTS AND SOCIAL STATUS

School sports teams combine the component of social status with athletics. On a school team, geeks are likely to play side by side with kids they never hang out with otherwise. You might think this is an area where a talented geek athlete can thrive regardless of his social status, but remember that hypercompetitiveness in sports actually has nothing to do with talent! If it did, a talented geek would never stand WIDE OPEN at the end of a basketball court waiting for an "über-jock" point guard to notice that he's WIDE OPEN and available to make an uncontested basket.

The fact is, if you are a geek and you play on a team with cool kids, you may not get the ball when you should. Even if you're open. Even if you're good. Sports are one more area where the social caste system plays out its unwritten rules. Certain kids always seem to pass the ball to certain other kids, and sometimes they do this on the admonition of their parents (insidious, but absolutely true). Also, since many coaches share the hypercompetitive spirit of the parents, it's not uncommon for rosters to favor "über-jocks."

This sort of thing can be frustrating, but it should not be a reason to quit the team. Perseverance often wins respect on the playing field (though that won't change the social structure off the field). Since sports teach strong character, even an unsatisfying athletic experience can ultimately be a rewarding one. I know this seems counterintuitive, but you're pretty far along in this book. By now that shouldn't surprise you.

The Long Ride Home

There's nothing quite as poignant as the moment I climb into the van with a disappointed athlete. All the promise and expectation that filled the air only a few hours earlier seem to melt into the silent recognition that a chance to achieve a measure of success slipped away. Sometimes there are tears, sometimes just exhaustion. Sometimes there is frustration so complete that it bubbles to an angry outburst. Most often there's just a quiet conversation about what went wrong.

I think I've done some of my best parenting in the van on those long rides home. Those are the occasions when I've used my children's sports experiences not only to encourage them in the short term, but to draw the connection to what lies ahead.

Through sports, my kids have shown that they understand what it means to fulfill a commitment, even when it felt like quitting a team might be the best way out. There's a lesson for lifelong marriage. Through sports, they've demonstrated that they'll make sacrifices for others. There's a lesson for a future parent. Through sports, they've taken on responsibility, been held accountable, and lived up to their potential. Those lessons will follow them to a job or to public service or voluntarism.

As athletes, they've felt the natural high of accomplishment, the fun of participation, and the love of friendships born of mutual effort and desire. Even on the worst day at a cross-country meet (and there have been plenty of those) or after losing a championship game or not making the cut, the intrinsic value of sports remains, no matter what the score at the end of the day.

I suppose if all this sounds corny, my geek-mom perspective is to blame. I think it's geek moms and dads who treasure the losses as much as the wins because those are the times when our roles as parents are needed most. Our children look to us for perspective. When we help them to view all of their contests as useful and necessary to the completion of their characters, then all of their endeavors have meaning and purpose.

The best rides home? The ones that end in the gentle realization that in life it's not what's lost on the playing field that matters, but what's found in the heart of a "team player."

Uncool Answers

My son loves sports and he's a fairly good athlete. More importantly, he works very hard and always does his best. Like all kids, he loves to win and gets frustrated when his teammates don't work as hard as he does to be successful. How can we help him from growing frustrated and angry at the other boys on his team?

Congratulations on having a son who has learned the value of dedicated effort! This is a crucial lesson and a skill he'll use no matter what he does in his life. Even though it's unlikely (statistically, anyhow) that he'll make his living as a pro, the perseverance and work ethic he is learning as a child athlete will serve him well.

COACH TOM IZZO'S INSIDE ADVICE
TO RAISE A CHAMPION

Tom Izzo's tenure as head coach of the Michigan State University men's basketball team is the stuff of legends. In only thirteen years, he has won one NCAA National Championship, four regular-season Big Ten Championships, two Big Ten Tournament titles, four Final Four appearances, four National Coach of the Year awards, and a Big Ten–best eleven straight NCAA Tournament appearances. Because of his consistent success, Coach Izzo's program was ranked second in the nation for the decade 1997–2007 by ESPN. Without a doubt, his career record of 302–128 proves his ability to coach champion athletes.

Recruiting is a big key to his success. Coach Izzo has attracted some of the nation's most talented high school players to MSU, including eight McDonald's All-Americans, along with seven Mr. Basketball award winners from Michigan, Illinois, and Minnesota in an eight-year span.

You might assume that Coach Izzo simply looks for the most talented up-and-coming players when adding to his roster each year, and it's true that talent is essential. But talent isn't everything. "I look for a well-rounded person," he says. "I figure anyone who is potentially playing at this level is pretty driven as an athlete. I want to see if they have people skills, if they are a multidimensional person. Most important, I want to see evidence of good character."

All kids love to win and some begin earlier than others to connect the dots between effort and outcome. Your son obviously has made this connection, but he must learn that others aren't always playing youth sports for the same reasons that he is. As well, he must learn that some kids actually are doing their best even if he believes they could do better.

Sounds to me like you have the makings of an excellent sports leader! Since your son already has discovered the positive feelings associated with

With strict NCAA rules about how much contact coaches can have with recruits, Coach Izzo doesn't get to know potential players and their families personally during the recruiting process. "I have very little time to spend with a recruit. I get one home visit and that's it." So what does the coach look for during that brief encounter in the athlete's home? "I look at how that young man treats his parents. Is he respectful? Is he polite? Does he use manners toward them as well as toward me?" Rather than focus on how a player has been parented, Coach Izzo looks at the result. "You can tell if the way a son treats his mother is genuine—there's no faking that relationship. I know if a son is respectful to his parents, he's been taught to respect his coach."

Coach Izzo says those parents who provide solid parenting to their children raise athletes who are easier and more fun to coach. "I'm looking for a player who has been raised to work hard but to keep his priorities straight. I also want to see strong people skills," he says. "Players have to be dedicated, but I want to work with athletes who keep life in perspective."

So what is Coach Izzo's inside advice to raise a championship athlete? "Don't try." Instead, instill in children the character of a champion and watch how far they'll go.

hard work and consistent effort, he can now learn how to inspire and motivate his teammates. For most kids, this doesn't come naturally. Their idea of showing leadership on the playing field is to dress down teammates for making a mistake. As we all know, "What'd you do that for?" is not an encouragement to someone who just threw the ball out of bounds.

Start role-playing with your son to teach him the language of encouragement and peer leadership. Explain to him that strong players have the power to motivate teammates by saying positive, admiring things to

COACH JIM HICKS'S TOP FIVE TRAITS OF A GREAT YOUTH ATHLETE

My husband, Jim, has coached youth basketball for all four of our children. As a former high school and college player (Williams College, Division III, 1976–1980), he knows the game inside and out. As the father of four, he has a parent's insight as well as firsthand experience motivating kids to work together as a team and do their best. He's also a teacher by profession, so Coach Hicks brings just the right skill set to the bench.

There's no record book for Coach Hicks's career. He can't give you his win/loss record for a single season, much less over the ten years since he began teaching children the game of basketball. The only statistic he points to with pride is 0. That's zero—the total number of times he's been confronted by an unhappy parent of one of his players. In a sports culture where parents are notorious for harassing coaches with complaints about playing time, starting lineups, and strategies to win the game, Coach Hicks's obvious commitment to fairness and helping all his players enjoy their team experience is evident to all.

He'll readily admit he has four favorites among the kids he's coached through the years (what a coincidence—they're all named Hicks!), but he's also worked with plenty of other kids who exhibit the traits every coach looks for in a young athlete. Here's what all his favorite kids have in common:

• **Supportive parents.** Coaches want to work with families who'll support the child's participation and the coach's leadership.

them. When a good player makes a point of telling a teammate, "Hey, great pass" or "Nice tackle," he can instill a desire to work harder. And as any coach will attest, peer leaders play a key role in motivating and inspiring their fellow players.

Teach your son that the role of a team captain is not to boss others around but to lead with positive comments, energy, and enthusiasm.

• Respectful attitudes. This may seem obvious, but coaches don't want to work with children who are rude, disobedient, or intentionally disruptive. Kids who can't behave appropriately make the team experience miserable for everyone.

• Enthusiasm. Some kids play sports only because their parents sign them up, not because they choose to play. A coach who's paying attention usually can learn how to motivate children who are willing generally to invest themselves in activities.

• Coachability. Coaches love the kids who are willing to do things the way the coach teaches them and to practice what's taught. Some kids may never do a particular thing very well, and that's okay. If they're willing to try, they'll improve and feel good about the improvement and the experience will be positive for everyone.

• Selflessness. It's a coach's job to teach children the joy and fulfillment of doing something together in a way that exceeds the sum of the things each of them could ever do alone. It's much easier to do this when every child, and particularly the best, most skilled athletes, are willing to do things in a way that includes everyone.

His team may not win any more games than they're winning now, but your son will be learning the leadership skills he needs to get that big promotion someday. How cool is that?

Guaranteed Geek: Tips to Help Your Geekalete Become a Winner

For Geeks of All Ages:

* Model physical fitness to your kids. Don't be just a spectator—let your kids see that physical fitness is an important lifelong priority.

* Put your money into family fitness. Get a driveway basketball hoop, buy bicycles for everyone, or put a tennis racquet for each person under the Christmas tree.

* When you recount your "glory days," be sure to tell stories of your hard-earned life lessons as well as your winning goals. Recount your failures and tell your kids how important—and beneficial—they were.

* Watch sports together on TV and not just football or basketball. Tune in to a college track meet or a women's lacrosse game to show kids the variety and skills in the world of sports.

For Elementary School Geeks:

* Sign your child up for instructional leagues only. Investigate the sports programs in your area to be certain the philosophy of the ones you choose fits with your values.

* Get involved as an assistant coach or parent leader. Even if all you do is coordinate the snacks, your child feels your support.

* Get to know the coach and support him or her when talking to your child.

* Don't coach from the sidelines. You'll confuse your child and stress him out!

* Remind your child to practice the rules of fair play in all venues, especially on the playground at school and in gym class.

For Middle School Geeks:
* As athletics become more competitive and your child's focus turns to winning and losing, keep sports in perspective. Keep the balance between supporting your child's strong interest in sports and helping him to understand what's truly important about playing.

* Don't gossip about the coach or other members of the team with other parents. If the conversation among parents makes you uncomfortable, sit elsewhere!

* Don't let your child tear down his teammates or coaches in conversations with you. Focus instead on positives about everyone involved in the team.

* Keep variety in your child's sporting life and continue to engage in lifelong sports such as running, tennis, and biking.

* If sports aren't your child's thing, encourage competition in other ways. Dance teams, "Odyssey of the Mind," 4-H, and other activities offer opportunities for healthy competition in areas that might better suit your geek.

* Evaluate your child's sports participation as a percentage of family time and resources. If most discretionary time and a large portion of discretionary money is spent on participation in organized sports, reconfigure your lifestyle for a healthier balance.

For High School Geeks:
* Encourage your high schooler to play at least one team sport every year. Physical activity is a known stress reducer for high school kids and those who participate in team sports exhibit fewer high risk behaviors than nonathletes.

* Support your athlete by attending her games and meets. Don't assume that a high school athlete is too old to care if a parent is cheering in the stands. They do care!

* Recognize that there's virtually nothing you can do to advance the possibility of your child receiving a college scholarship! If he is a gifted athlete who works hard and achieves athletic success, recruiters will find him without your assistance. If, like most kids, he's an average athlete participating in sports for fitness and fun, *nothing you can do* will increase his chances of getting a scholarship.

Rule #7

....

RAISE A TRUE FRIEND

The silence in the van broke with the muffled beeping of Katie's cell phone, tucked away in her purse on the floor. She fumbled to find it, flipped it open, and burst out laughing. "What is it?" I craned my neck while keeping my eyes mostly on the cars in front of me.

"Um...I'm not sure. I'm supposed to guess." The message was a photo from Katie's best friend, Chelsea. She and two other buddies, the inseparable Susie and Rachel, were gathered for a Friday-night sleepover (movies, popcorn, sugar in various forms). Katie was missing it for a college visit three states away.

The photo looked like a microscope slide of something plaid. Boxer shorts? Perhaps.

She sent a return text, flipped her phone shut, and sighed. "This is so typical," she said. "Just when things with my friends are going incredibly great, it's all coming to an end."

I let Katie's comment linger in the darkness for a mile or so. Clearly, she was starting to experience the characteristic nostalgia that engulfs the hearts of high school seniors—the sweet poignancy that inspires so many trite yet earnest graduation speeches and yearbook messages. Finally I said, "That's how you know it's time to move on."

We rolled along the highway, lost in our own thoughts. I imagined Katie was thinking about the things she and her girlfriends had yet to look forward to—prom, graduation, and the parties to follow. Me? I was thinking about Katie and Chelsea and the cheerleading class I had driven them to once a week in the first grade.

It was hard to conceive that the little girls who'd once learned pom-pom routines as six-year-olds now were contemplating their college careers.

Over the years, the relationship between Katie and Chelsea ebbed and flowed. Longing to be accepted, trying to fit in, they went their own ways at times, as most friends do over the long haul. Thankfully, they gravitated back to each other in high school, and together, toward a group of young women who shared their values, their strong faith, and a love of alternative rock. As a mother, I couldn't have asked for more wonderful friends if I'd chosen them myself.

We passed the miles talking about where her pals were going to college and the cool things she imagined they'll do when they "grow up." She spoke with the easy familiarity that comes when friends know everything about one another, the way high schoolers do.

As if on cue, Katie's cell phone beeped again with another mystery photo. She bantered by text with the gang at the sleepover, then finally typed, *Have fun guys. Thanks for thinking of me. I miss you.*

Friendship in the Culture of Cool

Katie's heartwarming night of text messages from the girls at the sleepover makes for a warm and fuzzy introduction to the subject of friendship, but I'd be lying if I said it represented the totality of her friendship journey. Remember back in the fifth grade? Katie-the-bookworm struggled to fit in and find a group of girls who accepted and appreciated her.

This is a good place to pick up that story where we left off. If you'll recall, Katie spent lots of time reading during the fifth grade because she simply didn't connect with the girls in her class. It's important to know that at the time our children attended a very small start-up school and Katie's class consisted of ten girls and no boys. All the other girls played soccer and hung out together constantly, going to practices, games, sleepovers, and yes, even a Back Street Boys concert. In contrast, Katie was an Irish dancer and spent most of her time outside of school playing in our neighborhood.

My husband and I concluded that as much as we loved the small school, there just weren't enough kids for Katie to find a few kindred spirits. Since we thought a larger social environment would be better for her as well as the rest of our children, we enrolled the whole gang at a larger school in the next town.

Talk about a change. In sixth grade, Katie was the "new girl" and was immediately absorbed into the popular group. Boy, did she feel cool! She loved the new school, but pretty quickly it was clear her new-found social prominence wasn't going to last. What happened to thwart her status?

A popular boy asked Katie to "go out" with him. *Going out*—the euphemism for an exclusive boy/girl relationship—wasn't something we permitted, and moreover, the very idea scared Katie half to death. It was one thing to hang out with the cool girls and eat lunch at their table. It was another thing entirely to have a boyfriend before you turned twelve. Katie sought my advice about how to handle the situation, and we decided the "parental scapegoat" was the way to go. She said she wasn't allowed to "go out." Thus, her fall from popularity began.

Soon enough, Katie found herself declining invitations to PG-13 movies and admitting she didn't watch MTV or *The Simpsons*. When cool kids started trading screen names and IMing the afternoons away, it was clear Katie wasn't actually one of them, but, in fact, was a geek. Our values about media, late blooming, and materialism impeded her ability to be cool.

The adjustment took a little time, but eventually Katie discovered she wasn't the only one whose parents limited access to a cool lifestyle. She gravitated toward a small group of articulate, fun, and caring friends and completed her middle school years in the security of a comfortable social circle.

As I write this, I'm almost amused at how easy it is to sum up my daughter's middle school friendship struggles in just a few paragraphs. It felt a lot more complicated than that as we lived through it! And not just Katie's experience, but Betsy's and Jimmy's, as well. By the time you buy this book, I'll be running alongside Amy as she sprints through those crucial years, and I don't expect her life to be any less emotional.

As every parent knows, finding friends in the culture of cool is one of the most challenging tasks a geek faces while growing up. It's also one of the most demanding aspects of bringing up geeks.

Friendships matter tremendously to kids as they grow—especially as they enter adolescence—and this is as true for geeks as it is for everyone else. I'm not suggesting that a kid raised this way should just pick up a book and ignore his yearning for friends. On the contrary, my experience as a mom (and a former adolescent) has taught me that good friendships are essential to healthy development.

The key word is *good* friends. By my definition, a good friend is one who is good *for* you—someone who affirms your self-esteem, appreciates your interests, grants you the freedom to be yourself, respects your values, and displays loyalty in times of need. And not for nothing, a good friend should be *fun*.

POPULARITY: THE HOLY GRAIL

Complicating the whole issue of friendship is the quest for popularity. Every parent will attest that kids know who the most popular are among their peers, and if kids aren't part of that social stratum, most wish they were. And who wouldn't? By all appearances, the popular kids have the most fun and everyone likes them best.

Popularity is important to parents, too. Recalling the opening scene of this book, you met a mom who truly believed popularity was paramount. She was literally horrified at my description of my kids as geeks. Others who have heard me mention the name of this book or heard me talk about this topic are aghast that I don't want popularity for my children. It's as if I'm advocating for them to be friendless loners, wandering through childhood with a set of encyclopedias to read between solitary distance runs and TV documentaries by Ken Burns! I am amazed at how many people must be educated to the idea that popularity does not equate with true friendship, nor does unpopularity condemn a child to loneliness.

And yet, the quest to be popular is very real. Just when does all this social awareness begin and how does it impact a growing geek?

As children become social creatures, they look around to see who are the most attractive, interesting, and fun friends. In short order— as early as kindergarten—children can identify the peers who seem to command the most attention and admiration. Even from this tender age, kids understand that fitting in and being liked by peers equates with the word *popular*. Being popular, then, stands for social acceptance and having friends.

There are literally countless studies about the process of emerging popularity in young children and the role popularity plays throughout childhood. I'm serious—countless. Too many studies to actually read—and many are written in a language that cannot be deciphered by mere mortal parents. Near as I can figure, however, many of them say similar things. To sum up: Popularity in very young kids is influenced by social competence, attractiveness, and natural leadership. At some point (pick your study, this varies), cliques form. In early adolescence, girls are cliquier than boys. Conflict surrounding the quest for popularity appears to peak in middle school as social status is clearly established. In high school, popular kids continue to set standards about what is and isn't cool, though popularity no longer is based on social competence, appearance, or natural leadership. Rather, access to media, evident materialism, and risk-taking behaviors define the popular group. In high school, kids who are entrenched in the upper strata live out their destinies as the assumed leaders of their sphere of influence.

It took me months of reading and research to learn all that. But quite honestly, having delved into all this research while also raising four children representing every critical age group one can study, my response was pretty much, "Well, *duh*." And yet there is much to learn.

As you might imagine, more attention is paid in psychological literature on the social status of girls than of boys. New classics such as Rosalind Wiseman's *Queen Bees and Wannabes: Helping Your Daughter Survive Cliques, Gossip, Boyfriends, and Other Realities of Adolescence* and Rachel Simmons's *Odd Girl Out: The Hidden Culture of Aggression in Girls,* offer insight into the patterns of behavior that seem to mark girls in adolescence. (The books about boys are frankly not as good or as interesting.) I couldn't begin to summarize the detailed depictions of girl cliques in these books, so I'll leave it at this: The politics of adolescent friendship are real and can have serious implications. All parents should learn how cliques operate in the culture of cool since the social lives of both girls and boys are affected. (Do read *Queen Bees.* It's a primer that will give you a framework to understand the basic structure of cliques. Read *Odd Girl* if you're facing more serious issues of loneliness or even bullying.)

What I've learned through all my reading and research is that there are good, logical reasons to eschew the mantle of popularity and instead seek out the safer social circles populated by geeks.

Popularity simply isn't the Holy Grail of friendship because, as you'll soon discover if you have not already surmised, there's more to the A-list than mere popularity.

THE TRUTH ABOUT THE A-LIST

While I was researching in order to learn all those commonsense things about social status in children, a couple things struck me as noteworthy.

One was the finding I mentioned in the introduction—that kids who are known by their peers as popular are statistically more likely to engage in high-risk behaviors. This affirmed my belief that an unpopular adolescence is a safer one, at least as a statistical probability. (Obviously, it's not a guarantee that a child won't engage in risky experimentation, but still.)

The other finding that fascinated me is one that substantiated the correlation between popularity and relational aggression (that's the term that describes nastiness). A 2004 study out of the University of Missouri–Columbia published in the journal *Developmental Psychology* found that "seventh- and ninth-graders perceived their relationally aggressive classmates to be more popular than meeker students...But while relational aggression, such as excluding other people or spreading rumors, correlated with popularity, the link between overt aggression, such as verbal insults or physical threats, and popularity was not as strong."

This is why bullies are not usually on the A-list, while the kids who egg them on and snicker in the background are.

I could write until my fingers fall off about the ways in which my children have experienced relational aggression at the hands of popular kids. My earlier story about Amy and the "it girls" is a pretty typical example of how it begins. In Betsy's case, the cool girls in fourth grade used to chant "the cow in the meadow goes moo!" every time she walked past—a taunt of her name in which they called her Bessy, not Betsy. Throughout seventh grade, Jimmy endured taunting and teasing that also centered on variations of his name. I learned somewhere along the line that because our names are so central to our egos, this sort of teasing, while seemingly inconsequential, is remarkably hurtful. Taunts such as these supposedly are done under the guise of humor. Kids who are targets of relational aggression often are told, "You're too sensitive. Lighten up."

The point of this book is not for me to rant about all the times my kids' feelings have been hurt or to deter you from a geeky life for fear you'll encounter much of the same. (I think you will, and I'll talk more about that shortly, but that's not what's important here.) Rather, I want to share that there is a moment of discovery for geeks that puts their lives into a new and positive light. It's the pivotal realization that *words have meaning and the word* popular *doesn't actually describe the coolest kids in school.*

I'll never forget a conversation in our kitchen among my kids about what it means to be popular. Amy, being the youngest, assumed being popular meant you were cool and everyone liked you best. That's when Katie, then a high school sophomore, set her straight: "Amy, there's a big difference between being cool and being popular. The word *popular* means most people know who you are and you're well liked. I have to say that by that definition, I'm popular. But the kids at school who are considered cool? To be honest, people don't like them. They're actually pretty mean."

Lightbulb! Understanding herself in terms of the dictionary definition of the word *popular,* Katie finally had grasped that she *was,* in fact, well-known and well regarded by the people in her world. She had put aside any concerns about her status because she felt confident and comfortable in her self-image. (Amy, being only a second grader at the time, simply jumped around the kitchen singing, "Katie thinks she's popular! Katie thinks she's popular!" Siblings. Sheesh.)

Katie had deciphered the difference between social prominence and genuine admiration. She also demonstrated my contention that kids who reach high school with a well-developed sense of self no longer worry about their place in the social hierarchy but instead focus on building healthy relationships and furthering their growth and maturity. Huzzah!

I realize four is not a statistically significant sample, but it's not a bad little child-development lab, don't you think?

GEEK VALUES AND THE SOCIAL LANDSCAPE

Time to get a little philosophical. Bear with me. Here I'm going to rely on the wisdom I've gained as a geek mom, and not so much on my bales of Internet research about children. I've laid out a premise through all my storytelling and now's the time to amplify it for you.

Time and again, I've illustrated how we make decisions in our home that cause our kids to be known as geeks. From locker decor to instant messaging to movie and TV choices, I've shared examples of times when my husband and I put our values first as we exercise authority in rearing our children. When we make decisions that reflect our values, those decisions by necessity impact the relationships we and our children establish outside our family.

Here's the premise: *If your values come first, before everything else, they even come before your child's friendships.* Holding fast to your values means your child will sometimes struggle to maintain friendships with others whose family values are profoundly (or at least practically) different from yours.

I've encouraged you in every chapter of this book to use *your* value system as the starting point for all the decisions you make with respect to your children. This is how you choose the movies you permit them to see, whether they may have access to the Internet to a greater or lesser degree, what clothes and toys you purchase for them, how you approach activities such as hobbies and sports—everything. *Every decision is a value-laden decision.* Even a nondecision is value-laden, meaning, when you don't think through a choice on behalf of your child but instead let social norms decide for you, you adopt the values those norms represent.

In all honesty, this is where my whole theory about geek parenting takes a fair amount of heat. I have had some pretty contentious debates with parents about the utility of keeping a child from seeing a particular movie, for example, when it means she'll miss out on a social function with a group of friends. Some folks can't believe that's what I'm advocating, but yes, I'm saying exactly that.

I think the only way to teach our children a value system is to show them how our values guide our day-to-day decisions. When we put our values first, ahead of social inclusion, we teach them that values are important and, as well, that it's possible to find friends who share or at least respect them.

In every section of this book, we find evidence of parents who say they value one thing, yet their decision making on behalf of their children betrays those values. How effective is a value system if you compromise it for the sake of peer acceptance? And how stalwartly will children cling to a set of values when all through their lives they've been taught that being included in activities with friends is more important than what you believe is right or wrong. Hello, peer pressure and high-risk behavior.

At about this point in those contentious debates, I usually hear something like, "You're discounting the importance of friends. Friends are more important to kids than anything else. Imposing our values on them isn't going to work because they only care about their social lives."

I've already acknowledged the importance of friends in kids' lives. So true! Kids need friends, and as parents, we can help them learn to be and find good ones. But kids need a compass to guide them through life—a compass to help them make friends, even. Acceptance by the peers they meet in third grade or middle school or high school ought not to be the compass they employ.

ABSOLUTELY EVERYBODY STRUGGLES

Now to tackle the issue of social struggle. I can pretty much summarize this in two words, proving that not every sentence in this book is a compound sentence. Ready?

Everybody struggles.

Every. Body.

There is no way to grow up without feeling embarrassed, excluded, unappreciated, betrayed, teased, confused, hurt, and generally pounded on. It stinks and it's not fair and it shouldn't happen, but it's life.

Every geeky kid will feel insecure and awkward at times and wish he were cool. But take note: Every cool kid will feel insecure and betrayed at times and wish he were a geek, since he knows the geeks are at least friendly!

The kids at the top of the popularity pyramid may look blissfully happy as they move about in thoughtless clumps through the mall, but the truth is, they're posturing and repositioning from moment to moment. You want struggle? Be a girl in a cool clique who battles to remain a size 0 and hears her friends laugh at her from the next dressing room. Be the first guy in the cool group to get acne. With the correlation between relational aggression and popularity documented, we can now acknowledge what we all know is true from our own adolescent days—*popular kids can be mean to one another!*

All kids, regardless of social status, fear being embarrassed by their peers. In 2003, the Girl Scouts did a study called "Feeling Safe" about the issues that most concern girls in our post-9/11 culture. The study looked at reasons why teen and preteen girls feel physically or emotionally unsafe. The number one fear of preteen girls by a huge margin? "Being teased or made fun of." This fear came way ahead of natural disasters, terrorism, or war. Among teenage girls, only "speaking or participating in class" ranked higher than the fear of being teased.

The process of self-discovery in childhood is always one that includes struggle. All kids work hard to fit in and feel accepted. To help them along, we need to coach our kids to become socially competent. But at other times—especially in middle school—we need to encourage them to just be themselves and wait for a friend to emerge.

My geek-parenting assertion always has been that one wonderful friend beats an army of meanies. And guess what? I actually found research that says I'm right about that! But the research isn't important. What is important is the sheer joy of hearing a child tell you all about her best friend and the fun, geeky things they do together.

GFFs: Geek Friends Forever

Since we know friendships are so important in our kids' lives, we need to help them foster friendships that are wholesome—that is, good for mind, body, and spirit. But how to help? Obviously we have a lot to do with our children's social circles when they're preschoolers since we're the ones arranging their playdates. It's easy at this age to focus on friendships that reflect your own comfort with a child's parents. After all, you have to feel you can trust these folks when your young son or daughter is in their care. You spend a fair amount of time with the parents of your child's preschool buddies, so my strategy was to make these friendships as worthwhile for me as for my kids.

When school starts, how do we continue to play a role in helping our kids make and keep good friends who are good for them?

As we've seen, kids enjoy a wide scope of friendships when they begin kindergarten. While social circles do begin to form even at this age, friendship groups still are fairly fluid. At this point and up through the third grade, I continued to make social arrangements for my kids and deliberately kept a variety of playmates on the calendar. I felt it was best for my kids to have lots of friendly playmates rather than promote the formation of a small group of "best friends."

After helping four children through this process, I've observed that third or fourth grade is about the time when kids truly establish themselves into specific groups. At this age, if I asked any of my kids to describe the social landscape at school, they could tell me which group spent recess on the swing set, which group played football, and which one occupied the four-square court. There was still some movement from group to group depending on the activity a child might want to do, but for the most part, well-defined social circles emerged.

This also is the age when friendship struggles seem to begin. Prior to eight or nine, I'd characterize the conflicts among kids as episodic—specific incidents about sharing or name-calling, for example. But when kids get to about third grade, I've observed that conflict usually is the result of a power struggle. This is because kids are starting to assert themselves in the social hierarchy.

Here I need to interject that there has been a marked difference between Jimmy's friendship journey and that of his sisters. No surprise there! Jimmy's social life chugged along in complete equilibrium for many years. No conflicts, no upheavals, no problems whatsoever save the problem of whom to choose for a weekend sleepover. He was friendly with most of the boys in his class, and he found himself in a large group of pleasant, playful little guys. Typical of boys, Jimmy's social encounters were all about doing fun stuff and having fun. He never lost a moment of sleep over the issue of friends until the seventh grade (more on that to come). I have to hand it to him; he's a textbook example of the male of the species.

The girls have been another story. By the fourth grade, all of them came home from school and wanted to talk about "a problem" about friends. As cliques took shape, my girls had to figure out where they fit in. In this effort, they needed to learn the skill of discernment in order to identify the traits of a good and loyal friend.

Discernment means the exercise of good judgment, but this doesn't mean I taught them to be judgmental of others in a negative way. Rather, it means I taught them that some kids would make better friends than others. In discerning which groups would be best for each of them, they had to figure out what traits they valued in friendship and who exhibited those traits most consistently.

For a child to learn discernment, we need to keep the lines of communication wide open. Our kids are bound to make mistakes along this road—some that we as parents might feel embarrassed about. ("You said what!?") Best to keep our egos in check so our kids don't clam up on us. Only in viewing "girl world" through my daughters' eyes was I able to help them figure out where they best belonged.

The next step after discernment is to promote social interaction. This is what we all do when we help our kids generate playdates and sleepovers and such. You probably don't need much advice on this score, though my one suggestion would be to invite your child's friends into your family's geeky lifestyle. Outings to museums, parks, and the library (as opposed to the mall and to PG-13 movies) can include your child's pals and are great ways to engender geek friendships that make life fun.

FRIENDSHIP UPS AND DOWNS

I've already shared Katie's particular friendship struggle in the fifth grade, and of course that was somewhat unique given the limited social opportunities of an extremely small school. If there's a lesson there, it's to be open and flexible to make big changes in your life when you feel that's what's best for your child.

Other than her experience, it's been pretty smooth sailing until about the seventh grade. You'll recall at the outset of this book I described that year as the "line in the sand." Obviously the onset of puberty and the implicit impact of raging hormones play a role at this age, as I've also discussed. However, another factor, and a huge one in my experience, is the divergent styles parents take with respect to freedom, media, and behavioral expectations.

Where friendships are concerned, this is the time when my kids all have encountered the "morphing" of a few close friends. Kids with whom they journeyed lovingly and reliably for several years took a "cooler" path, and my kids had to accept that these friendships by necessity took on a new and disappointing character. It's a bummer.

Fortunately, as I've already described, when old friends swim off for cooler waters, geeky friends do rise to the surface. Sometimes it's an old pal from first grade; sometimes it's someone unexpected whose lifestyle we discover mirrors our own. From a geek parenting point of view, the thing to know is that periods of loneliness are normal for all kids as they master the art of making and keeping friends. Since this is a lifelong quest, it makes sense that it takes years to learn.

The most important lesson we can teach our children during the natural ups and downs of friendship is to be the kind of friend to others that they hope to find for themselves.

BULLYING FROM THE GEEK PERSPECTIVE

Every so often, the "ups and downs" of friendship take a significant downturn because of bullying.

There's been a ton of media attention in the past several years to the problem of bullying, in part because of the violent behavior of some kids whose victimization caused them to snap. It's tragic that it seems to have taken an event such as the Columbine shooting to raise our national consciousness about the problem of bullying. While I'm not asserting by any stretch that retaliatory violence is understandable (since most kids who are bullied don't resort to gun violence), it's certainly important to note that bullying can produce acute emotional problems.

Geeks, being notably different from the cool norm and sometimes even a little quirky (in a good way!), can find themselves targets of bullying. There's nothing more maddening or confounding than watching your child suffer from the mean, heartless behavior of his peers. I speak from experience.

Since I admit my kids have, at one time or another, been victims of both relational and overt aggression, it's fair to question whether my geek-parenting theory isn't just a manual on how to raise the class target. Aren't I proving the point that it's unsafe and unhealthy for a kid to grow up as a geek?

Consider these startling statistics that I found on the Web site www.bullystoppers.com: 90 percent of kids in fourth through eighth grades report they have been the victims of some form of bullying. *That's 90 percent!* Bullying peaks in middle school, with up to 7 percent of eighth graders staying home from school at least once a month to avoid a bully. The problem of bullying is so rampant that it's obviously not directed only at kids whom others consider unpopular or uncool. Rather, it's a cultural norm of adolescent behavior.

By now you know that just because something is a cultural norm doesn't mean I think it's actually normal. Bullying is a great example of something that is prevalent and pervasive, yet everyone knows is wrong. The causes and implications of widespread bullying have prac-

FRIENDSHIP STRUGGLES: ALL
PART OF THE GAME

The back door slammed shut, and seconds later, Jimmy stomped across the kitchen and into the dark living room, where he sank dejectedly into an easy chair. "What's wrong?" I asked, since obviously something was wrong.

"Nothing," Jimmy said from the shadows in the next room.

"Well, clearly there's something wrong or you wouldn't be so upset. What happened?"

"Just the same thing that always happens," he said, trading his seat in the dark for a chair at the kitchen table, where I sat with Katie and Betsy.

Jimmy's face was red and sweaty and he fought back a lump in his throat as he talked. "What always happens?" I ask, disconcerted that something was happening with the frequency of "always" and I was completely unaware.

"Whenever there are three guys playing, it always turns out that the other two start picking on me and giving me a hard time. It's always two against one. No one ever takes my side. Never."

Jimmy explained that he and two seventh-grade pals were playing outside. One started picking on Jimmy. The other friend laughed along. Jimmy got defensive and emotional, so naturally, they teased him for being defensive and emotional. Then they went inside to play a board game. The teasing cycle started anew until finally Jimmy gave up and ran home in anger and frustration. "They didn't even care about the Monopoly game," he anguished. "I had to move their pieces around the board and everything!"

And they say girls are melodramatic.

Of course preteen drama and friendship struggles aren't reserved just for girls. Virtually all children feel the sting of teasing from their pals, prompting some parent in history to conjure the phrase "sticks and stones may break my bones but names can never hurt me." Whoever thought that up may have meant well, but we modern parents know that nothing could be further from the truth.

I was just about to kick into high parenting gear and lead a brainstorming session on "things Jimmy could have done other than get mad at his friends," but it turned out my skills as a facilitator weren't needed. Instead, my teenage daughters jumped into the conversation with stories meant to comfort their younger brother. Pretty soon they were playing "can you top this," generating giggles from Jimmy as they recounted similar friendship struggles as preteens. Their funny stories helped ease the tension, but only a little. He was upset and annoyed—and anxious about what to expect when he went outside to play the next day.

I listened while my children talked about Jimmy's alternatives—finding other guys to play with, ignoring the teasing, dreaming up snappy comebacks. One of the girls even suggested the standard caveman response: "Why don't you just haul off and punch them? I thought that was the advantage to being a boy."

I raised an eyebrow. "Thanks, Katie. That's really helpful."

Just then the phone rang. Jimmy jumped to answer it, and sure enough it was his neighborhood pal calling to apologize for the teasing. Jimmy said he was sorry, too, for overreacting and getting so mad. They agreed to lighten up and to hang out the next day. A thirty-second phone call resolved the situation far better than my maternal musings about friendship.

When he came back to the kitchen, Jimmy was a new person; his pessimism was gone and instead he was filled with the confidence that comes when friends reassure you that they care about you. Unfortunately, adolescent friends don't usually call to say they're sorry. This is why it's essential for kids to learn the rules of the friendship game: forgiveness, good humor, kindness, and empathy—and apply those rules even when their pals don't. It's not easy and it doesn't happen overnight. It takes maturity and experience to learn that even good friends might sometimes hurt your feelings. Hard as it is to imagine, kids discover they can even look back one day and laugh about it.

tically become a unique discipline within psychological study. I hope the experts get it figured out, but as a mom, my take is that kids who behave as bullies are missing some fundamental values about how to treat other human beings.

My point is that virtually *all* kids (sans that lucky 10 percent)—not just geeks—at some point must deal with a bully. If there are traits of kids who are targets, they must be so diverse as to describe a full 90 percent of all children. So I'm not willing to concede that raising a genuine, enthusiastic, empowered kid is the route to victimization.

Rather, I think bullying is an area that requires us to focus on the geek meaning of *empowerment*. By coaching kids to handle themselves in the face of bullying, we teach them that they needn't feel like victims. On occasion we must advocate for them with school administrators and teachers. Whenever it occurs, parents must respond swiftly and firmly to get the behavior stopped.

In our experience, however, my husband and I have impressed upon our children *their right to be exactly who they are*. The key issue to address is the effect of bullying on the spirits of our children. We must never let them conclude that their self-worth or self-esteem is wrapped up in the words or actions of a cruel or brutal peer. Ultimately, while our kids' experiences of bullying have been hurtful, they also have been very instructive.

There's a saying I learned that fits here: "Prepare the child for the path, not the path for the child." That is the wisdom that has guided us when our kids suffer the cruelty of their peers.

How to Raise a True Friend

Around our house, whenever we discuss any friendship issue, we talk about the attributes of a good friend. This is how we instill the skills of discernment and, as well, how we teach our children to be a good friend to others. Here's what we focus on in conversations about friendship:

It Takes One to Be One

Geeks need to learn to be open, trusting, and available to their friends. By their nature, children are fairly self-centered, so our job is to teach them to be other-directed. Little ones need to learn the basics of sharing and fair play; as they get older, issues center on sharing power and the right to make suggestions and decisions that affect everyone. Along with tactics to play equitably, kids need to learn what it means to be loyal. It's never too early to teach the pitfalls of gossip, backstabbing, and criticism. Also, when they make inevitable mistakes in friendship, kids need to learn to ask for forgiveness (and to give the same to their friends!).

Accept That Friendships Change over Time

One reality we have encountered while raising geeks is that friendships change over time, especially because of our geek lifestyle choices. We make it a point not to judge other families, but to simply state that we do things differently around our house. To the extent that our rules and decisions impact friendships, we offer our support. Heck, sometimes our kids are downright mad at us and we understand! Still, they accept that our decisions reflect our love for them and they believe us when we reassure them that they'll find other friends in time. Not only has that always come to pass, but their geek friends are simply awesome.

Know the Players

It's imperative that we know our children's friends. This is easier when kids are young and their social lives depend on us. It gets more difficult as kids get older and they socialize away from home. All the more reason to know the players in your children's friendship circles. It's not possible to guide our kids toward safe and wholesome life choices if we don't know the people they're hanging with. To this end, my husband and I open our home to parties and always offer to do the driving when our kids make plans with friends. It's also crucial to get to know the parents of their pals. Happily, those who share your geek lifestyle may become your close friends, too!

Quality Not Quantity

Especially as kids age, we need to teach "quality over quantity" where friends are concerned. Some parents worry when their middle schooler or high schooler has a small social circle. They reason that few friends may mean lonely nights at home when pals aren't available. Not to worry—geeks are comfortable at home, as you'll learn in the next chapter! Rather than lament a small social circle, encourage your child to find those two or three kids who make him feel free to be himself. These are the people who are truly good for him.

Repair When Broken

Not a child on the planet will grow up without making a friendship faux pas. In fact, most kids invariably will do something hurtful toward a friend out of selfishness or insecurity. (Adults do this sort of thing from time to time, too!) Kids don't want to admit they're in the wrong and they also don't tend to come to us and tell us they've messed up. Usually I find out about these things when I ask, "How come you haven't called your pal lately?" After a roundabout excuse, it's pretty clear they've done something to cause the pal to be angry. These mistakes are the stuff of "teachable moments." Coach your geek on how to make amends and repair a broken friendship. Even if the friend isn't among the primary pals your child seeks out for companionship, working things out is the right thing to do.

Recognize the Benefits of Adversity

When social struggles surface—and invariably they will—realize that children grow through adversity. No, we don't want our kids to suffer or to feel bad. Nothing is more heartbreaking than watching a child walk to the van at the end of a school day with his shoulders drooped and his spirit injured. But loving adults—parents—can mend that heart with encouragement and insight. Our job isn't to keep our children from ever experiencing adversity in life or difficulties in their relationships. Our job is to support our kids as they muddle through; to advise, enlighten, and empathize. This is how they learn that no matter what the world throws at them, they can survive and thrive.

Geeks and Peer Pressure

It might seem irresponsible of me to write a book about raising kids and leave the issue of peer pressure to the end of a chapter about friendship. But in the geek lifestyle, this is where it rightly belongs because raising a geek is a major impediment to the power of peer pressure over your child. By asserting your parental authority to set limits on your child's freedom and his access to the culture of cool, you coincidentally thwart the peer group from its capacity to tempt and corrupt your child. The only peer pressure my children have ever experienced is the pressure to excel in school or sports as a way to maintain their place among their geeky friends. This isn't exactly the kind of pressure that worries me. Honestly, that's about the only issue we've faced, and it's not just my family. It's true for most of the geek families we know.

Geeks in a Gaggle

Recalling the night Katie and I drove out of state for a college visit while her girlfriends sent photo messages to her phone, the most tender moment came when she finally closed her phone and sighed, saying "Mom, I just love my friends."

Love. That's what friendship is really all about—the chance to love others with selfless abandon; the chance to feel love from others that's freely given.

For children, the unconditional love of parents and siblings is the foundation upon which they build a sense of self. The love of friends— generously given and affectionately returned—expands a child's self-image to include a warm and kindly spirit. On the chance our children aren't always certain of our assurance that they're lovable, friends are the proof that it's true.

In my home, perhaps no sound delights my heart as much as the giggling of geeks in a gaggle. I think I treasure my children's friends as much as my children do because I know how much happiness friends bring to their lives. Happiness...and love.

Uncool Answers

Now that she's heading into middle school, I can see how the girls in my daughter's friendship circle are changing. There's a heightened interest in boyfriends, makeup, and clothes and lots more freedom than I am comfortable permitting my child. I think it's time for new friends! How can I help my daughter move to a new social group?

Middle school is the time when geeky values have a serious impact on friendships. The good news is this is the age when other geek families start to show their true colors, which means, good friends shouldn't be too hard to find.

You describe a problem that has two parts. First is detaching from the former social circle, which probably will be heartbreaking for your daughter to a certain extent. If these are the pals she's had since elementary school, the fact that they're now "way cool" middle schoolers means you rightly must pull back. There's nothing you have to do to detach your daughter from the pack. This happens naturally as you live day to day within your values about media, clothes, behavior, and the freedom you will or won't extend to a preteen.

The second issue—finding new friends—also emerges somewhat naturally as other geek families also maintain their value-driven geek lifestyles. Believe me, you are NOT alone out there, even if it sometimes feels that way! Geeky kids tend to gravitate to one another in middle school as they discover who else hasn't seen a certain movie or doesn't hang out on certain Web sites. Your job is to keep the communication open about friendships and offer lots of fun, appealing avenues for hanging out with her new pals. My kids were pleasantly surprised to discover that our "stricter" standards about media and other cool things had no impact on their social lives once they found a great group of friends. On any given weekend, there are hosts of kids sleeping in my basement to prove this fact. It's just that the kids in my basement are geeks.

Guaranteed Geek: Tips to Help Foster Geek Friendships

For Geeks of All Ages:

* Facilitate social opportunities for young children. Look for pals in the neighborhood and through preschool or church for regular playdates.

* Get to know their pals. Use open-ended questions that give kids a chance to say more than yes and no. "What's the best lunch you ever had?" is a better question than "Do you like grilled cheese?"

* Get to know the parents of your children's friends.

* Keep getting to know the parents of your children's friends. You can never know them well enough.

For Elementary School Geeks:

* Periodically ask your child to describe recess to get a feel for how cliques are developing.

* Comment whenever you notice a peer who behaves kindly or with compassion. These are the kids you want hanging around your house.

* Facilitate playdates and help direct your child to friends who share your geeky values. These friendships are likely to grow over the years.

* When they make a mistake, teach kids to ask for forgiveness, not just say they're sorry. There's a difference! Children need to learn the power of a genuine apology, which includes seeking the forgiveness of the person whose feelings they hurt. Friends are quick to forgive and forget because they want to get back to having fun!

For Middle School Geeks:

* Keep communicating. Be open and approachable so your middle schooler can talk to you about friendship issues.

* Recall stories of friendship struggles you went through at the same age. Also, encourage an older mentor such as a former baby-sitter or cousin to share stories of middle school struggles. Everyone has angst at this age and kids need to be reassured it will be okay.

* Maintain your geeky values about media and socializing rather than try to straddle the fence to fit in. Only by embracing your geeky lifestyle will you discover who else is sharing your path.

* Hang on! It's a bumpy ride for everybody, but middle school doesn't last forever.

For High School Geeks:

* Before high school starts, have some frank conversations about what you anticipate with respect to socializing. Assert your expectations about behavior and convey to your high schooler that your geek lifestyle will continue through these years.

* Open your home to your high schooler's friends as much as possible. Maintain a wholesome, fun environment where kids feel comfortable hanging out. Don't be naive—keep a healthy suspicion that prompts you to supervise teens appropriately.

* Get to know the parents of your high schooler's friends. (It's

worth repeating!) Parental unity is crucial in upholding geeky values.

* Allow your relationship with your teen to grow naturally into a mature parent/child friendship. This is not the same as trying to be an über-buddy. Rather, as you stay close through the teen years, let the relationship unfold into a friendship where mutual respect, admiration, and love grow through young adulthood.

Rule #8

....

RAISE A HOMEBODY

I recall the precise moment when I realized we were in a battle with our calendar. Katie was in the eighth grade, Betsy was in sixth, Jimmy was a third grader, and Amy was a kindergartner.

It was exactly 7:27 on a Monday morning and someone hurled that week's first salvo: "Clarinet lesson in three minutes!" (I'm pretty sure the person who announced this was not the kid who actually played the clarinet.) The words had an explosive effect. Lunch boxes flew, backpacks and coats launched like so many hand grenades across the kitchen.

I peeled off my fuzzy pink robe and jumped into fatigues—sweats over my pajamas—and in seconds we mobilized our assault vehicle— my Honda Odyssey minivan. At 7:35, we lurched to a stop in front of the school, where the music teacher waited patiently for the untimely arrival of his student.

Was he surprised Betsy was late for a Monday-morning lesson? No. In truth, he was probably surprised she showed up at all.

That we were overbooked was obvious. The calendar on the fridge posted cryptic reminders of our various activities. On a Tuesday, I wrote *A/4/Gym*, the little one's gymnastics class. It was a ten-week session, except in week six and week eight, when spring break schedules prevailed. Also on a Tuesday, *J/7/Bball* to assure that my son attended basketball practice. My husband was his coach, so you'd think we would remember, but you never knew.

Back when the older girls were still babies, I wondered about families who operated like whole groups of Energizer bunnies, running here and there in an endless sprint to make lessons, practices, and games. Smugly, I held a toddler on one hip and a newborn on the other, smiling the knowing smile of "The Mother Who Would Do It Differently." I would say no to the fast pace that robs families of unity and cohesiveness and dinners 'round the table.

Fat chance. By the time I had four kids, I had about as much hope of avoiding a busy calendar as I had of avoiding trips to the grocery store with barefoot, filth-covered, sticky children in pajamas. (I said I'd never do that either. Live and learn.)

Now, like most families, our calendar rules the day. Cross-country season becomes the spring musical, which becomes track season. Basketball, basketball, and more basketball. Practices, games, tournaments. Team party? Sure! We'll host!

It's even worse if kids actually have talent in one area or another. We've been caught up at times in music, theater, dance, and art activities that added beauty and richness to life, but also mayhem to our family schedule.

It would be interesting to contemplate the effect of busy schedules on the fabric of family life. But who has time to think about it when you're barreling down the street on the way to a dentist appointment for which you're already late? Honestly.

Frenzied Family Life

The Hicks family calendar no longer hangs on the fridge. It became impossible for me to keep our schedules in my day-timer and also on the poster-size magnetic calendar I bought at the start of every school year. Plus, with commitments posted in two locations, the calendars never were in sync. Appointments usually were missing from whichever one I consulted, and as a result, so were we. These days I keep our central calendar in my laptop. Every child is color-coded, as are Jim and I, with family events highlighted in bright yellow.

As you might imagine, there aren't as many bright yellow entries on the calendar as I would like. Still, we manage to maintain a sense of family unity because of our geeky lifestyle.

THE TIME CRUNCH

Carving out family time poses a challenge for all of us. In fact, studies show American parents feel generally rushed, with working moms leading the pack feeling short on time. We scratch and claw for virtually every spare minute to exercise, prepare and share meals, read, walk our dogs, and pray. I'm not going to bore you with a bunch of statistics about how busy we all are. Heck, you're a parent—you barely have enough time to finish this book.

Suffice to say, the vast majority of us are working parents, in either one- or two-career households. If we're able to choose full-time parenting, we're working just as hard but in a different way. We're all juggling the demands of our roles as well as our commitments in our communities. Between the activities of daily living and the stuff we pile on just to add "quality" to our lives, we're frenzied.

Studies about strong families and successful kids prove that time spent sharing family meals, doing chores and homework, and sleeping contribute to kids' general health as well as to their school success. But we all know that overloading the calendar robs families of the time to do those things, in particular.

SOCIAL LIVES OUTSIDE THE HOME

All our busyness is part of the problem, but not the whole problem. Another factor I've observed is the primacy of an outside social life for all family members. In the last chapter we discussed how crucial it is for kids to have friends and to enjoy social relationships. But at the same time I think the culture of cool promotes the idea that friendships are the *most* important relationships in a child's life. They're not.

Now remember, I'm no expert. But my experience leads me to conclude that family relationships ought to come first, even (perhaps especially) during those all-important adolescent years. Sadly, by the time they reach adolescence, children often adopt the cultural message that their families are woefully uncool and unimportant. And parents, perhaps unwilling or unable to compete with this attitude, seem to accept that a participative family life ends when kids are old enough to answer their own cell phones and make their own plans.

In my view, this mind-set is what drives overactive childhood social lives. In the culture of cool, kids expect to be out and about with their friends anytime they're not being carted to or from school, a lesson, a practice, or a sporting event. Out of concern that kids are socially well adjusted, parents don't set standards about unstructured family time. Instead, family time is reduced to mundane or routine tasks such as an orthodontist appointment or a trip to the store, or else major events such as holidays.

Ironically, it appears the notion that tweens and teens don't want to hang out with their families is actually a myth. Adolescents report that they like hanging with the family. (Maybe kids are geekier than they want to admit!)

FAMILY STRENGTH IN *BEING* AND *DOING*

Balancing time commitments is a topic that's almost clichéd, and yet we can't deny that time—a finite commodity—must be parceled out carefully if we're to assure a healthy, wholesome family life for ourselves and our kids. If we lose sight of our values about family time, or worse, if we confuse shared busyness for a genuine experience of relationship, we miss our opportunity to build strong families.

There's a big difference between *being* together and *doing things* together. A family can do a whole lot of stuff together, and shared activities are definitely a source of family unity and fun. If you surf the Web for articles on "family time," you'll find literally thousands of sites offering suggestions for special things to do together. The problem I have with this notion is that family time becomes just one more structured activity. It's something else *to do*. Theoretically, if the focus is on the activity and not on the family, it doesn't much matter who is involved, does it?

Researchers describe strong families as those that reinforce the ideas of both *family behaviors* and *family relationships*. This is why my geeky contention is that families ought to spend time at home, doing nothing but being a family at home! All relationships need an investment of time—unstructured, unplanned time. Even though we may recognize this need and perhaps crave downtime with our families, our culture doesn't allow us or encourage us to carve out much time to simply *be*.

CREATING FAMILY IDENTITY

Very little attention seems to be paid to the idea of family identity, perhaps because our culture's definition of *family* has evolved to encompass such a broad range of living arrangements. The traditional family consisting of lifelong-married couples and their children continues to decline, while blended families, single-parent households, and grandparented households increase.

Family dynamics are altered drastically with parents' changing relationships, so the concept of a single identity by which a family is known becomes difficult to establish. (Nonetheless, as you'll read shortly, I believe every family—no matter how traditional or unconventional— can and should establish a distinct family identity.)

Despite statistics that portray American families in a state of flux, the family remains the primary social unit to which we all belong.

Belonging is especially crucial for children as they develop a sense of self. Kids need the support and encouragement of their families as they explore and establish their personalities and character. Even into adulthood, our families of origin remain the foundation of our selves. Functional or not, our families are the keys to our perspective on all things.

The culture of cool isn't focused on family identity. In fact, as I noted a few chapters ago, in the cool culture it's "all about me." It sometimes seems that the media promote this mind-set, paying more attention to the notion of children separating from the family than it does to growing closer and more intimate. In my view, however, we've confused the concept of healthy separation with an unhealthy and dangerous isolation from loved ones.

Connection to family members is fostered when we build strong and discernible family identities, which I define as the unique personality and character of a particular family. Identity communicates to a child, "You are one of us."

In an online article, author Elisa Medhus, M.D., affirms what many of us know instinctively about family identity: "Creating a family identity is an effective way to instill our children with a sense of permanence, belonging and stability, paving the road for raising confident, independent, moral children. Since the family is our children's first 'pack,' it's important to do all we can to satisfy that intense pack animal urge to belong—to feel accepted by others."

That pack mentality starts early, as very young children naturally are drawn to the idea of family identity. Even as preschoolers, for example, they love to point out which house on the block belongs to their family. They naturally brag about family activities and vacations. The say "we do this" and "we do that," not only to describe specific tasks, but to define the habits and traditions unique to their families.

As children grow, parents need to promote the idea of family identity to include the traits of loyalty and pride. In this way we foster solid family relationships for the long term.

A Geeky Home Sweet Home

Glancing at the Hicks family calendar, our geeky existence doesn't look appreciably different from the lifestyle others choose. But underlying our frenetic scheduling are some core values that characterize our home and family life, making us a little bit different from other folks:

* We believe time to *be* a family (as opposed to doing things as a family) is essential to promote our children's healthy development (as well as our enjoyment of our parenting journey).

* We believe socializing outside our family must be balanced against the emotional need for us to *be together.*

* We believe while they are growing, our kids need the security and comfort found *only at home.*

* We believe family loyalty is fostered when children are *obligated to be present* and to support one another.

As in all things, the geek perspective regarding family life prompts my husband and me to apply our values as we make decisions about how we spend our precious time.

Our geek mentality is that the home must be the central focus of our family's life. It's the command center, the emotional HQ. We think our kids have to be here—a lot!—in order to absorb the strength, support, and values that form their personalities and character. By focusing on home and family, geeks also develop loyalty to and from the loved ones who will sustain them in the years ahead.

These values combine to create Rule Number Eight for bringing up geeks: Raise a Homebody.

HANGING OUT

Homebodies enjoy and appreciate time spent with their families. Raising a homebody means both establishing family time as a responsibility for each member, and also creating a home environment that's positive, inviting, and fun. Sounds great, huh?

Don't get the wrong impression. There are times when we mandate that our kids need to be at home for no other reason than *to be at home*. Sometimes this requirement is met with something less than enthusiasm. Yes, I'll admit it, sometimes our kids get downright honked off, especially when they have to get on the phone and decline an invitation to hang out with a friend.

Our point is this: If hanging out with friends is worthwhile because such unstructured time allows for easy conversation and relationship building, the same is true about hanging with family. There have been times when one of my kids argues about staying at home by reasoning, "We're not *doing* anything. What's the point?" The point is we're at home. Period.

I don't think family life should feel like we're perpetually on a cruise ship. I don't want to be a cruise director, constantly drumming up group activities to entertain the patrons. Personally, when I hit Web sites about building family relationships, they just exhaust me. They seem to presume we can't be together unless we're tie-dyeing shirts or building a birdhouse or playing Monopoly.

Without apology, we convey instead to our kids that they benefit and our relationships grow by the sheer fact of being together in our home. The cool thing is that hanging out together produces moments of spontaneous fun and casual intimacy that we simply couldn't engender any other way.

"THE HICKS FAMILY PHRASE OF THE YEAR"

Family identity is what makes us unique. It's the combination of rituals, traditions, stories, jokes, and memories that define our journey together. Identity reflects our history and our preferences. It's everything that makes our house exclusively our own.

Some of our identity comes from Mom's and Dad's families of origin. For example, we've adopted the tradition of lining up from youngest to oldest and singing "Jingle Bells" as we file down the stairs on Christmas morning to open our gifts. I swear. We really do this. I did it as a child, and now it's something my family does as well. (I think some of my siblings adopted that tradition too. Hokey, aren't we?)

Jim grew up in an extended family led by his maternal grandmother, a tiny but formidable woman who emigrated as a child from Sicily to Brooklyn. His family culture was influenced by her Italian roots. So we eat a lot of pasta, and because Jim has a phenomenal sense of humor, we make a lot of jokes about organized crime.

Humor is a huge element in family identity. At our house, for example, we have established something called "The Hicks Family Phrase of the Year." It's our way to recognize the most hilarious or memorable phrase uttered by one of us in a calendar year. Once it was Jimmy's classically indecisive response to nearly any question he was asked: "Sort of, but not really." The best one was Betsy's mafioso greeting to her dad while slowly spinning in his desk chair to face him, "Daddy...you're like family to me." One year we couldn't decide. Just when we thought the year had come and gone without a phrase, we were driving to Midnight Mass and Jimmy lashed out at one of his sisters, "Shut up! It's Christmas Eve!" Talk about your seasonal greeting. We howled all the way to church.

Some folks call this sort of thing "family lexicon." We give an award for it.

Another aspect of our family identity is that we're all very talkative. When our kids' friends come around (which is very frequently—we're a gathering house), they comment on how much we talk to one another. A few kids who come from quieter homes are especially fascinated by the loquaciousness at the Hicks house. We used to be self-conscious about it, but it turns out the quiet kids think we're a lot of fun.

Family identity doesn't mean everyone turns out the same. Belong-

DAD IS MORE FUNNIER

When Amy was only six, she summarized with exceptional clarity the differ-ence between Mom and Dad. "Dad is more funnier."

So true.

Dad is the parent who composes rap songs about doing dishes and wails the "I've got too much homework" blues.

Dad cheerfully chats it up before school in the morning while all around him mayhem erupts. Some would call him oblivious. In fact, I would call him oblivious. But others—our children, for example—call him "more funnier."

I used to rant about the injustice of his role as the "more funnier" parent. Why did he get to be "more funnier"? Why couldn't we take turns being "more funnier"? It seemed unfair that his place in our children's lives will forever conjure memories of midnight basketball and Mafia humor, while thoughts of me will recall complex schedules executed with military preci-sion—not to mention an unkind depiction of my neat-freak neuroses.

Admittedly, I never invested myself in a "more funnier" capacity. As soon as the kids were old enough, Jim was the one to launch Saturday-morning games, an activity in which I never participated (I was folding laundry). Clad in pajamas and surrounded by anyone small enough to play, he prompted shrieking through the house in an elaborate hide-and-seek ritual known as "Heffalumps and Woozles." The theme required players to claim a Winnie-the-Pooh character as his or her identity, and then hide somewhere in the "Hundred Acre Wood" (our house). Jim, singing the "Heffalumps" theme song (there is one) conducted an exaggerated search to "find" Pooh, Piglet, or other characters, some of whom played the game in plain view. He pre-tended not to notice.

Who wouldn't find him "more funnier" than the parent who broke up the game and sent the players upstairs to get dressed and brush their teeth, there being a soccer game in forty minutes?

The "more funnier" dad in our house also fostered an appreciation of *The Godfather*, a movie classic whose dialogue all four of our kids can recite, yet none had seen until TNT ran a sanitized version that Katie watched in high school.

The Godfather became Jim's all-purpose parenting script. Trouble with a friend at school? "Ya gotta ask yourself, 'What would Don Corleone do?' " he counseled. Thanks to their dad, our children often shrug their shoulders and with diction that sounds as if their mouths are full of marbles ask, "Whadayagonnado?"

Sometimes he's "more funnier" without meaning to be. Like the family dinner when someone innocently asked, "What's a mortgage?" What followed was an eye-glazing description of the Federal Reserve, mortgage interest rates, credit ratings, locking in at the bottom, and what happens when the bank sells your loan to a mortgage company and how the service from these places usually stinks. This went on for quite a while—the kids actually ate vegetables just to pass the time—and then someone said, "So a mortgage is a piece of paper?"

Our inherent differences as Mom and Dad ensure balanced parenting. Neither my role nor his is more or less important, but simply the completion of the circle of our family identity that encompasses form and function, content and character.

And besides, if I ever tried to be the "more funnier" parent, I know what the kids would say: "Mom...Fugeddaboudit."

ing to the Hicks family is the foundation upon which our kids build their unique personalities. Each one is different and we encourage them all to be themselves—wholly distinct persons apart from their parents and siblings. Yet no matter how they carve out their individuality, all four of them can claim their Hicks family identity as both the launching pad for individuality and the support network to become the person they're each meant to be.

TIME WELL SPENT

Perhaps the only thing that works better than hanging out at home to foster family identity and genuine relationships is to go away. Together, I mean.

Family trips seem to almost magically transform us into a pack. Venturing out into the world, we necessarily rely on one another to execute the basic tasks of travel as well as to entertain one another. Taking a break from the routines and activities of daily life frees us up to focus on our relationships, though we don't frame it like that with the kids. We just say, "We're going camping!"

Jim and I heard somewhere that a child's most memorable family experiences surround camping and cottages. We've been lucky enough to enjoy both.

The first time we ever camped, it rained. Not the light mist that waters the fauna and flora. It rained buckets, sheets, cats and dogs—choose the metaphor you like best. Not only did it rain, but the tent we had borrowed leaked. This was the moment I discovered I am a fair-weather camper.

Still, my introduction to camping wasn't all bad. I realized a campground is a place where kids may play games with siblings while the adults sit on collapsible chairs encircling a roaring fire. Not all bad!

After that first camping expedition, I decided we could be a camping family—but only if we owned the proper gear. I discovered there are entire aisles at Target devoted to camping. Not only that, but they make lots of cool stuff to set up a temporary residence in the wild. Over the years, I've turned our camping equipment into a prop trunk for a Martha Stewart photo shoot, all in the name of "atmosphere." The tiki torches are especially nice, but even I will concede that the outdoor rug is a bit over-the-top.

Our camping adventures always generate stories and memories for our kids. When they were young, we camped at Assateague Island National Seashore on the Maryland coast, where wild ponies roam free among the tents and RVs. A few times we camped with my siblings and their families, creating memories with cousins, aunts, and uncles. One year involved a skunk and a footprint in Katie's birthday cake. The best campout was just a couple summers ago when the six of us split into three two-man teams for meal planning. Each team was responsible for two meals over the course of the weekend, from choosing the menu to cooking to cleaning up. The food was wonderful; the cooperative atmosphere was even better.

A cottage produces a different sort of family experience. Whether it's a weeklong rental or several weeks in the summer, cottages tend to mean living in a smaller space, sharing only one bathroom, and working together to make meals and do laundry. Days are filled only with the "work" of recreation—walking the beach, reading, or lingering at a lakeshore.

Vacations of all sorts can spirit us away to a place of family cohesiveness. We've done a few big ones—Disney World, Washington, D.C., and even a trip to the Caribbean, where we swam with dolphins. And no, we're not superrich. But Jim and I decided long ago that we'd rather end up with a vault full of memories and a close family than a fortune in our retirement. (That plan appears to be working.) Once again, this is a matter of establishing our priorities with respect to limited resources.

Family travel doesn't have to be pricey, however, and I think any family that doesn't travel on the assumption it's too expensive is being penny wise but pound foolish. We've asked ourselves, "Can we afford *not* to occasionally share the world with our children? Can they afford not to build sibling relationships with one another, free of interference from their social circles?" For us, the investment of time and money comes back to us in shared memories and richer relationships. There's nothing like a swimming pool or a lake to melt away the eight years between our eldest and youngest children, fostering the kind of friendship that can't be found anywhere else in their lives.

I don't want to paint some unrealistic picture that makes my family sound freakishly happy and harmonious. In fact, at the start of every trip there's some sort of blowup as we gradually get into the groove of being together in tight quarters for an extended period. We have four kids—naturally there's conflict! By the end of our family trips, we're all eager to get back to our daily lives—especially if we've been camping (admittedly, that's a hygiene thing).

I suppose the reason we're eager to return is that for geek families like ours, there's no place like home. But my mom always liked that phrase *Home is where the heart is.* Hokey as it may sound, wherever we're together as a family feels like home to us.

"At Our House . . ."

No one can tell you how to create the unique identity that marks your family as special. Only you can weave together the rituals, traditions, and personality that your children come to appreciate as your family's unmistakable fabric. Some of your identity may reflect your cultural or ethnic heritage, or it might convey your particular passions. One of my dearest friends is a fitness fanatic—her family's identity reflects the healthful lifestyle she and her husband maintain. Another dear friend's family identity is wrapped up in their passion for horses—it's a big part of who they are and how they spend their time together.

Regardless of your family's particular makeup, you still are the head of your household and it's both your right and your responsibility to create a family identity your kids can embrace. Think "we" and "us"; not "you" and "me." When you approach family life as the advocate for the unit known as "our family," you naturally promote the personality and character of your home.

Family First

When family comes first, all the members understand that time must be reserved for family activities, gatherings, and just hanging out. Never feel sheepish about saying no to others in order to enjoy time with your kids. In fact, be sure your children know when you make the choice to spend your leisure time with them rather than do something social outside the home. Don't let kids develop social priorities that put the family last on their list either. If the calendar makes it hard to be together, reserve time for your family just as you would other important activities. You might just declare it's a "Saturday night in" when everyone stays home for the evening with no particular plan. Some families schedule regular nights for dinners, games, a movie (in or out), or a special activity like bowling or minigolf. Of course big events such as holidays and reunions give you the chance to make and enjoy your family traditions. At holiday time, try to focus on the people, not the trappings.

A Comfortable Retreat

Look around your house—is it a comfortable retreat for everyone? Is it a place your kids want to hang out? Is it a place they feel comfortable bringing their friends? A child's home needs to be a welcoming place. A house that's too fancy and elaborate isn't child friendly; while a house that's in a shambles makes a child feel depressed and embarrassed. When your home reflects your pride in your family, it naturally feels like a place your kids want to be.

Home and Away

Make it a priority to spend time at home, but also to gather up your clan for occasional trips together. Family travel offers opportunities for shared problem solving, exploration, and fun. Cheap trips are as beneficial to family relationships as expensive ones, so don't let money deter you from suspending reality in the name of family time.

Rites of Passage

Among your family rituals and traditions, find special ways to recognize milestones in the lives of your growing geeks. Celebrations of birthdays and graduations are the obvious rites of passage that come to mind, but others such as getting a first job, making the honor roll, or being named first chair in the band are all reasons to applaud one another. Siblings need to be taught to encourage one another's efforts, as well. Even with busy schedules, they should attend an occasional game or concert in which the other is participating. Simply being there for one another builds the bonds of family love.

The Family That's Geeky Together...

...stays together. Supports one another. Understands one another. Annoys one another, yes, but forgives one another too. The family that's geeky together spends a lot of time laughing together, talking together, and most importantly, just *being* together. Geeky families protect time in their busy lives for group activities, and as well, geeks invite others into their homes to enjoy the comfortable, caring atmosphere within.

Geeky families are strong families because they stand on a foundation that puts family unity at the forefront. Because of this strength and unity, geeks feel secure in who they are and how they fit into the larger world. It's belonging to a strong family that gives geeks the confidence to present themselves to the world in all their uniqueness. Being different from the culture of cool isn't a big deal to geeks who know that walking in the front door at home, they'll meet with unconditional acceptance and love.

Uncool Answers

My eighth-grade daughter belongs to a busy social circle. All the girls go to one of their homes each day after school to do homework together.

My daughter comes home for dinner but then spends the evening IMing and texting her pals until bedtime. We spend about fifteen minutes a day together and that time usually is spent going over the plans for the next day or the weekend ahead. There is a sleepover every weekend at one of their homes—we host it about every six weeks. She's a good student and a pleasant girl. Is her social life appropriate?

To be clear, I absolutely support and encourage kids of all ages to have friends and to engage in healthy, wholesome social lives. For an eighth-grade girl to spend every waking hour with her friends strikes me as neither healthy nor wholesome! Consider that your measly fifteen minutes each day can't compete with the overwhelming influence of her friends on her values and behavior. You need to rein her in!

Declare After-School Study Sessions a Once-per-Week Option

The fact that your daughter is getting good grades is nice, but I'd be concerned about whether she's really doing all her work on her own. Require her to come home each day after school, but allow her to choose one afternoon each week to study with friends. She could look ahead to see when there's a test or quiz and plan to work with friends to prep for those.

Call "Time" on IM and Text Messages

If you allow her to use IM or text messages after school, set a time when both must be turned off. Allowing unlimited communication means her friends are always encroaching on your time together.

Limit Sleepovers to Every Other Weekend

I'm one who thinks sleepovers each weekend are unnecessary. They make kids overtired and they promote mischievous behavior. Remember you're not committed to the social demands of a group of eighth graders. Regulate the number of nights out per month and use the time instead for family outings or hanging out at home.

Require That She Socialize with Her Friends at Your Home More Frequently

If you're hosting only once every six weeks, you don't see much of your daughter's friends. Geek parenting encourages more hands-on supervision and one way to do this is to be the gathering house for her friends.

Be the Fun Alternative

Don't just demand that your child be at home. Make home a place she wants to hang out!

Recognize That Your Rules Will Change Her Social Status

Your daughter may feel less connected to her friends, but she'll be more connected to you and your family. It won't take long before her friends realize she's still available, just not quite so excessively. And don't be surprised if your insistence that she spend more time at home results in a similar pattern among her friends. I've found lots of parents are looking for one courageous mom or dad to step up and do what they themselves believe is right. When that happens, it's "parental dominoes."

One of the healthiest, most wholesome social activities a child can enjoy is time at home. Raising a homebody means keeping kids around the house—oftentimes with their friends—so that you can be an integral part of their social development.

Guaranteed Geek: Tips for Geektime at Home

For Geeks of All Ages:

* Make your house as homey as it can be. Kids need to feel that home is both a comfortable retreat from the busy outside world, and also a place where they can bring friends.

* Get a kid-friendly item at home such as a trampoline, Ping-Pong table, or pool table.

* Declare a Friday or Saturday night as "home time." Make no specific plans except to turn off the electronics in your home. Watch what happens!

* Remember even a brief amount of unstructured time with the family is invigorating for kids. Even a half hour on a Saturday morning to lie around in pajamas before the day's activities is beneficial.

For Elementary School Geeks:
* Limit outside socializing to a few events each week.

* Kids thrive on routine. Keep your life as organized as possible and give children a sense of stability through regular family rituals.

* Tell and retell your family stories. Kids need to adopt the family's history as their own.

* Refer to your family with pride. Kids need to feel connected and empowered by the notion of "our family."

For Middle School Geeks:
* When kids reach middle school, reassess whether your home offers opportunities for adolescents to hang out. Consider converting a basement space into a recreation room for geeky preteens.

* Continue family traditions even if they make your child feel embarrassed. We still sing "Jingle Bells" no matter how silly a young teenager feels doing it. It's part of our identity!

* Introduce the notion of family pride when talking to a preteen about the choices he may face. While reinforcing unconditional love, teach him that his actions reflect on his whole family. Instilling loyalty and pride can encourage kids to uphold the family reputation for genuine, enthusiastic, empowered kids.

* Middle schoolers make wonderful travel agents. Get yours involved in plotting a family vacation.

For High School Geeks:
* Don't assume high schoolers aren't interested in time with the family. Continue to offer and expect family participation.

* Remind an older teen that younger siblings probably sat through countless games, concerts, and events on his behalf. Ask him to reciprocate at least occasionally to express appreciation and love for the younger sibling's past support.

* Open your home to high schoolers. Offering them a fun, comfortable place to hang out keeps your teen around the house but also facilitates his desire to hang out with his friends. Plus, geeky teens are fun to have around. (Really!)

* As teens graduate and get ready to leave home, remind them that their departure will have an emotional impact on everyone. Encourage them to be sensitive and caring even as they express their excitement to move on.

Rule #9

RAISE A PRINCIPLED KID

One evening Betsy was helping me make dinner. She grabbed a knife and an onion and sidled up to the cutting board. "French was interesting today," she said.

"How so?" I asked.

"Well, this kid, Dan, made a really rude comment to my friend Sarah. He pointed to her stomach and said, 'Sarah, put those rolls away. It's not time for dinner.' So I sort of went off on him."

Ouch. Comments about a teen girl's physical flaws are off-limits. No wonder Betsy got mad. "What do you mean, you 'went off on him'?" I had visions of Betsy pummeling Dan with an English-to-French dictionary and yelling, "*ferme-la!*"

"I stood up and said, 'That was a horrible thing to say to a girl. You might think you're funny, but nobody else does. Everyone else thinks you're rude and mean.'"

"Wow," I said. I didn't know whether to be impressed or afraid, but I was glad I wasn't the onion she was chopping. Recalling the episode had caused her to dice furiously. "What did everyone else do?"

"Nothing. But later in the cafeteria some kids said that was the best French class ever."

This wasn't the first time Betsy had spoken up for someone. Back in middle school, several classmates prided themselves on their ability to bring a particular teacher to tears by making nasty comments and refusing to cooperate with her. Betsy lamented the cruelty she witnessed, but she didn't know how to help or what to do. On the one hand, she was bothered by the bullying she saw—enough to report it to me and consider whether she could intervene. On the other hand, a thirteen-year-old girl who stands up and shames her peers for teasing a teacher is a hopeless geek. She was savvy enough to appreciate what this tactic would say about her.

Still, that was the approach I encouraged her to take. "Look," I said, "you can sit there and watch those kids, and you can think it's terrible, but if you don't speak up, you're no better than they are." She agreed with my logic, but that didn't mean she was convinced.

Then one day she couldn't tolerate it any longer. She said to the whole class, "I can't believe how disrespectful and rude you guys are. This is an adult and it is really inappropriate to tease her and talk back." Even the teacher was shocked.

Just as she figured, taking a stand solidified her place in the Geek Hall of Fame. Not only was she a notorious teacher's pet, she was a teacher's pet whose motives were pure—she wasn't just sucking up to get a good grade.

By the time she reached high school, Betsy's reputation as an outspoken geek had preceded her, but she didn't mind. She had discovered it felt good to do the right thing, like speak up when someone gets hurt at the hands of a bully, even if her tirades didn't change things much.

Then again, standing up in French class to defend her friend Sarah somehow came across as pretty cool, even to the popular crowd. In my book, though, what's important is that Betsy speaks up even when nobody thinks it's cool but her.

Principles of Popularity

I'm always proud when I think of the times Betsy has stood up for others, but ironically, it was her one and only foray into unprincipled behavior that (briefly) got her noticed by the "cool crowd." Looking to protect her A average in eighth grade English, she asked a friend for an answer on a homework assignment, only to be charged with cheating. (The bad news was she *was* cheating; the good news—she was so inexperienced at it, she did it right in front of the teacher).

Suddenly, Betsy wasn't perceived as the Goody Two-shoes who reprimanded her peers for taunting an adult. She was just a flawed middle schooler, taking a shortcut to get her homework done—no better than anyone else. Her reward? A spike in social status and a place at the lunch table with the popular people. Weird, huh?

Betsy's popular phase didn't last long. She never felt comfortable flipping her hair and talking about "hot guys," and her career as a homework cheater ceased after one unsuccessful episode. She obviously wasn't the real deal as far as the cool group was concerned. More than that, Betsy understood the disappointing reality that her weakest moment—an act of unprincipled convenience—gained her more admiration than speaking out for the just treatment of another person.

Such is the twisted moral code of the culture of cool.

WHAT'S COOL ISN'T ALWAYS WHAT'S MORAL

Throughout this book, I've illustrated the irony of modern American parenting—knowing, on the one hand, what's best and good for kids; yet on the other hand, doing exactly the opposite. Now get ready because I'm going to show how the consistently incongruous behavior on the part of parents plays out in the moral development of children.

In 2006, the Josephson Institute of Ethics conducted its biannual survey on ethical behavior in teens. It's a huge sample—some thirty-six thousand high school students participate in it—and it covers a wide range of circumstances in which ethics could or should drive behavioral choices.

Here's what the institute's October 2006 press release said about the results:

> *According to the Josephson Institute's 2006 Report Card on the Ethics of American Youth, today's young people reveal deeply entrenched habits of dishonesty. The report reveals high rates of cheating, lying and theft. More than one in four (28%) of the 36,122 high school students surveyed admitted stealing from a store within the past year. Twenty-three percent said they stole something from a parent or other relative; 81% confessed they lied to a parent about something significant and 39% said they lied to save money. Cheating in school continues to be rampant. A substantial majority (60%) cheated on a test during the past year (35% did so two or more times) and one in three (33%) said they used the Internet to plagiarize an assignment.*
>
> *As bad as these numbers are, it appears they understate the level of dishonesty exhibited by America's youth as 27% confessed they lied on at least one or two questions on the survey. Experts agree that dishonesty on surveys usually is an attempt to conceal misconduct.*
>
> ***Despite these high levels of dishonesty, these same kids have a high self image of their ethics. A whopping 92% said they were satisfied with their personal ethics and character and 74% said that "when it comes to doing what is right, I am better than most people I know."*** [Emphasis added.]

There it is, folks. The next generation of teachers, law enforcement officers, physicians, pharmacists, lawyers, judges, politicians, and clergy. *The next generation of parents.*

The culture of cool—the dominant popular culture of our day—is a culture in which it apparently is morally acceptable, or at least common, for more than a quarter of teens to admit they are thieves and way more than half to admit they are regular cheaters. No wonder Betsy's cheating episode made her feel like one of the gang. She finally was!

What's most important in my mind is the paragraph that says nearly every teen surveyed—92 percent—feels happy with his or her ethics and morals. On the face of it, this seems impossible to comprehend. How could that many kids be lying, cheating, and stealing with such frequency and yet report feeling good about their ethical and moral fiber? Confusing, isn't it?

I would be confused too, except that I read Betsy Hart's extraordinary book, *It Takes A Parent: How the Culture of Pushover Parenting Is Hurting Our Kids and What to Do About It*. Hart discusses a widespread fallacy in child rearing today, namely, "one of the most tenaciously held pieces of accepted wisdom in today's parenting culture: Criticize the behavior, not the child." Experts counsel that parents should avoid criticizing children at all costs because it makes kids feel bad about themselves. To this, Hart replies, "Well no doubt. This used to be called developing a conscience. But we modern parents are so desperate for our kids to feel good about themselves *all the time,* no matter what they do or don't do, that we are loath to let them feel bad about themselves, even when they *should* feel bad about themselves. What a terrible disservice to them." [Emphases in the original.]

The experts who warn about bruising a child's self-esteem through criticism have somehow convinced parents not to speak up even when kids behave unethically. Thanks to this backward notion, we're stuck with a generation of teens who are capable of separating their own behavior from their intrinsic character. Consequently, they routinely engage in unethical behavior but still feel great about their ethical and moral selves. Cool!

I'm siding with Ms. Hart here. Separating a child from his behavior impedes the formation of a conscience. Self-esteem? Kids have plenty of that. But a conscience that might sometimes produce guilt or remorse? Not so much.

The whole vocabulary of moral behavior seems to be uncool. I've noticed the word *morality* gets a bad rap. Being "moral" is something people are accused of as if it's akin to selling snake oil. Call someone a "moralist" or say they're "moralizing" and watch the response you'll get. "How dare you. I would never moralize. I would not impose my morals on someone else." (Of course people who say this are standing on moral high ground, but don't mention that. It only generates a circular argument.)

As a culture, we need to remember that morals are not viruses.

VALUES VERSUS MORALS

In each chapter of this geeky-parenting book, I've shown how my husband and I impose our values on the decisions and choices we make on behalf of our children. As well, I've encouraged you to use *your* values as the guideposts for child-rearing choices you must make. Values are unique to us. They're the expression of our moral and ethical beliefs, and for most of us, they also reflect some tenets of religious belief. Values also might reflect our heritage and traditions as well as our political and civic opinions. My point is, the values we hold about the culture and its place in the lives of our kids may vary.

Morals are something different. A moral code asserts right and wrong in assessing conduct.

Imagine that values are the ingredients we each like in our salad. I'm a fan of bib lettuce, ripe tomatoes, and purple onions. You might like romaine, avocado, and scallions. Either way, we're both eating salad.

If values are the salad, morals are the *bowl* in which you mix the salad. They're the hard-and-fast container that holds the food. Salad bowls might *seem* to vary—some are wooden, some are glass, some are pottery—and this variation might confuse folks into thinking there are lots of kinds of morality. But no. A bowl is a bowl is a bowl.

In the same way, some things are always right; some things are always wrong. And a bowl is always a bowl.

From a parenting perspective, though, moral relativism has encroached into the home, leading kids to believe that their moral codes are entirely subjective. Not only are parents neglecting to teach right from wrong, they're adding to the confusion by stressing positive self-esteem regardless of a child's behavior, leaving kids without the conscience to evaluate their own choices against a moral standard.

To develop authentic, good character, children need to learn what's right and wrong. If they don't, they take on the relative morality offered by the culture, in which any expedient or desired behavior is cool. Given the overwhelming results of the Josephson Institute's report card on youth ethics, behavior that's commonly considered cool needn't always be moral.

MORAL TEACHERS: MEET THE FACULTY

We've all heard it said, "Parents are a child's first teachers." Sadly, too many parents are failing to recognize that the most important lessons they must teach revolve around moral and ethical behavior. We spend scads of time helping our kids to become stellar athletes or outstanding students, but comparatively little time developing their characters. In the same way that raising a great pitcher is the result of throwing baseballs on the driveway night after night, raising a principled child is the result of teaching, talking about, and practicing strong ethical principles.

We need to teach about ethical choices all the time—not just when kids make mistakes. Unfortunately, parents often assume their kids should know what's right and what's wrong. Kids need to be told!

When children choose unethical behavior, parents' reactions reinforce the lesson, sometimes in insidious ways. Parents who are embarrassed about the things their kids do try to cover up for them or shift the blame elsewhere. The new cultural norm is for a kid to get into trouble and for his parents to raise hell and blame the teacher, administrator, or police officer who brings the behavior to light. Ask any teacher what the most common response is when confronting a parent: "My child would never do that." Apparently, no one wants to accept that we all are raising human beings who do foolish and sometimes destructive things.

Some parents believe it's hypocritical of them to come down on their kids when they themselves made similar mistakes as children. They make the excuse, "We all cheated when we were kids," or "Everyone shoplifts when they're young," sending the strong message to their children, "Your unethical behavior isn't a big deal." Kids come away from episodes in which they're caught cheating or lying with the impression that the worst part was getting caught, not choosing the unethical behavior.

Some parents do a terrific job teaching about ethics, but they're teaching how to be unethical rather than ethical. For example, doing homework for their kids, writing notes to teachers full of falsehoods and fabrications *(Carl had the flu last night and couldn't do his homework),* and in other ways assisting their kids to live an unprincipled life. As an example of how widespread this problem is, my children's fourth grade teacher insists that any student who turns in a paper that is typed must also have a note from his parents swearing that the child typed it himself. I think this begs the premise if a parent is so unethical as to type the paper for the child—which is against school policy—would not that parent also be willing to write a note to lie about it?

Some parents, when helping their kids to do something without principle, say, "We're only doing this because it's an emergency." These folks are teaching their children something more complicated: situational ethics.

If parents are the first teachers of their children, other adults quickly join the faculty. Extended family, teachers, coaches, neighbors, and friends all add lessons about ethical behavior. Are these folks always teaching kids to do what's right? Maybe, maybe not.

In 2007, the Josephson Institute released the results of a survey of more than five thousand high school athletes that revealed that more than 90 percent of them admire their coaches and believe coaches want them to do the right things. At the same time an alarming number of athletes said they would be comfortable breaking rules, ignoring a scoring mistake that favored their team, or otherwise unethically gaining a competitive advantage to win a game. Suffice to say, coaches ought to mention these things in the locker room when giving pep talks on playing like winners.

Teachers, similarly, send dicey messages about ethics. Kids see their teachers looking the other way when cheating takes place and playing favorites among the students in class. Kids further conclude that all adults skirt around the rules.

And of course the ever-present media message is that unethical, immoral, and even illegal behavior is nothing but glamorous! As I write this, for example, the inexplicably famous heiress Paris Hilton luxuriates on a beach in Hawaii, contemplating the scores of lucrative opportunities through which she can exploit her experience of incarceration. What message did our children take from the video footage of Ms. Hilton's release from jail, with literally hundreds of photographers and reporters capturing her humble walk from the county jail to her waiting limo? Never has a probation violation been so enticing.

The impact of media role models is debatable, since geeks know all about Paris Hilton but find her repugnant, if not laughable. But the cool culture makes icons out of people whose ethical choices are often questionable, at best.

A Geeky Code of Moral Excellence

To teach a geek about morality and ethical behavior, we need a basic lexicon. As I researched this topic, I decided the garbled vocabulary around morality is part of the reason why kids don't understand how it works in their daily lives.

For example, this came from the Web site www.familyeducation .com: "Moral behavior means different things to different people. For our purposes, morality means treating ourselves and others with respect. Empathy, compassion, and a sense of justice are central components of this kind of moral behavior." Empathy, in particular, is a word that gets lots of play in parenting literature about teaching morals. Using empathy, I gather, kids should focus on the feelings of others when deciding if their behavior is considered moral.

As a moral code, it strikes me this thinking boils down to: *Be nice.* But there's more to morality than being nice, isn't there? We could agree that the majority of teens who admitted on that survey to cheating are perfectly *nice*, and yet we have a problem with their moral conduct. I think the 92 percent of teens who feel good about their moral and ethical codes really just consider themselves nice people.

Unfortunately, nice isn't what this is about.

Moreover, when teaching children how to decide what's moral, we can't confuse them with emotions. "How would someone else feel?" isn't an accurate moral compass. Feelings are fluid—they change from person to person and day to day. Not only that, but feelings are easily projected and not accurately understood. How often do we say to someone "You shouldn't feel that way"? Who are we to decide?

This is also why the writer at www.familyeducation.com acknowledged a morally relativist view. If feelings are the measure of right and wrong, then right and wrong depend on the person.

But morality is the assumption that some things are simply right and some are simply wrong and that these standards are true all the time, for everyone. Ergo telling the truth is right, lying is wrong; doing your own homework is right, cheating is wrong; respecting the property of others is right, stealing is wrong; respecting the feelings of others is right, abusing them is wrong.

As teaching tools, the words *right* and *wrong* are underrated. Come to think of it, so are *good* and *bad*. (And while I'm at it, I think the word *nice* ought to be banished from the universal parenting dictionary—anyone can be nice, after all. Heck, even felons are "nice" to the people they love.)

Doing "right" and being "good" are signs you've internalized a moral code that guides your behavior and judgment.

Being "nice" means…well…it means you're nice. Not that there's anything wrong with that.

ELEMENTS OF GOOD CHARACTER

When my kids were small, we had a sizable collection of videos that I permitted them to watch instead of regular TV. One of these was called CHARACTER COUNTS!$_{SM}$, a production of the CHARACTER COUNTS! Coalition. It featured an introduction by actor Tom Selleck and a team of child singer/dancers who introduced the Six Pillars of Character$_{SM}$: trustworthiness, respect, responsibility, fairness, caring, and citizenship. Each pillar was illustrated through a vignette, short story, or scene such as a Barney episode or an animated *Babar* story.

My kids loved the video, except for the lengthy introduction by Tom Selleck. I didn't mind the intro because, let's face it, Tom Selleck is hunky. Also, I felt reassured that a Hollywood actor was involved in character education. It was a pretty long video too, so I could usually get several loads of laundry folded while the children were occupied.

That video did a great job of introducing some lofty ideas about morality in a way that made sense to my kids. But of course teaching a moral code is a long process; we have to keep the subject at the forefront if we expect them to know how to act when faced with the infinite number of choices life presents.

As a lexicon for morality, the Six Pillars of Character outlined by CHARACTER COUNTS! (www.charactercounts.org) provide a thorough checklist for geeky ethical behavior. Since I can't improve upon them, I'm including them. Take note of how many behaviors on this list *do* consider the feelings of others, and yet cast an even wider net for ethical behavior choices:

Trustworthiness
* Be honest
* Don't deceive, cheat, or steal
* Be reliable—do what you say you'll do
* Have the courage to do the right thing
* Build a good reputation
* Be loyal—stand by your family, friends, and country

Respect
   * Treat others with respect; follow the Golden Rule
   * Be tolerant of differences
   * Use good manners, not bad language
   * Be considerate of the feelings of others
   * Don't threaten, hit, or hurt anyone
   * Deal peacefully with anger, insults, and disagreements

Responsibility
   * Do what you are supposed to do
   * Persevere: Keep on trying!
   * Always do your best
   * Use self-control
   * Be self-disciplined
   * Think before you act—consider the consequences
   * Be accountable for your choices

Fairness
   * Play by the rules
   * Take turns and share
   * Be open-minded; listen to others
   * Don't take advantage of others
   * Don't blame others carelessly

Caring
   * Be kind
   * Be compassionate and show you care
   * Express gratitude
   * Forgive others
   * Help people in need

Citizenship
   * Do your share to make your school and community better
   * Cooperate

* Get involved in community affairs
* Stay informed; vote
* Be a good neighbor
* Obey laws and rules
* Respect authority
* Protect the environment

SEIZING THE MOMENT TO TEACH
RIGHT AND WRONG

As parents we must always be on the lookout for "teachable moments." These are the unplanned life lessons usually precipitated by a bad decision. No doubt, trial and error is the most effective learning tool, though sometimes it's costly. Betsy's cheating episode taught her a lot about what it means to have integrity and how valuable her good reputation is. Unfortunately, it cost her an A in English and a chance for the honor roll that semester. Small price to pay for a lesson well learned.

Lying is perhaps one of the most frequent unethical acts we parents face. Kids have a millions excuses for lying, and to a child they all seem reasonable. Sometimes kids lie for absolutely no discernible reason. We have to remember that some unethical behaviors, such as lying, become habit if we don't nip them in the bud. (Jimmy once lied and told me he'd put the dog out. Problem was, it was winter. No yellow snow. Kids are lousy liars and they need to be told this time and again.) Look out for complacency on your part. I think sometimes, rather than hunt down the truth and make a child face his dishonesty, we play along or turn a blind eye to avoid conflict.

Mistakes are a given. We can't keep them from happening, but we can help our kids make the most of their errors by teaching them to take responsibility and make amends. If we run to our kids' rescue, argue with others that they're not at fault, and seek to reduce the ill effects of their actions by smoothing things over, our kids miss out on the chance to learn difficult moral lessons.

Children need concrete experiences to internalize a moral code, which means they need their mistakes. But they also need to figure out how to apply their ethical standards in day-to-day situations.

Using circumstances of daily life, we can find plenty of opportunities to review moral and ethical choices:

* When a term paper is assigned, review what constitutes ethical research and attribution.

* If there's a school dance on the calendar, talk about the ethics of accepting or declining a social invitation in a way that considers others' feelings.

* If kids at school are known to be cheating, talk about how this affects all students and discuss a child's ethical obligations and options.

* If a child sees a friend steal something from another friend's locker, discuss whether there is a moral obligation to talk to the friend and/or report it to a teacher.

* If a child feels a friend is being treated unfairly by a teacher or coach, discuss what to do and whether there is an ethical question.

* When talking about playing on the playground, discuss what's right and wrong when kids ignore the rules of a game.

* If a child hears gossip or rumors about a friend, talk about what he should do. Discuss ways to stand up for the friend and also consider any ethical obligation the situation implies.

* When watching TV or using the Internet, discuss the ethical choices of celebrities and others portrayed in the news.

Geek parenting includes lots of conversations about what constitutes right and wrong, and as well about how to exhibit a strong character by choosing what's right. This is how we help our children develop moral intelligence, the capacity to view their choices through the prism of standards of right and wrong.

STANDING ON PRINCIPLE IN THE LARGER COMMUNITY

Principled kids tend naturally to gravitate to community service, causes, and politics. This is why I've always contended that geek parenting is not a "red" or "blue" issue, since principled children from every political viewpoint can and do become geek activists.

Developing a strong sense of right and wrong, geeks realize that justice and fairness must be protected—not just for themselves but for others. Show me a news story about a young person who mentors poor kids or works for a clean environment or volunteers at a soup kitchen and I'll show you a geek—a young person who appreciates from a tender age that the world needs the active response of those who love what's good and right.

Geeks also stand on principle for individuals. This is why Betsy spoke up for a teacher and a friend, and why all of my kids are known for befriending and advocating for others who seem less able to protect themselves.

To be clear, it's entirely possible and likely that some cool kids are morally upright and exhibit strong ethical conduct. I'm not suggesting that all cool kids are morally bankrupt! I am saying, however, that the culture of cool doesn't put a big price tag on principled behavior. Standing up for what's right most definitely is a trait of a geek.

How to Raise a Principled Geek

Of all the things that make my children geeky, perhaps none makes me prouder than the fact that they are principled young people. They may not always do the right things—no one does—but they usually know what the right thing is. They also show guilt and remorse when they choose what's wrong, and out of those feelings of regret, they turn things around. In my mind, that's the basis for an ethical life (and a geeky lifestyle). Here's how we've helped our kids internalize a moral code and exhibit principled behavior:

Model Moral Behavior

We have to be principled parents to raise principled kids. Children can sniff out a phony a mile away. We can't say, "Always tell the truth," and then let our kids hear us on the phone lying to a neighbor about why we won't be coming to her cookout. Our own ethical behavior speaks louder to our kids about how to behave than any lecture or life lesson we can offer. In every situation they ever observe, are our children seeing an example of moral leadership?

Connect Behavior to Character

Children want to do good and they want to *be* good. If we connect their behavior to their character, we show them how their actions speak for the intentions in their hearts. When they make mistakes, it's okay for kids to feel bad! In fact, they ought to sometimes be ashamed of their choices and show remorse. This is how their consciences help them to see right and wrong in all things.

Praise Moral Conduct

Kids are faced with countless opportunities to make immoral and unethical choices. When they choose what's right, we need to recognize them and praise their good character. Telling kids, "I'm proud of you for going back to the store to pay for a missed item" or "I'm impressed that you spoke up against a bully" reminds them that their good behavior is valued. In the same way, we need to praise kids when they correct their mistakes. I never dress down kids who admit to a lie, since I want them to learn that telling the truth is always the right road.

Practice Through Hypotheticals
Good judgment and moral behavior don't come naturally—they have to be learned. We need to teach discernment in all situations so kids develop the moral intelligence to know right from wrong. This takes practice and lots of interesting conversations about real, as well as hypothetical, ethical dilemmas. When chatting with kids, pose ethical problems such as, "Suppose you found a diamond ring on the ground in front of a jewelry store..." Ask what a child could do, but offer variations on the problem as well. ("Now suppose your dog needed an expensive operation...") Kids love to consider their ethical options!

When No One Is Looking
Teach the adage "Character is what you do even when no one is looking." Help kids develop a sense of pride based on integrity and authentic ethical behavior. Remind them that no one might know about an unethical choice such as lying or stealing, but the child in the mirror knows everything.

Principles in Action

Principled kids often face uncool tasks, such as speaking out on behalf of a friend who's being teased or confronting peers who are cheating. They don't just look the other way to avoid the wrath of the popular crowd; they stick by their principles because they have strong personal character. It takes courage to uphold principles in childhood—kids might see how taking moral shortcuts would make them popular and get them included in the cool crowd. When we convey to our kids how much we admire their ethical choices and moral behavior, we give them incentive to keep choosing what's right. When they make mistakes and feel badly about themselves, we can teach them that righting their course is the way to authentic self-esteem.

A principled child is one who understands how his actions can hurt or help others. Raising a geek who stands on principle isn't easy, since

MORALITY AT BARNES & NOBLE

There's an old parenting adage on the subject of kids and morality: Just when you think you've done a great job of teaching your children right from wrong, someone will ask for a ride to the bookstore to drink smoothies and read the books for free. Here's what happened:

Betsy asked if she could go to Barnes & Noble. I asked if she needed to buy a book. Betsy admitted she didn't want to buy a book; she just wanted to buy a smoothie and a scone and read a book for free. "I figure after about four trips to the store, I can read an entire book, so I don't need to actually buy it."

I was horrified! Not only because I had just published my first book and now understood all too well the ramifications of low book sales. Rather, I was aghast that I'd raised a kid who didn't know this was wrong.

She didn't get the problem. "It's not like I'm breaking the spine or anything," she argued. This wasn't the point, but I have to admit I was relieved.

"Betsy, reading an entire book at the bookstore without buying it is stealing," I said.

I didn't know where to start my lesson on morality, so I tried the Golden Rule. "How do you suppose those authors would feel knowing you are enjoying their work but you're not willing to pay for it?"

"They probably would feel great. At least they'd know how much I like their books."

"What about the bookstore owners?" I asked. "How do you think they feel about people who come in to read but won't spend any money in the store?"

She got defensive. "Hey, I'm getting a snack. There's money involved."

I explained that buying a Frappuccino and a muffin from the bookstore's coffee shop doesn't send cash flowing into the pockets of the people whose work she was enjoying for free.

"What about the person who actually does purchase that copy of the book? How will that person feel when she finds the crumbs from your scone inside?"

"There are no crumbs, and besides, she'll never notice the book has been read."

Betsy thought we had hit on a "gray area"—a moral question that could be argued either way. The problem is, in our culture nearly every issue lands in the proverbial "gray area."

I finally realized why Betsy was confused about the moral question at hand. I was proposing all sorts of empathetic reasoning, but I never actually used the only two words that would help her understand the context in which she needs to evaluate her behavior: *right* and *wrong*.

"Betsy, it's wrong to read a book in a bookstore that you haven't paid for and have no intention of buying."

"Oh," she said.

Children crave clarity. Betsy craved clarity and books, which is not a bad thing, come to think of it. I was somewhat chagrined that the conversation even needed to take place since I'd have thought by then she knew the difference between perusing and consuming. But the fact that we had the conversation at all struck me as a moral victory—or at least a victory for morality, which in my mind was a darn good thing.

the culture of cool offers so many attractive, unethical choices. But a kid who grows in moral intelligence sees himself as an agent for goodness in his own world and, later, in a "real world" that desperately needs more principled geeks.

Uncool Answers

The kids in my son's seventh-grade class cheat on their homework. They pass assignments around at lunchtime and fill in the answers on math worksheets and maps for social studies. He does his homework on his own at home, taking his time and doing it right. It really bugs him that so many kids get full credit when he knows they're not doing their own work. What should he do?

It's hard to convince a child of that adage "Cheaters never prosper" when they're surrounded by kids getting great grades on work they didn't do. I don't blame your son for his anger. It's not fair.

This is one of those situations in which I would focus on two things: First, he's responsible for his own behavior. He should take pride in the fact that he works ethically on his own homework and is actually learning the math! At some point there will be a math test, I would guess, and the fact that he actually understands the material will pay off.

Second, he needs to learn in this situation that life isn't fair when it comes to people cheating. Some folks will do anything to gain an advantage—he'll learn this is true in school, and later, in his professional life. Focus on the value of his reputation for integrity and let him know that people who cheat generally pay a price eventually.

I wouldn't encourage your son to be the one to report the cheaters. I would, however, encourage you to mention it during your regular parent–teacher conference. Simply say that your son has expressed concern and frustration about other kids sharing their work. If you alert the teacher to look out for it, the problem may come to the surface.

Schools understand that they are in a constant battle against rampant cheating and they need support from principled kids to do the right thing, no matter what others are doing.

Guaranteed Geek: Tips for Geeky Moral Development

For Geeks of All Ages:
* Adopt a vocabulary for moral behavior. Tape it to the fridge!

* Talk about ethical choices. Be sure to use the word *ethical* so kids understand it's a question of right and wrong.

* Applaud moral behavior whenever you see it.

* Model moral choices and get your kids' input when you are faced with a moral dilemma at work or in the community.

For Elementary School Geeks:
* Watch or read the children's classic *Pinocchio* and talk about the important role played by Jiminy Cricket. (He served as the boy's conscience, but he didn't do a great job for much of the story.)

* When reading books, talk about "the moral of the story..."

* Define behaviors as "right" and "wrong." Encourage kids to make choices that are "good" and not "bad."

* If a child makes an ethical mistake such as cheating, stealing, or lying, teach him how to correct it by taking responsibility and making amends. Don't just say, "Never do that again." Take back the stolen item, make him admit the lie or confess the cheating and suffer the consequences.

For Middle School Geeks:
* Make it tough to cheat. Stay on top of schoolwork and be aware if homework is done at home.

* Discuss moral dilemmas in friendship struggles. Talk about how to be an ethical friend.

* Set rules for Internet use that convey your ethical standards. Ask your middle schooler how she can use the net ethically.

* Talk about themes presented in movies and TV shows. Consider the ethical problems involved in the plot and discuss whether the characters choose right or wrong.

For High School Geeks:
* Talk seriously about the ramifications of cheating. Make sure your high schooler knows the school policy about cheating and consider setting one of your own, as well.

* Establish a "truth bonus," an understanding that telling the truth about a mistake will minimize the consequences, while lying will make the outcome worse.

* Discuss the importance of hanging with ethical friends. Encourage your child not to straddle the fence by hanging out with kids who make poor choices. Remind him he's known by his friends.

* Let your child know when people tell you they admire his good character. (They will!) Tell him how proud you are of him and thank him for upholding the family's good name.

....

RAISE A FAITHFUL KID

Every year, on the night before school starts, I announce that it's time to take a walk. All six of us fan out throughout the house to find our flip-flops, someone gets a leash for Scotty the dog, and we set out in a disorganized band up our street. Usually it's pushing nine o'clock, so while the sun still washes the sky with color, twilight has set in, suspending us in an envelope of growing darkness. As we stroll past our neighbors' houses, we notice the glow of lamplights and the blue flicker of their televisions. It's a peaceful, poignant time. We all know why we're there.

One by one, we confide our goals for the coming school year. Starting with Amy and working our way up the line to Katie, our children tell us what they hope to accomplish and how they expect the year to unfold. We'll hear, "I want to win an award at sixth-grade camp" or "I plan to complete all the levels for Reading Month in March." There always are goals about school performance—"I plan to make the honor roll at least one semester" or "My goal is to get an A in all my classes for at least one quarter."

It's typical to hear a few athletic goals such as setting a new personal best in running or helping a team win a league championship. Upcoming milestones are mentioned—the first chance to be in the band or go to the prom, perhaps—and of course seminal events like starting or graduating from high school are acknowledged.

Jim and I also share our plans. Our kids want to know about our professional goals and also about how pursuing these might affect our family life.

Before the walk is over, though, we shift the focus to our true agenda: reminding our children that we were created for more than our own goals and desires. Somewhere in the planning, we need to dream of what God wants for us—imagine that our place in creation is meant for more than our own achievements. Somewhere in the planning, we have to set a goal about being the person God wants us each to be—a person who may be asked to suffer, to sacrifice, and to search for meaning not only in our accomplishments but in our failures. As they look at the year before them, we want to instill a sense of responsibility for its outcome, but more than that, remind them that the outcome ultimately will reflect a living faith in God.

As inspirational as we might be, six people and a dog cannot walk far on an August night without being discovered by mosquitoes. Invariably one of the children complains of being eaten alive, and at about this time there will be a tiff because someone will have stepped on someone else's flip-flop. I'll realize it's bedtime for the younger kids. And thus the magic of the moment fades with the last of a deep orange sunset.

But as traditions go, our annual walk on the last night of summer vacation strikes me as uniquely instructive: It connects us to our individual futures and our responsibility to create our own realities; it connects us to one another and to our obligation to support the dreams we each hold dear; and it connects us to our Creator, whose vision of us we know to be perfect and purposeful, yet remains ours to discern.

The cool thing is it only takes about a half hour. And also, it's really fun.

Spiritual Yearnings

Up to this point, I've written about the geek-parenting perspective in most of the practical ways in which we confront the culture of cool. We've talked about how to promote a child's intellectual curiosity, how to protect his innocence, how to help him discover his passions and relate to family and friends. In the last chapter, we talked about the geek perspective on principled behavior. So it might seem we've hit the high points in the effort to bring up geeks.

Yet in my mind, it's difficult—impossible, actually—to approach the notion of geek parenting without knowing about the foundation upon which my whole theory rests: my belief in God's plan for us and for our geeky children.

Before you conclude that I'm about to promote a specific religious agenda, please know that's not the case. This book does not advocate a particular faith expression—the tenets I'm expressing apply to *any* family in which a religious or spiritual belief or practice is present. Just as I have pointed out that geeks come in all political stripes, they also come in all religious traditions. My family and I happen to be practicing Roman Catholics, but it's not our Catholicism or even our Christianity that influences our geeky lifestyle.

In fact, when it comes to children and religion, my geek-parenting experience convinces me that it's not *which* religion we practice and teach our children, *but that we teach them one.*

Children naturally yearn to feed their spiritual selves. Caring for the whole child, we rightly must consider his physical, intellectual, emotional, and spiritual dimensions. I came to this conclusion on my own while studying the four "subjects" within my personal "child-development lab." But it turns out one of the world's foremost authorities on children's psyches learned this same thing over the course of thirty years of interviews and research. Dr. Robert Coles, psychiatrist and Harvard professor, concluded in *The Spiritual Life of Children* that his life's work had helped him to "see children as seekers, as young pilgrims well aware that life is a finite journey and as anxious to make sense of it as those of us who are farther along in the time allotted us." Having studied children of the three great world religions—Judaism, Christianity and Islam—as well as children who grow up in a secular belief system, Coles concluded that soul-searching and the yearning for a sense of spirituality exist from a young age in virtually everyone.

BEYOND SPIRITUALITY: RELIGIOUS PRACTICE

Pollsters from the Gallup Organization confirm that 86 percent of us say we believe in God. (Interestingly, 81 percent of us believe in heaven, while only 69 percent believe in hell. Clearly there are a whole lot of folks who have never been to Target on Christmas Eve. Hell is real, people.) Doctrinal belief among that vast majority obviously varies, but overwhelmingly we view God as real and, therefore, an entity with whom we can relate in both a "spiritual" and "religious" way.

Perhaps we should start with the difference between those two concepts before we jump into a discussion of a geeky faith perspective.

The word *spirituality* refers to a sense of connection to God—an intimate relationship as expressed through personal prayer and contemplation. Understanding ourselves as spiritual beings, we see the world around us as an expression of God's creative energy. We see ourselves connected to God and to one another in some purposeful way. We put our faith in God (or a "higher power" or a "creative being"—spirituality doesn't put a form on the face of God) and we look to Him for guidance and to give our lives meaning.

Religious practice is the expression of faith in a structured way. Learning the tenets of our specific belief systems, going to church, reading the Bible and other books about faith, belonging to a youth group or prayer circle, wearing religious jewelry, or keeping religious artwork in the home—all of these are outward expressions of an inner faith. We get to pick the one that works for us.

Just as kids long for a sense of spirituality, they also respond to structure and rituals to relate to God. Little children intuitively know that God is more than just an imaginary friend. As they grow, kids accept that God sets standards about how to behave and how to treat others. They want to go to God with requests but also with gratitude and praise. Through religious practice, children work out some of their spiritual questions, but they also establish a religious framework through which to view the world.

I think geeky kids need both a spiritual and a religious point of view. Supporting their spiritual journeys, we help them establish intimacy with God; offering them a religious structure enables them to incorporate God into their daily lives.

Obviously, the *reason* for religious practice is the belief that it's the *right thing to do*—it's what God wants us to do. If we're religious, it's because we accept that this is the avenue to best promote our relationship with God as we love and serve Him.

Coincidentally, though, researchers have demonstrated time and again that those who engage in a regular religious practice benefit in some specific ways. For example, there's a strong correlation between religious practice and overall happiness in family life—people who regularly attend a church, synagogue, or mosque report being happier with their lots in life than folks who don't. One study shows that kids whose parents engage in a regular religious practice are better behaved and well adjusted than other kids. The survey of parents and teachers of more than sixteen thousand children (mostly first graders) by researchers from the University of Mississippi found that kids whose parents regularly attended church and talked at home about their religious beliefs showed better self-control, social skills, and approaches to learning than kids of nonreligious parents. Another study proves that religious teens engage less often in high-risk behaviors than their nonreligious peers.

It's important to note that these findings support religious practice, not just an avowed sense of spirituality. It may be good for us just to be believers, but it's better—empirically, anyway—to be religious.

More on all this shortly. First, we have to look at where God stands in the culture of cool.

GOD IS (SORT OF) COOL

Ironically, God is extremely cool in the media, but living a "godly" life is very uncool.

Now, I'm not a cultural commentator. I'm a wife, a mother, and a newspaper columnist, and as I've stressed time and again, none of that qualifies me as an expert on anything except laundry. So it's probable that my assessment of God's place in the culture is going to come across as anecdotal at worst, provincial at best. But here goes: I think God got cool when Madonna started wearing giant crosses as earrings. She was followed in close succession by rap stars, professional athletes, actors, and heiresses in their pronounced affection for religious symbols as jewelry, body art, and good-luck charms. In addition to outward symbols of traditional faiths, the culture likes to point to any form of spirituality as denoting God's coolness. So, for example, we see red strings on the wrists of Madonna and other stars who have adopted Kabala as their belief system, as well as notable conversions such as Katie Holmes's switch from Catholicism to Scientology.

Celebrities invoke God whenever they make big mistakes, and I'm not questioning the sincerity of these spiritual awakenings since God has a reliable way of making Himself known to all of us in moments of humiliation and despair. Yet generally, shortly after celebrities announce their profound gratitude to God for helping them see the light, they resume whatever lifestyle it was that got them into trouble in the first place. The culture of cool may love God, but it looks from a distance as though they don't view Him as having a stake in their moral choices. I'm just saying.

While portraying celebrities as having strong spiritual connections, the media depicts organized religion in a decidedly uncool light. Admittedly and without a doubt, lots of folks within organized religion don't need the media to help them look bad. From televangelist and Catholic-priest scandals to religious fanatics of all flavors, our cultural experiences of various churches invite scrutiny and even criticism.

Having said this, we live in a culture in which it is necessary for virtually every faith tradition to have its own antidefamation organization. Bashing religions is commonplace—and funny—in the culture of cool. Even if people say they're personally offended by the overt cynicism and disdain directed through the media toward institutions of faith, the media's overarching view of religion is having an impact on beliefs and morality. For example, hard evidence suggests a strong relationship between heavy TV viewing and waning morality, which is to say people who watch a ton of TV tend to have lower standards about what constitutes ethical behavior. Conversely, light TV viewers report higher standards for what is and isn't ethical. These findings correlate with the scads of statistics and studies I mentioned in "Raise a Sheltered Kid," where we learned of the impact of media on behaviors in adolescents.

It's worth noting that while a vast majority of people profess a belief in God, less than half report regularly attending any sort of religious services. Actually, if it's accurate, the 40 percent who say they go to church would be viewed as a healthy portion of the population. Unfortunately, studies to verify whether folks *really do* go to church suggest that 40 percent figure probably is inflated. Why is this disconcerting? Because it means people are lying to pollsters about going to church. I just think that's ironic, is all.

And further, while adults say they have strong religious beliefs, studies suggest folks don't really have a grasp of what their faith actually teaches. David Kinnaman, president of the respected Christian research firm the Barna Group, explains, "Most Americans do not have strong and clear beliefs...That is, they lack a consistent and holistic understanding of their faith." Results of the firm's research show that people professing to be Christians don't understand basic biblical principles. Kinnaman attributes the watered-down belief system in part to "increasing pressure on Christians to bend and shape their views into something that's popular, something that fits the pop culture's view of what spirituality ought to be."

As a Catholic Christian, I certainly agree there's pressure to articulate a faith that's not just tolerant, but politically correct. From what I read and see in the media, I think the same is true for other religions too. Our cultural efforts to respect diversity and practice tolerance seem to have resulted in weak strains of doctrinal belief, on the off chance that a strong and obvious religious conviction will offend others.

So how do all these observations converge on the spiritual and religious development of youth in the culture of cool? Professors Christian Smith and Melinda Denton examined this question in their seminal report, *Soul Searching: The Religious and Spiritual Lives of American Teenagers,* based on the most extensive research ever conducted with teens on the subject of religion—the ongoing National Study of Youth and Religion (NSYR). Smith and Denton learned that "the vast majority of American teenagers are *exceedingly conventional* in their religious identity and practices... When it comes to religion, they are quite happy to go along and get along." [Emphasis in the original.]

The authors point out that teens, contrary to popular stereotypes (but in keeping with what I said earlier in this book!) are not necessarily rebellious, disgruntled, or snarky when it comes to religion. In fact, the data demonstrated that "there are a significant number of adolescents in the United States for whom religion and spirituality are important if not defining features of their lives." However, even among teens who said their religious beliefs were a central focus, knowledge about their faiths proved to be limited, at best.

Instead, what *Soul Searching* documented is a new "belief system" among American teens: "moralistic therapeutic deism." It's a term coined by Smith and Denton to describe these five basic "tenets" of belief:

* God is distant. He created the world and watches over us, but He's not really involved in history or world events.

* God wants people to be nice to one another.

* God wants us to be happy above all else. Happiness and feeling good about ourselves are the primary goals of life.

* God helps us when we have problems.

* Being a good person is the measure of a person's life. If we're good, we will go to heaven.

Ah, yes...be good and happy and nice. These are lovely ideas, indeed. The problem is life is full of lots of other stuff, namely evil, suffering, pain, envy, and anger. Life is not all warm and fuzzy, and a religious system that focuses on the warm and fuzzy without addressing the existence and purpose of genuine human anguish seems to short-change its believers, indeed!

More to the point, the belief system described by Smith and Denton reflects ignorance of religious tradition—*any* tradition! Rather than adopt or reject a well-articulated theology, teens today have surmised that religion is only about feelings.

So what can we conclude? Media messages convey that God is pretty cool, but organized religion is lame. Consuming exorbitant quantities of media, cool kids ascertain this message. Since their parents don't practice much religion and can't themselves articulate the beliefs on which their faith stands, kids don't learn much beyond the cool cultural message that God wants them to be happy, nice, and good. Amen to that.

One last conclusion: Once again, the pattern emerges—we know that religious practice would benefit us and our kids, but...well...you know.

Geeks Before God

The risk in writing this section is coming across as sanctimonious. That's the last thing I want to do. (Frankly, if you met me at the grocery store or out walking my dog, you'd see I'm just your basic flawed and feeble woman, working hard to get things right.) Rather, I'm trying to make a case for paying attention to our kids' spirituality and supporting them in establishing a religious point of view because I believe these things are in their best interest. Faithfulness is part of the geek lifestyle because faith in God is what's real and lasting and beneficial.

Believing we're always in the presence of God, my geeky family accepts that we're made for more than popularity or social status or high achievement or material comfort. Even if we help our children to be bright, accomplished, hardworking, and successful, the purpose isn't for their glory or our pride. It's bigger than that. To borrow a phrase that shows up in countless online articles, "We're raising kids for heaven, not for Harvard."

Our geek-parenting perspective begins with the belief that being mother and father to our four children is both a blessing and a responsibility. Our faith tradition views parenthood as a vocation—not a job or a hobby but a calling to serve God by shepherding His children. We view ourselves as our kids' stewards, charged with helping them toward independence and responsibility, which ultimately will allow *them* to serve God in whatever capacity He calls them. Our entire geek-parenting strategy reflects this belief about our role in the lives of our children, and of their purpose in creation—*to know God, to love Him, to serve Him, and to live with Him for all eternity.*

But how does all this play a role in bringing up geeks? Well, when it comes to raising geeky kids, religion is both the chicken and the egg:

* Kids who are known to believe and profess a strong faith are viewed as geeks in the culture of cool; and,

* Kids who are known as geeks need a strong faith to help them through childhood.

IN THE BEGINNING . . . THERE WERE GEEKS (JUST KIDDING)

It's never too early or too late to begin a spiritual journey with our children. Kids of all ages are curious about God! When they're little, they want to know what God looks like and how God feels about things. As they grow, they want to know why God does things—why did God make bugs that bite and why does God make it snow on Saturdays but not school days? (Those are good questions, actually.) Eventually, understanding that the world contains a fair amount of pain and suffering, kids want to know why God lets loved ones get sick or die, and what kind of God allows war between the very peoples he created (another good one).

Not only do kids have questions of this sort, they also want to know what God intends for them personally. Why would God permit someone to exclude them from a social event; how could God be loving and care for each one of us if He won't answer a simple prayer for family harmony or that Mom or Dad would find a job? Children appreciate instinctively the paradoxes of belief in God—being "love" on the one hand, and allowing us to suffer, on the other.

Through a religious experience in childhood and by standing on a foundation of faith to assess and understand life's ups and downs, geeks incorporate a spiritual dimension that gives them purpose and power.

What can parents do to promote a spiritual and religious geek lifestyle? Teach our children to look *up*, look *out,* and look *in.*

EYES UP—TO HEAVEN

Looking up to God, we teach children the essential truths of our respective faiths. This should be the easy part, since the great world religions stand on history and tradition. Yet as research proves, we parents aren't always so sure of what we ourselves believe! Many adults realize after having children that they don't know as much about their religion as they need to know in order to pass it on to their kids. In this way, children have a lovely capacity to lead their parents (back) to God. As geeky moms and dads, we may need to rekindle our practice of faith or revisit the basic tenets of our beliefs so we're able to teach them to our children.

All religions have in common the idea of service to God. Such a lofty, spiritual goal can be meaningful even to a child. We can inspire our kids in this way by teaching them about the historical foundations of their faith, including lessons of courage from believers in history and in modern times.

The beauty of organized religion is ritual. All faith traditions incorporate rituals that include praise, thanksgiving, and intercession to God. Childhood is the time to get kids involved in worship and religious education. Milestones help kids assimilate more deeply into their faith, so make the most of these! In fact, make a bigger deal out of religious milestones than any others—this is how we send a message to our children about what's most important.

EYES OUT—TO OTHERS

Looking out to the community, we teach children how our faith traditions should influence our relationships. Religion teaches us that there's more to relationships than being nice—in fact, I'm pretty sure "nice" is not even a biblical concept! First, religion teaches the primacy of parents as surrogates for God, so the notion of obedience to Mom and Dad takes on a spiritual meaning. In this context, it makes a lot more sense than just blindly doing what you're told, doesn't it? An eye toward others also calls us to respect the dignity of each person and to live a moral life—not just because others will think highly of us, but because God commands it. Relationships—especially friendships—must be viewed in this spiritual context.

The idea of community service comes from this other-directed facet of spirituality. Engaging in service as a family teaches children the value of humbling ourselves before others. Whether through religiously affiliated service programs or secular ones, kids learn that caring for the needs of others is intrinsically joyful. As they grow, teens discover that service projects and commitments give life a lot more depth than just hanging out with friends at the mall. (Oh wait. Geeks don't do that very often anyway.)

EYES IN—TO THE HEART

Looking inward toward the heart, we teach children that their faith can sustain them regardless of their circumstances. When life has meaning beyond the material world and when relationships have meaning beyond the ego, the pain and frustration of growing up are viewed in religious and philosophical contexts. This aspect of spirituality focuses on "personhood" and is the source of true self-esteem. Kids can learn to look inward for God's presence by learning to pray and by seeing God in the natural world.

Children and teens say they pray in a host of ways—while listening to music, playing with a pet, getting ready for a test, doing chores, even in the bathroom!—anytime can be prayer time. To support a prayerful life, we can get kids devotional materials written for their ages and, as well, put a journal by the bedside. We also can tell our kids about our prayer lives and model for them a regular spiritual practice. Seeing religious reading material by your bedside or noticing a spiritual CD in your car will prompt conversation about the role of your faith in your day-to-day struggles.

STRUGGLES FOR GEEKS AS SEEN
THROUGH THE PRISM OF FAITH

A child who grows up with a faith perspective has coping skills that support the geek lifestyle. That's borne out in the research about religious kids generally.

Now, I've made it pretty clear there are social implications in choosing an uncool path, and when I'm challenged about my geek-parenting strategies, it's usually this aspect that makes parents leery. And I agree, since the geek lifestyle can be seen as the hard road, we geek parents face a difficult task making sense of our choices.

Faithfulness makes sense.

What do you say to a child whose friends tease and exclude her? How do you frame the loneliness and heartache that come with taking a stand or living out your values? When the culture tells you your personality, interests, clothing, music, movies, and lifestyle are unappealing and uncool, how does a child learn to be optimistic and self-confident? In my home, the answer to these questions is "Look to God for perspective and comfort."

I believe—and I communicate to my children—that God calls them to live in a way that's wholesome and healthy. I believe the hard times they experience in childhood are part of growing in genuine character to become strong, faithful adults. And I believe by making the hard choice for a geek lifestyle, we're using the gifts and opportunities given to us by God to be the people we're meant to be.

Finding Faith in All Things Geeky

In the nine preceding rules for raising geeks, we've looked at the many ways in which our parenting decisions affect our children. Now, adding the dimension of faith, we can see that each facet of the geeky lifestyle enables us to teach our children to be grateful for the incredible gifts God gives each of us:

* *To be a brainiac* is to accept God's gift of intellect; to use our abilities to discover and enjoy God's awesome creation—our universe.

* *To be sheltered* is to accept God's gift of innocence; to see the world through unspoiled eyes and to appreciate life with a sense of wonder.

* *To be uncommon* is to accept God's gift of uniqueness; to claim our own interests and passions and to follow our own paths, not just follow others.

* *To be liked by adults* is to accept God's gift of civility; to exhibit respect and maturity in our relationships.

* *To be a late bloomer* is to accept God's gift of dignity; to refuse to be exploited by others.

* *To be a team player* is to accept God's gift of activity; to enjoy our capacity to be challenged and to learn to cooperate with others toward a shared goal.

* *To be a true friend* is to accept God's gift of community; to understand ourselves as loved and loving and to find God in the hearts of friends.

* *To be a homebody* is to accept God's gift of family; to uphold the bonds of unconditional love that illuminate God's love for us.

* *To be principled* is to accept God's gift of integrity; to live responsibly and to be accountable for our actions and for the world around us.

* *To be faithful* is to accept God's gift of Himself; to know that we were created for a purpose and to live as we believe God intends.

FELLOW TRAVELERS ON THE JOURNEY

Perhaps the most gratifying moments for faithful, geeky parents are the ones in which we realize that our children are sharing a faith journey with us. True, we may begin and end our travels at different points, but for the period of time we're entwined as parent and child, we get to experience the trip together. From a geek perspective, this is what's cool. Very, very cool.

Nothing has been so humbling as to realize that my personal experience of faith is so wrapped up in my role as mother to my four children. From contemplating my first pregnancy to birthing my fourth child, the miracle of their arrivals provided the irrefutable truth of God's benevolent existence. My motherhood journey now takes a new and nostalgic twist as I begin the process of launching them one by one into a waiting

A LETTER FOR KATIE TO READ ON RETREAT...

February 2006
My darling Kate,

As I write this letter, I can picture you at the retreat house, only a few miles away from home, but on a very big adventure, indeed. I imagine you sitting by the fire...I imagine you listening and laughing, shedding some preconceptions along with many tears as you discover what your faith is really all about. I suspect at times you have felt overwhelmed with emotion, and maybe you've been amazed at the things you didn't know about yourself and others and God.

It's not unusual for me to imagine what you're doing when you're on a new experience. Because you're the oldest, everything that's new for you is new for me, too...and while you may not realize it, you have carried my heart along each time you venture into the world. I confess I've sometimes wondered—and always prayed—that I've prepared you for whatever you might encounter, but you've never failed to surpass my fondest hopes for you.

That's because you are more than I ever dreamed a daughter could be, Kate; you are the daughter God dreamed you could be. And now to see how eager you are to grow in your relationship with God fills me with even greater pride and admiration for you.

In this yearning, you'll find you are complete. For while you may think something has been missing in your life, being on "God's time" may show you that your Creator already gave you everything you need to be united with Him.

He gave you parents who adore you and a family to uphold you no matter where your path may lead. He gave you sisters and a brother who idolize you. (No, really.)

He gave you friends who appreciate your wit and wisdom, who seek your advice and support your endeavors, and who listen to your stories even if you ramble a little.

He gave you an inquisitive mind and a love of learning, and more than these, the capacity to understand.

He gave you a kind heart; a caring and compassionate spirit that enables you to show empathy to others and inspires you to serve.

He gave you willingness to love and a sense of loyalty that conveys your devotion.

He gave you a conscience to guide you, and a desire to please Him that directs you.

He gave you a countenance so lovely that your smile literally radiates His presence.

He gave you optimism to dream of the life you envision for yourself

He gave you the grace to accept that dreams sometimes don't come true; and the hope to dream yet again.

He gave you the deepest blue eyes—windows to a soul burning with the fire of faith—longing for connection with the One whose breath caused you to be.

More than anything, Kate, He gave you His constant presence—through His Holy Spirit in your soul, through His Son in the Eucharist; through a mom and dad who committed to God long ago that we would help you know Him and love Him and serve Him.

Not that the journey of faith won't permit you to believe that He left something out.

We all feel inadequate when faced with risks; we all struggle with fears that sometimes hold us back from doing what we ought to do, or from loving as we should. And we all sometimes fail to live in the awareness of God's loving presence and the appreciation of the gifts that make us whole.

But those are the detours that bring us back to Him, aren't they?

There is so much to discover about your relationship with God and about the life He has called you to live. I can tell you that answering His call is the singular purpose for which we all were created. Yet it's also the central issue in a struggle with God that prompts us all to ask: His purpose or mine? His dreams or mine? His will or mine?

I hope while on "God's time," you glean some insight into His purpose for you and also that you learn to trust Him—not with the trust of a child—but with the trust of mature faith, knowing that He's leading you in places you can't imagine.

Trust Him, Kate, because He can imagine. And believe me when I tell you His dreams for us are so much bigger than our dreams for ourselves.

After all, I dreamed of just a daughter...and God, in His infinite Love, gave me you.

I love you with all my heart,
Your Mom

world. In every day and through every phase, I have understood myself as an agent of God's love. To be sure, I could never love my children as much as they deserve to be loved. My imperfect, often selfish, and sometimes inept attempts to lead them lovingly toward their Creator only highlight the difference between Him and me. I'm only human...He's divine.

Yet there are those instances when I'm certain I'm sending the message He wants me to deliver; times when only His inspired wisdom could explain my unintended profundity. Conversations whispered in the dark at bedtime, silent hugs so tight they nearly hurt to give and to receive, hands held together in prayer—all somehow convey more than my habitual "I love you's."

Journeying together with our children on a spiritual pathway rocks. It's especially exciting to watch our kids take steps toward the mature faith that will mark them as adults. Case in point: Katie's first Kairos retreat. *Kairos*—the Greek word meaning "God's time"—is a four-day sojourn to discover God's friendship. The format for the retreat takes participants through a learning process intended to bring God closer and make faith a more vibrant source of strength and support. When Katie returned home from Kairos, she hugged me and said, "I don't want to hurt your feelings, Mom, but I realize now that I love God even more than I love you."

"Not to worry," I told her. "Same here."

Uncool Answers

How should I respond to my son's complaint that his prayers for a best friend have gone unanswered? His faith is wavering because he thinks God is letting him down.

I'm with your son—God does have a bad habit of holding out on answers to prayers! The thing to do is remind him that God has three answers and He uses them at His discretion: Yes, no, and wait. The trick is to convince your son to wait patiently for the friend God most certainly is sending his way.

Sometimes when my kids complain that God is leaving them high and dry, I have to remind them of the other ways in which He clearly blesses them. This is especially true when friendship struggles take center stage, since these tend to be emotionally grueling and all-consuming. With four geeky children, I've noticed that friendships naturally ebb and flow as kids get older and the culture inserts itself into our choices. It's those times when I put a bigger focus on our family relationships and on spending time together as a family.

When the problem is something you can't control, such as wishing for a best friend, look to the other aspects of your geeky lifestyle that you can promote. Is your brainiac child ready for a challenge such as space camp or a local museum seminar? Is your uncommon geek ready for a new hobby? Is your team player looking to learn a new sport? Does your homebody geek need a family adventure? Finding ways to nurture some other aspect of your child's development takes the focus off the friendship problem in the short term.

In the long term, if the issue isn't one of natural friendship cycles but in fact reflects a deeper problem, take action. Your son's complaint about unanswered prayers could be a sign that he's depressed and needs help. See his teachers and the counselor at school; talk to a pediatrician and to your clergyman. Figure out if there's a problem with bullying or aggressive behaviors at school and make certain you haven't missed any signals. If so, recall my earlier advice—don't be afraid to make big changes if they're necessary to ensure a healthy, happy environment for your child.

But do remember that every child sometimes feels lonely, and every person sometimes feels that God neglects prayers! Waiting on the Lord is a time-honored geek tradition. So tell your son to hang in there. Geeks tend to blossom at just the right moment.

Guaranteed Geek: Tips for a Geeky Faith Life

For Geeks of All Ages:

* Read "The Book"—or the Torah or the Koran! Know what you believe *and why,* so you can teach your faith to your children.

* Get books and movies about your religion and include these in the regular rotation of nighttime reading and entertainment. (Animated stories for children about heroes of faith are as fun to watch as Disney princesses.)

* Convey that religious services are a priority. Plan around them and make them a part of your family's routine.

* Teach children the proper etiquette for religious services. Kids need to learn early how to behave at their own churches and, as well, how to act when visiting the church of a relative or friend—especially one of another faith. If you're going to a religious ceremony unfamiliar to you or your child, do some research in advance to find out what's expected.

* Bring your clergyman home! Inviting your pastor, rabbi, or imam to dinner with your family helps children assimilate into the faith and also teaches them that faith leaders are people too.

For Elementary School Geeks:

* Teach and celebrate the rituals of your faith. Help kids to understand that sacraments and religious milestones are important to the whole family.

* Celebrate religious holidays *religiously*! Help children learn their importance in a spiritual sense, not only a cultural one.

* Teach about other religions that friends may practice so your growing geek learns tolerance and appreciation of others' beliefs.

* Add a spiritual or faith dimension to conversations about school, friendship, sports, and media.

* Give religious gifts to kids for birthdays and other gift-giving events.

* Pray together!

For Middle School Geeks:
* Convey your faith's teaching about morality. Help your geeky child understand his moral choices against the backdrop of his religious traditions.

* Keep piling on religious celebrations. Confirmations, bar and bat mitzvahs, and Ramadan all allow children to grow in participation because of their advancing age.

* Get kids in a youth group to help them practice their faith in a fun, supportive setting.

* Continue religious education either formally or at home so kids can articulate the tenets of their beliefs.

* Pray together!

For High School Geeks:
* Talk about religious issues throughout the world. Help teens understand how their faith tradition fits into the moral and political landscape.

* Invoke God's help when teens struggle with decisions about risky behaviors. When talking about your expectations regarding drinking, smoking, drugs, and sex, give kids your religious perspective and discuss the spiritual issues involved.

* Discuss your faith perspective on relationships between guys and girls. Make sure you share your spiritual beliefs about sex and marriage. This is best done long before there's an actual boy- or girlfriend in the picture.

* Encourage your teen to be as involved in church life as he is in other areas. Look for retreats and teen trips offered by your church and encourage teens to take advantage of these as ways to explore their spiritual development.

* Promote (or even require) some regular community service during high school.

* Pray together!

CONCLUSION

Throughout my parenting journey, I've read a fair number of parenting books. Some of them are helpful and offer wisdom and solid strategies. Some of them are just a lot of hooey, to be completely honest. As parents, we get to choose the paths we want to follow to develop our skills and philosophies. This is how we can best serve our children.

I've tried to articulate the parenting strategies my husband and I have developed based on the experience and education we've gained over more than eighteen years. By presenting "geek parenting" to you, I hope to encourage you in your own journey, one that asks for your most thoughtful and courageous effort.

There's no way I could address all the issues that might arise in your family life. And anyway, the point isn't to glean my specific advice for what to do in every situation, but rather to incorporate a geeky worldview when it comes to your kids. I hope I've given you some things to think about.

Every family is special. If yours is a geeky family, I happen to think you're very special, indeed!

Your Uniquely Geeky Family

Geek families have much in common, but we also are unique. We all face issues that reflect our personalities, education, and life experiences, as well as the makeup of our families. It's these unique aspects that often cause us to ponder how we can parent more effectively.

Whenever I speak to groups about geek parenting, it's typical for question-and-answer sessions to delve into these family variations so parents can learn how to apply geek principles in their particular circumstances. The more I learn about families, the more convinced I am that a geeky lifestyle can suit anyone who wants to raise genuine, enthusiastic, empowered kids.

Single-Child Families

Only children make wonderful geeks! My husband is a perfect example of an only child who lived a geeky lifestyle, and in fact, his boyhood experiences have significantly shaped our parenting style and influenced our family life. The biggest pitfall of parenting an only child in the culture of cool is to keep materialism in check. When you have just one child, you're more able to afford to give him all the latest gadgets and gizmos that make for a cool existence. Resist materialism by evaluating your purchases on the basis of what's best for your child, not what you can afford. Another area of concern is in friendships, since you may be tempted to allow an extremely active social life on the grounds that your geek is always home alone with Mom and Dad. Don't permit more socializing than you believe is healthy and necessary. Also, make sure your home is a place where your child's friends can congregate.

Because of their frequent exposure to adults, only children tend to have terrific manners and are confident conversing with their parents' friends. Since they must often entertain themselves, only children frequently are good readers. And since parents of only children aren't juggling the activities of several kids, they tend to be hands-on and involved parents—an essential element in geeky living. Raising an only child most certainly can be a geeky endeavor!

The Sibling Factor

As a mother of four children, I've seen how our geek lifestyle has become a part of our family identity. As they grow, our younger children have certain expectations about the sorts of things they can and can't do as they get older based on the decisions they've seen us make regarding the older siblings. They know our house rules and tend to just accept that there are certain things that make us geekier than other families.

A struggle for parents is to keep the level of supervision strong with younger children while the older ones gain greater freedom and flexibility because of their advancing ages. This is particularly true when regulating media content, for example. Parents often ask me, "How do we keep the younger one from seeing the video that we only allow for the older one?" The answer: Get ready for a few years of vigilance. One way we've dealt with this concern is to include the older siblings in the mission of protecting the innocence of their younger brother and sister. By investing them with responsibility in this regard, they help monitor and supervise what's coming into the house via TV, radio, and Internet. Also, older kids are very annoyed if their younger siblings get a lot of freedom that they didn't have. They tend to keep us on our toes!

Not that this is always easy or that we're always successful. Amy and Jimmy most certainly display greater awareness of pop culture than Katie or Betsy did at the same age. To a certain extent we can't avoid this—after all, the older ones didn't grow up in a house with teenage girls, while the younger ones can't escape them. I try to remember that each child's experience is unique, and therefore my duty is to approach each one with a new eye toward geek parenting. For example, Katie and Betsy only knew the Olsen twins as child actors in the TV series *Full House*. Amy knows they are wealthy young adults and that one of them has had an eating disorder. Nonetheless, she watches *Full House* reruns a lot (and loves the show).

Siblings provide a lot of geeky support for one another. It's been incredibly gratifying to see our older daughters reassure Jimmy and Amy when the inevitable friendship issues arise, for example. They're able to vouch for our parental advice and offer strength and support during difficult times.

Single Parents

Some of the best geek parents I know are single parents, so clearly Mom or Dad's marital status doesn't impede a geeky lifestyle. As with all issues involving divorced parents, the more communication, the better. When both parents have a geek vision for what's best regarding their children, decision making is smoother. Issues arise when one parent is committed to the geek lifestyle but the other wants to engage in the culture of cool (or at least, doesn't see any harm in it). This tends to come across as one parent being the strict one, while the other is lenient. (By the way, this issue can arise in two-parent homes just as easily.)

Kids need consistency to the extent that adults can provide it. We know it's always in a child's best interest if Mom and Dad are on the same page, especially regarding the influence and impact of the culture in daily life. It's worth spending some time discussing and may even be a subject for some adult counseling sessions.

Regardless of the attitude of the other parent, a geek dad or mom should maintain geek standards in his or her home. Period. Your rules apply in your home; it's both your right and your responsibility to set limits that you think will benefit your child. Let the rules speak for themselves, though, rather than trash the other parent's lax standards. Kids will get the message about what's important to parents simply by living your geek lifestyle.

Special-Needs Families

Parents of special-needs kids have much to think about in addition to the impact of the cool culture. Some might try to keep up with what's popular and cool as a way to help a special-needs child fit in better with his social surroundings. This might seem like a compassionate strategy, but I would caution that it may not be. Instead of working harder to conform (possibly sending the message to a child "I want you to be like everyone one else"), parents can instill the geeky values of uniqueness and individuality. A special-needs child already knows what it's like to be different from others; he needs to find kids who *choose* to be different from the norm. In hanging with geeks, a special-needs child can discover the power and pride of developing genuine self-esteem based on who he is, not what others may think of him.

Special Circumstances

Children living in special circumstances need lots of loving care. The kind of attention and supervision advocated in geek parenting is especially needed as caregivers help children confronting difficult life situations. Losing a parent or sibling to death, awaiting adoption, living in foster care, or living with grandparents are all examples of special circumstances that kids may face. Each of these situations presents challenges in which it may seem trivial to make a fuss over the cool culture and its impact on innocence or materialistic attitudes. But the contrary is true—as we monitor the content of a teen's iPod or put controls on his spending, parents and caregivers send the strong message "You are precious to me, and even though I know your life is tough, I'm committed to doing what's best for you no matter what." That's a powerful message to a child in pain! The harder a child's life, the more attention we must pay to his healthy environment. Rather than use his challenging situation as a reason to indulge him, parents and caregivers need to offer their most thoughtful and participative supervision.

Depression

The issue of depression in children and families is a critical one. You won't be surprised by my considered opinion that our culture is partly to blame for the fact that a growing number of children and teens cannot seem to find a way to feel content and happy, despite the fact that ours is the most prosperous, most pampered culture in history. Bombarded as they are with images and information that tell them "the world is a mess," our kids understandably struggle to find optimism and a sense of purpose. Depression is more than this, of course, but I can't help but question whether our steady diet of media, consumerism, and premature adulthood isn't at least partly responsible. Certainly, the research I did to write this book has convinced me the culture is relevant in this regard.

As far as the geeky lifestyle is concerned, I want to be clear that it should not be a source of depression. Involved and attentive parents who set reasonable limits and standards for their children's behavior, and who also provide loving, stable family relationships, ought not to worry that their parenting style will cause unhappiness. The opposite is true!

Having said this, depression is a real medical issue and must be taken seriously. Kids who suffer the emotional turmoil of depression need clinical, emotional, and spiritual support.

Happily Uncool Ever After

Thinking back on that conversation all those years ago at the school picnic, I realize that my insignificant comment was actually the first moment I stood up for geek parenting. Gradually, I started asking other parents how they did things and what motivated them, and I discovered there's a movement among us to recapture some important aspects of childhood for our children—and at the same time improve the quality of our families. Over the years, as I admit to folks that I'm bringing up geeks, I have concluded that others need justification, support, and ideas to lead their children toward a wholesome, healthy geek lifestyle.

To be sure, it sometimes feels like we're the only ones working against the culture of cool. Jimmy let me know he is the only guy in his eighth-grade class without a cell phone; Amy insists she's the only girl among her fifth-grade friends who doesn't have an iPod Nano. Not that I sit around worrying about the impact of my decisions about such things, but it's illustrative of my children's sense that we're very different from other families. Even though it's not true that we're the only ones, it feels to them, as it does to me, that the cultural tide runs mightily in only one direction.

We have to ask ourselves why that is. Why is the culture able to exert such a wallop on our children's innocence? Why does the culture rob our kids of a childhood filled with discovery and wonder and replace it with materialism and celebrity? Why do we go along with the culture's values, which could exploit our kids, rather than with our own values, which would empower and encourage them?

Maybe it all boils down to happiness.

Assuring that children are happy strikes me as the only logical explanation for what I view to be incongruous parenting. It's the only reason I can come up with when I see the documented disconnect between what adults believe and what they do in raising their kids. It's the only thing I ever hear when talking to parents who try to rationalize decisions they themselves can't justify.

In the end, everyone just wants their kids to be happy.

Maybe we view their contentment as a measure of our love, or at least a measure of our competence. Maybe we just figure if they're happy, then everything's okay.

I want my kids to be happy too. Believe me, I do. But more than mere happiness, I want them to experience true joy, genuine contentment, and peace during times when happiness is simply not attainable. I want them to be happy with who they are, even when they're not happy about the way things are going. Most of all, I want them to know how to find happiness within themselves and through a faith that both stands them firmly on the ground while propelling them toward their dearest dreams.

It's not enough for me that my kids seem happy. It's certainly not enough that they be considered cool or that they feel popular. It's emphatically not enough to sell them short on character development in the name of social standing. My obligation to my children and to the God who created them calls me to expect much more.

Certainly, I've learned in the past few years that I am not alone! As I articulate my commitment to shielding my kids from the cynicism and exploitation that permeate our culture, I realize there's a desire among parents to resist what's *cool* in favor of what's *good*. Now I'm suggesting that it's not enough to cower in the shadows of the culture of cool, feeling unsupported and misunderstood. By saying loudly and proudly, "I'm bringing up geeks!" we stand for our kids' individuality; for their right to be themselves in a world that would have them conform to something less.

As a parenting trend, I believe bringing up geeks will rejuvenate our society's value on childhood innocence and afford our kids the chance to grow to be the people they are meant to be. As a lifestyle, I hope bringing up geeks results in a more joyful experience of parenting and family life.

In childhood, it may not seem cool to be a geek, but adults know better.

In the end, geeks become the coolest adults but also part of an important cycle. After all, it takes a cool adult to raise a happily uncool kid.

Resources

Introduction

Gray, John (1999). *Men Are from Mars, Women Are from Venus, Children Are from Heaven*. New York: HarperCollins.

Hatchett, Glenda (2004). *Say What You Mean and Mean What You Say! Saving Your Child from a Troubled World*. New York: Perennial Currents.

Levine, Madeline (2006). *The Price of Privilege: How Parental Pressure and Material Advantage Are Creating a Generation of Disconnected and Unhappy Kids*. New York: HarperCollins.

Rule #1—Raise a Brainiac

(2001, April 12). Brainy Students Least Likely to Engage in Risky Behaviors While "Burnouts" and "Non-Conformists" are at Highest Risk. Retrieved 2007, from Science Daily Web site: www.sciencedaily.com/releases/2001/04/010412080741.htm.

Perry, Bruce. Curiosity: The Fuel of Development. Retrieved 2007, from Scholastic Web site: teacher.scholastic.com/professional/bruceperry/curiosity.htm.

Fact Sheet Overview. Retrieved 2007, from National Institute for Literacy Web site: www.nifl.gov/nifl/facts/facts_overview.html (2003).

Hofferth, Sandra (2000, April 17). How American Children Spend Their Time. Retrieved 2007, Web site: ceel.psc.isr.umich.edu/pubs/papers/ceel012-00.pdf.

(1966). Reading Is Fundamental. Retrieved 2007, Web site: www.rif.org/

(2006, June). Kids and Family Reading Report. Retrieved 2007, from Scholastic Web site: www.scholastic.com/aboutscholastic/news/reading _survey_press_call_2.pd.

(1998). Why Teach Current Events? Retrieved 2007, from Education World Web site: www.education-world.com/a_curr/curr084.shtml.

The Facts: Highlights of Arts Education Research. Retrieved 2007, from Art USA Web site: www.artsusa.org/public_awareness/facts/.

(1997, July). Student Interest in National News and Its Relation to School Courses. Retrieved 2007, from Archive Web site: web.archive.org/ web/20040627072424/nces.ed.gov/pubs97/web/97970.as.

Rule #2—Raise a Sheltered Kid

Hansen, Chris (2007). *To Catch a Predator: Protecting Your Kids from Online Enemies Already in Your Home.* New York: Dutton.

Singer, D. G. & J. L. (eds.) (2001). *Handbook of Children and the Media.* Thousand Oaks, CA: Sage Publications.

Strasburger, V., & Wilson, B. (2002). *Children, Adolescents, and the Media.* Thousand Oaks, CA: Sage Publications.

(2005, August 17). APA Calls for Reduction of Violence in Media Used by Children and Adolescents. Retrieved 2007, from APA Online Web site: www.apa.org/releases/videoviolence05.html.

(2004). Center on Media and Child Health. Retrieved 2007, from Center on Media and Child Health Web site: www.cmch.tv/.

(2002, July 8). Children and Advertising. Retrieved 2007, from National Institute on Media and the Family Web site: www.mediafamily.org/ facts/facts_childadv.shtml.

Roberts, D. F. (2005, March). Generation M: Media in the Lives of 8–18 Year-Olds. Retrieved 2007, from Kaiser Family Foundation Web site: www.kff.org/entmedia/upload/Generation-M-Media-in-the-Lives-of -8-18-Year-Olds-Report.pdf

Marketing to Children: An Overview. Retrieved 2007, from Campaign for Commercial-Free Childhood Web site: www.commercialfreechildhood .org/factsheets/ccfc-facts%20overview.pdf.

Lenhart, A. (2001, June 21). Teenage Life Online. Retrieved 2007, from Pew Internet and American Life Web site: www.pewinternet.org/pdfs/PIP_Teens_Report.pdf.

Retrieved 2007, from Wired Safety Web site: www.wiredsafety.org/.

Retrieved 2007, from Media Research Center Web site: www.media research.org/Welcome.asp.

Retrieved 2007, from Missing and Exploited Children Web site: www.missingkids.com/.

Retrieved 2007, from Nielsen Media Research Web site: www.nielsenmedia.com/nc/portal/site/Public/.

Facts and Figures About Our TV Habits. Retrieved 2007, from Turnoff TV Network Web site: www.tvturnoff.org/images/facts&figs/factsheets/FactsFigs.pdf.

Retrieved 2007, from FamilyEducation Web site: www.familyeducation.com/home/.

PTC Condemns Ultra-Violent TV Content and Calls on Industry to Shape Up. Retrieved 2007, from Parents Television Council Web site: www.parentstv.org/.

Statistics. Retrieved 2007, from Protect Kids Web site: www.protectkids.org/statistics.htm.

(2004). Study Finds "Ratings Creep": Movie Ratings Categories Contain More Violence, Sex, Profanity Than Decade Ago. Retrieved 2007, from Harvard School of Public Health Web site: www.hsph.harvard.edu/news/press-releases/2004-releases/press07132004.html.

Baig, E. C. (2005, January 30). Study Shows Some Teens Not as Web-Savvy as Parents. Retrieved 2007, from USA Today Web site: www.usatoday.com/money/industries/technology/2005-01-30-teens-usat_x.htm.

Collins, Rebecca (2004, September 3). Watching Sex on Television Predicts Adolescent Initiation of Sexual Behavior. Retrieved 2007, from Official Journal of the American Academy of Pediatrics Web site: pediatrics.aappublications.org/cgi/content/full/114/3/e280.

Perle, L. (2007, January 4). Watching the News. Retrieved 2007, from Common Sense Media Web site: www.commonsensemedia.org/parent

_tips/commonsense_view/index.php?id=191&utm_source=newsletter
&utm_medium=weekly&utm_campaign=168&utm_content=QA.

What Do I Need to Know about Children and TV? Retrieved 2007, from
University of Michigan Health System Web site: www.med.umich
.edu/1libr/yourchild/tv.htm#presence.

Rule #3—Raise an Uncommon Kid

Levine, Madeline (2006). *The Price of Privilege: How Parental Pressure
and Material Advantage Are Creating a Generation of Disconnected
and Unhappy Kids*. New York: HarperCollins.

The Commercialization of Toys and Play. Retrieved 2007, from Campaign
for Commercial-Free Childhood Web site: www.commercialfreechild
hood.org/factsheets/ccfc-facts%20toysandplay.pdf.

Roberts, S. (2004, September). New American Dream Survey Report.
Retrieved 2007, from New American Dream: More of What Matters
Web site: www.newdream.org/about/Finalpollreport.pdf.

Kids and Commercialism. Retrieved 2007, from New American Dream
Web site: www.newdream.org/kids/index.php.

(2002, May). Thanks to Ads, Kids Won't Take No, No, No, No, No, No,
No, No, No for an Answer. Retrieved July 9, 2007, from New American Dream Web site: www.newdream.org/kids/poll.php.

Child Development. Retrieved 2007, from Campaign for Commercial-Free
Childhood Web site: www.commercialexploitation.com/links.htm.

Borba, M. (2006). The Big Brat Factor. Retrieved 2007, from Family Magazine
Group Web site: www.lafamily.com/display_article.php?id=539.

Gibbs, N. (2001). Do Kids Have Too Much Power? Retrieved 2007, from
Time Web site: www.time.com/time/covers/1101010806/cover.html.

(1995, July). Yearning for Balanced Views of Americans on Consumption,
Materialism, and the Environment. Retrieved 2007, from Sustain-
able Consumption and Production Web site: www.iisd.ca/consume/
harwood.html.

Drummond, T. (2000, February 7). Harlem's Chess Kings. Retrieved
2007, from *Time* Web site: www.time.com/time/magazine/arti
cle/0,9171,996016-1,00.html.

Golin, Josh (2005, July). Marketing and Parental Responsibility. Retrieved 2007, from *Mothering* Web site: www.mothering.com.

Rule #4—Raise a Kid Adults Like

Cohen, Jon (2006, February 13). Poll: Rudeness in America, 2006. Retrieved 2007, from ABC News Web site: abcnews .go.com/2020/US/story?id=1574155.

Aggravating Circumstances: A Status Report on Rudeness in America. Retrieved 2007, from Public Agenda Web site: www.publicagenda.org/ specials/civility/civility.htm.

We're Ruder Than We Used to Be, Americans Say. Retrieved 2007, from *USA Today* Web site: www.usatoday.com/news/nation/2005-10-14 rude amercians poll_x.htm.

American Manners Poll. Retrieved 2007, from *USA Today* Web site: www .usatoday.com/news/nation/2005-10-14-rudeness-poll-method_x.htm.

Talking Back. Retrieved 2007, from University of Pittsburgh Web site: www.pitt.edu/utimes/issues/30/110697/18.html.

Rule #5—Raise a Late Bloomer

Marikar, S. (2007, January 17). Some Say It's OK for Girls to Go Wild. Retrieved 2007, from ABC News Web site: abcnews.go.com/US/Health/ story?id=2798436&page=1.

Hymowitz, K. S. (1999, October). Kids Today Are Growing Up Way Too Fast. Retrieved 2007, from Manhattan Institute for Policy Research Web site: www.manhattan-institute.org/html/_wsj-kids_today_are _growing.htm.

Kendrick, C. Mother Unhappy About How Son Dresses. Retrieved 2007, from FamilyEducation Web site: www.life.familyeducation.com/teen/ discipline/41548.html?detoured=1.

Kendrick, C. Teen Wants to Pierce Navel. Retrieved 2007, from Family-Education Web site: www.life.familyeducation.com/teen/independence/ 41660.html?detoured=1.

Hopson, K. (2007, March 5). Childhood Obesity May Contribute to Earlier Puberty for Girls. Retrieved 2007, from University of Michigan

Health System Web site: www.med.umich.edu/opm/newspage/2007/
puberty.htm.

Ginty, M. (2007, March 30). U.S. Girls' Early Puberty Attracts Research
Flurry. Retrieved 2007, from WUNRN Web site: www.wunrn.com/
news/2007/03_07/03_26_07/040107_usa.htm.

(2001, February 12). Early Puberty: Obesity, Environment Suspected.
Retrieved 2007, from *USA Today* Web site: www.usatoday.com/news/
health/2001-02-12-early-puberty.htm.

Jayson, S. Media Cited for Showing Girls as Sex Objects. Retrieved
2007, from *USA Today* Web site: www.usatoday.com/news/health/
2007-02-19-sexualized-girls_x.htm.

Rule #6—Raise a Team Player

Dellasega, Cheryl (ed.) (2005). *Mean Girls Grow Up: Adult Women Who
Are Still Queen Bees, Middle Bees, and Afraid-to-Bees.* Hoboken, NJ:
John Wiley and Sons.

Alsever, J. (2006, June 25). A New Competitive Sport: Grooming the
Child Athlete. Retrieved 2007, from the *New York Times* Web site:
www.nytimes.com/2006/06/25/business/yourmoney/25sport.html
?ex=1308888000&en=a3e8cf4552249fe6&ei=5088&partner=rssnyt
&emc=rss.

(2007, June 4). Soccer Mom Alert: More May Not Be Better. Retrieved
2007, from MSNBC Web site: www.msnbc.msn.com/id/19027225/.

Stenson, J. (2005, April 12). Keeping Kids in the Game. Retrieved 2007,
from MSNBC Web site: www.msnbc.msn.com/id/7288461/.

(2007, June 24). More Kids Turning to Personal Fitness Trainers.
Retrieved 2007, from MSNBC Web site: www.msnbc.msn.com/id/
19403443/.

Langendorf, L. (2003, January 23). Basic Rules for Parents. Retrieved
2007, from Sports Esteem Web site: www.sportsesteem.com/word
press/index.php/archives/25.

(1997). The Citizenship Through Sports Alliance. Retrieved 2007, from the
Citizenship Through Sports Alliance Web site: www.sportsmanship.org/.

Rule #7—Raise a True Friend

Winerman, L. (2004, June 6). Among Young Teens, Aggression Equals Popularity. Retrieved 2007, from APA Online Web site: www.apa.org/monitor/jun04/among.html.

Houtman, N. R. (2000, September). Finding a Friend: Children's Friendships Are Training Ground for Adult Relationships. Retrieved 2007, from Science and Engineering at the University of Maine Web site: www.umaine.edu/mainesci/archives/Psychology/Friendships.htm.

Schoenberg, J. (2003). Feeling Safe: What Girls Say. Retrieved 2007, from Girl Scout Research Center Web site: www.girlscouts.org/research/pdf/feeling_safe.pdf.

Statistics on Bullying. Retrieved 2007, from Bullystoppers.com Web site: www.bullystoppers.com/statistics_on_bullying.htm.

Rule #8—Raise a Homebody

Moore, K. A. (2002, August). Family Strengths: Overlooked but Real. Retrieved 2007, from Child Trends Research Brief Web site: www.childtrends.org/files/FamilyStrengths.pdf.

Medhus, E. (2001, August). The Importance of a Strong Family Identity. Retrieved 2007, from Woodbury Reports Archives Web site: www.strugglingteens.com/archives/2001/8/oe03.html.

Rule #9—Raise a Principled Kid

Coles, Robert (1998). *The Moral Intelligence of Children: How to Raise a Moral Child*. New York: Plume.

Hart, Betsy (2005). *It Takes a Parent: How the Culture of Pushover Parenting Is Hurting Our Kids—and What to Do About It*. New York: G. P. Putnam's Sons.

Geer, J. (2007, February 20). Survey of High School Athletes: What Are Your Children Learning? The Impact of High School Sports on the Values and Ethics of High School Athletes. Retrieved 2007, from the Josephson Institute's Report Card Web site: www.josephsoninstitute.org/sports_survey/2006/.

Jarc, R. (2006, October 15). The Josephson Institute's Report Card on American Youth. Retrieved 2007, from the Josephson Institute of Ethics Web site: www.josephsoninstitute.org/pdf/ReportCard_press -release_2006-1015.pdf.

CHARACTER COUNTS! and the Six Pillars of Character are service marks of Josephson Institute. The definitions of the Six Pillars of Character are reprinted with permission. © 2008 Josephson Institute www .charactercounts.org.

Rule #10—Raise a Faithful Kid

Coles, Robert (1990). *The Spiritual Life of Children*. Boston: Houghton Mifflin.

Gray, H. T. (2007, July 7). Study Shows Beliefs Aren't Strong, Clear Among Americans. *Lansing State Journal*, p. 3D.

Harper, J. (2007, February 5). Poll Finds Solid Ties Between Faith, American Well-Being. Retrieved 2007, from the *Washington Times*: National Weekly Edition Web site: www.americasnewspaper.com/ ME2/dirmod.asp?sid=&nm=&type=Publishing&mod=Publications% 3A%3AArticle&mid=8F3A7027421841978F18BE895F87F791&tier =4&id=AE762ABD48C445F2B02659EEF66DE01D.

Newport, F. (2007, June 13). Americans More Likely to Believe in God Than the Devil, Heaven More Than Hell. Retrieved 2007, from the Gallup Poll Web site: www.galluppoll.com/content/default.aspx?ci=27877.

Wenner, M. (2007, April 24). Study: Religion Is Good for Kids. Retrieved 2007, from LiveScience Web site: www.livescience.com/health/070424 _religion_kids.html.

Smith, C. (2005, September 9). Soul Searching: The Religious and Spiritual Lives of American Teenagers. Retrieved 2007, from National Study of Youth and Religion Web site: www.youthandreligion.org/news/2005 -0929.html.

Mohler, R. A. (2005, April 18). Moralistic Therapeutic Deism—the New American Religion. Retrieved 2007, from Regent University Web site: www.christianpost.com/article/20050418/6266_2_Moralistic_Thera peutic_Deism—the_New_American_Religion.htm.

Murray, B. (2004, October 6). Understanding the Religious and Spiritual Lives of Teenagers. Retrieved 2007, from FACSNET Web site: www .facsnet.org/issues/faith/youth.php.

Vitagliano, E. (2005, November 15). A Strange Faith—Are Church-Going Kids Christian? Retrieved 2007, from Agape Press Web site: www .headlines.agapepress.org/archive/11/152005a.asp.